THE CHURCH OF ROME
at the
BAR OF HISTORY

THE BANNER OF TRUTH TRUST
3 Murrayfield Road, Edinburgh EH12 6EL
PO Box 621, Carlisle, Pennsylvania 17013, USA

*

© William Webster 1995
First Published 1995
ISBN 0 85151 673 4

*

Scripture quotations are taken from the
New American Standard Bible © 1960, 1962, 1963,
1968, 1971, 1973, 1975, 1977 by The Lockman
Foundation. Used by permission.

*

Typeset in 11/12 pt New Baskerville
Printed and bound in Great Britain
at The Bath Press, Avon

THE CHURCH OF ROME
at the
BAR OF HISTORY

William Webster

THE BANNER OF TRUTH TRUST

THIS BOOK IS DEDICATED TO
ART NUERNBERG AND DAN JOHNSON
IN DEEP APPRECIATION FOR THEIR FRIENDSHIP
AND MINISTRY IN MY LIFE

CONTENTS

	Introduction	ix
1.	*The Authority of Scripture*	1
2.	*Scripture and Tradition*	15
3.	*Tradition and Roman Catholicism*	22
4.	*The Papacy and the 'Rock' of Matthew 16*	34
5.	*Papal Authority and Infallibility: The Test of History*	56
6.	*Marian Dogmas*	72
7.	*Salvation and the Sacramental System*	90
8.	*The Eucharist*	117
9.	*Faith and Justification*	133
10.	*Truth: The Defining Issue*	145

APPENDICES

1.	*The Fathers on the Meaning of Tradition and its Relationship to Scripture*	155
2.	*Vatican I and Vatican II on Papal Infallibility*	162
3.	*The Bull* Unam Sanctam *by Boniface VIII*	165
4.	*Vatican I and Vatican II on Papal Primacy*	168
5.	*Writings of the Fathers on the Meaning of the Rock and Keys of Matthew*	174
6.	*Letter of Gregory the Great to John of Constantinople Objecting to his Adoption of the Title Universal Bishop*	184
7.	*The Official Teaching of the Roman Catholic Church on the Person of Mary*	187

8.	*The Fathers on the Real Presence and the Eucharist*	191
9.	*The Fathers on the Eucharistic Sacrifice as not being Propitiatory in Nature but a Memorial of Thanksgiving and Praise*	196
10.	*Thomas Aquinas on the Nature of Faith*	200
11.	*Martin Luther and John Calvin on the Relationship Between Justification and Good Works*	202
12.	*Comments of the Fathers on the Nature of Justification*	205
13.	*The Teaching of the Council of Trent on Justification*	208

Notes   215

Index   236

INTRODUCTION

In the on-going debate between evangelical Protestants and Roman Catholics, one of the fundamental points of disagreement is centred upon the relationship between Scripture and tradition. The evangelical view is that Scripture alone is the Word of God and the final authority and ultimate standard of appeal in all matters related to faith and practice. The Roman Catholic position, on the other hand, while agreeing that the Scriptures are the Word of God, does not limit inspiration to Scripture alone. It holds that the Church's 'Tradition' is equally as inspired as the Old and New Testaments. Consequently, tradition is also a standard of authority with regard to doctrine and practice.

The Roman Church asserts that there is a body of teaching which has been handed down orally from the apostles as a separate source of revelation from the Scriptures. This oral tradition has been preserved complete through the apostolic succession of bishops, and is guaranteed to be free from error because of the assurance given by Christ of the presence of the Holy Spirit in the Church in all ages. This source of truth is supplemental, but in no way contradictory, to the inspired Scriptures. According to official Roman Catholic teaching, the revelation contained in the Bible and in tradition complement one another and share an equal authority:

There exists a close connection and communication between sacred tradition and sacred Scripture. For both of them, flowing from the same divine wellspring, in a certain way merge into a unity and tend toward the same end. For sacred Scripture is the Word of God inasmuch as it is consigned to writing under the inspiration of the divine Spirit. To the successors of the Apostles, sacred tradition hands on in its full purity God's Word, which was entrusted to the Apostles by Christ the Lord and the Holy Spirit. Thus, led by the light of the Spirit of truth, these successors can in their preaching preserve this Word of God faithfully, explain it, and make it more widely known. Consequently, it is not from sacred Scripture alone that the Church draws her certainty about everything which has been revealed. Therefore both sacred tradition and sacred Scripture are to be accepted and venerated with the same sense of devotion and reverence. Sacred tradition and sacred Scripture form one sacred deposit of the Word of God, which is committed to the Church.[1]

The Roman Catholic Church claims ultimate authority, therefore, on the grounds that it produced the Scriptures and it alone possesses the key to the proper interpretation of them. While officially holding to the position that it does not believe in new revelation or the introduction of new doctrines—since the oral tradition is simply the preservation of the teaching of the apostles handed down through successive bishops—the reality is quite different. For, as we will see, numerous teachings of the Church of Rome which it claims are revealed by God are not found in Scripture, nor in the tradition of the early church.

In this book we want to consider the whole issue of Scripture and tradition. We will review the claim of Scripture to be divinely inspired and the scriptural teaching about tradition. We will then examine some of the Roman Catholic Church's distinctive and traditional doctrines, and in particular the claim that these doctrines are based on a tradition which has been handed down from the apostles to the bishops in an unbroken succession to the present day, to see if this claim can be verified historically.

The ultimate question to be addressed is this: Is Scripture the final authority in matters related to faith and practice or has God also inspired tradition, as the Roman Church claims, as the unwritten Word of God which is to carry an equal authority?

---

[1] Walter M. Abbott, S.J., *The Documents of Vatican II* (Chicago: Follett, 1966), p. 117.

1

The Authority of Scripture

Scripture has authority, as both Roman Catholics and evangelical Protestants will agree, because it is the Word of God. But Scripture is not the Word of God merely because the Church says it is. Scripture's authority is derived from its intrinsic nature as a communication from God to man—it has an authority independent of the Church. In this chapter we want to examine the nature of that authority and the claim that Scripture is inspired by God and thereby trustworthy.

The basis on which Christians accept the inspiration of Scripture is because the Scriptures themselves make that claim. This is significant because if they did not claim divine inspiration for themselves then we would have no right to claim it for them. However, in 2 Peter 1:20-21, the apostle writes: 'But know this first of all, that no prophecy of Scripture is a matter of one's own interpretation, for no prophecy was ever made by an act of human will, but men moved by the Holy Spirit spoke from God.' Peter is unequivocally claiming that the prophetic Scriptures are not a human but a divine work, that the authors wrote under the control of the Holy Spirit, and therefore that the Scriptures come from God.[1]

The fullest statement on the divine inspiration of Scripture, however, is found in Paul's second letter to Timothy (3:15-17):

From childhood you have known the sacred writings which are able to give you the wisdom that leads to salvation through faith which is in Christ Jesus. All Scripture is inspired by God and profitable for teaching, for reproof, for correction, for training in righteousness; that the man of God may be adequate, equipped for every good work.

Paul clearly states here that *all* Scripture is inspired by God. He is referring specifically to the Old Testament since the New Testament canon was not complete at the time he wrote, but the New Testament must also be covered by this statement for in 2 Peter 3:16 Peter refers to Paul's writings (including this epistle to Timothy) as Scripture. The apostles were confident to make such claims for their own writings because Jesus had promised them that the Holy Spirit would guide them in all truth, thereby enabling them to write the New Testament Scriptures (*John* 16:13).

The words from 2 Timothy 3:15-17 are very important. The word used for 'inspired' literally means 'God-breathed'. Though men wrote the Old and New Testaments, it is God who worked through them to write exactly what he wanted. By their own testimony the Scriptures are not merely the product of man, but are authored by God himself. This does not mean that men are not intimately involved in the process but rather that God, working through the personalities of the authors, so controlled the process and the individuals that the final product was exactly what he wanted said. And therefore, the Scriptures are infallible and inerrant because they are given by God and are an authoritative expression of his will and truth.

In his letter to Timothy, Paul tells his young co-worker of the functions of the Word of God in the light of its divine inspiration. The Scriptures are 'profitable' or 'useful'[2] for instruction in doctrine—that is, they teach us what we are to believe and practise with respect to God and godliness—and they are also given to reprove and to correct false doctrine. The Word of God checks us where we are wrong and shows us how to correct ourselves; and this whole process of teaching, reproving and correcting trains us in righteousness. As we submit to the Word of God we are instructed in truth and directed how to live, and this makes us 'adequate' for every good work and for doing the will of God. The word Paul uses for adequate is *artios*, which means 'complete' (or 'perfect').

So Paul is arguing that the Scriptures are sufficient for an individual to be perfectly equipped for knowing and doing the will of God in the areas of faith and morals, because they are authoritatively given for that purpose.

The Roman Catholic Church, as already shown, teaches that Scripture alone is *not* all-sufficient—it must be supplemented by a tradition which is equally inspired. But, as we shall see below, the Apostle Paul never claims that tradition is inspired, authoritative and profitable in the same way as the Word of God. If the Scriptures are not sufficient and God has indeed given the Church tradition as a separate source of revelation, why is this never mentioned in Scripture itself? After all, Paul is writing about the Old Testament in this passage and there existed, beside Scripture, an extensive Jewish tradition, directly related to it, to which he could have referred. But he did not do so. So while we are told in unequivocal terms that Scripture is inspired, the Word of God is completely silent about the inspiration of tradition.

To argue, as the Roman Catholic Church does, that 2 Timothy 3:15-17 says that Scripture is profitable but not sufficient as a rule of faith is to twist its meaning in order to defend a man-made tradition. This is not a new phenomenon. The Pharisees, according to Jesus, misinterpreted Scripture in order to adhere to their tradition and he condemned them for it (*Matt.* 15:1-9). But in both cases the Bible's clear statement remains—Scripture is sufficient 'for teaching, for reproof, for correction, for training in righteousness; that the man of God may be adequate, equipped for every good work'.

The fact that Paul does not use the precise word 'sufficient' in the text just quoted in no way invalidates our statement. The sufficiency of Scripture, and therefore '*sola scriptura*', is implicit in what he says and in the rest of biblical testimony.

The truth contained in the word 'trinity' stands upon exactly the same basis. The word itself is not found in Scripture. But it is a convenient term for summing up the general teaching of the Old and New Testaments on the nature of God. The teaching for which the word stands is in Scripture and therefore the use of the term is warranted. In like manner the terms 'sufficiency' or '*sola scriptura*' sum up the overall teaching of Scripture about itself. Specific scriptural descriptions of the Word of God, which speak of its nature and function, lead us inescapably to this conclusion. The following are some of the words which tell us how God would have us regard his Word:

pure—perfect—sure—truth—eternal—forever settled in heaven—it sanctifies—it causes spiritual growth—it is God-breathed—it is authoritative—it gives wisdom unto salvation—it makes the simple wise—it is living and active—it is a guide—it is a fire—a hammer—a seed—the sword of the Spirit—it gives the knowledge of God—it is a lamp to our feet—a light to our path—that which produces reverence for God—it heals—makes free—illuminates—produces faith—regenerates—converts the soul—brings conviction of sin—restrains from sin—is spiritual food—is infallible—inerrant—irrevocable—it searches the heart and mind—produces life—defeats Satan—proves truth—refutes error—is holy—equips for every good work—is the Word of the living God (*Psa.* 119:9-11, 38, 105, 130, 133, 160; *Psa.* 19:7-11; *Psa.* 111:7-8; *Isa.* 40:8; *Eph.* 5:26; *2 Tim.* 3:15-17; *Jer.* 5:14, 23:29; *Matt.* 13:18-23; *Eph.* 6:17; *Psa.* 107:20; *Titus* 2:5; *1 Pet.* 1:23, 2:2; *Acts* 20:32; *John* 8:32, 10:35, 17:17).

It is impossible to find a more convincing argument for the sufficiency of Scripture than these descriptions. And no such language is ever used about tradition in the Scriptures. Nowhere does it receive such commendation. We are told in explicit terms that Scripture is inspired, but never is that said of tradition. On the contrary, when the New Testament speaks of tradition it does so in words of warning (*Matt.* 15:2-6; *Mark* 7:3-13; *Col.* 2:8; *1 Pet.* 1:18; *Gal.* 1:14). When we look at the overall teaching of Scripture about itself and tradition, it is surely clear that it teaches that Scripture is sufficient.

Any claim that such belief in Scripture was created by Paul and the other disciples must also be rejected. It is the express teaching of Jesus Christ himself. Christianity is founded upon the person and work of the Lord Jesus Christ, the Son of God. His attitude to the Scriptures is supremely important. Since he is God, then all that he teaches must be true and authoritative.

The Authority of Scripture

Jesus clearly taught that Scripture is inspired by God. He regarded it as truth—infallible, inerrant, historically reliable, authoritative for living, and an all-sufficient rule of faith. He could say, for example, when speaking with the Pharisees or Sadducees, 'Have you not read what God said?' and then quote from Scripture (*Matt.* 22:31-32). In Matthew 4:4-10, Jesus repeatedly answers Satan by using the Old Testament as the Word of God, saying, 'It is written.' He maintained that not one jot or tittle would pass from the law until all was accomplished (*Matt.* 5:17) and that the Scriptures cannot be broken (*John* 10:35). In the prayer to his Father on the night before he was crucified, Jesus declared that 'Thy word is truth' (*John* 17:17). He affirmed the historicity of Adam (*Matt.* 19:4), Cain and Abel (*Luke* 11:51), Noah (*Luke* 17:26), Jonah (*Matt.* 12:40), the creation account (*Mark* 10:6-9), and the reality of heaven and hell (*Mark* 9:44-46).

Jesus also used the Word of God as an ultimate standard of authority when he came into conflict with other people. He rebuked men with Scripture; correcting their false concepts, teaching and misinterpretations of Scripture by using scriptural proofs. Matthew 22:23-33, for example, describes how Jesus told the Sadducees that they were greatly mistaken in their denial of the resurrection because they did not know the Scriptures or the power of God. Then he quoted a passage from the book of Genesis as an authoritative declaration from God to correct them. It is highly significant that Christ never appealed to tradition as a standard of authority; instead he used Scripture to correct the errors of tradition.

As Jesus is Lord over the Church, the Church must not only accept his teaching on the Scriptures; it must also adopt the same attitude towards them that he did. His entire life was submitted to the authority of Scripture. In quoting passages from the Old Testament during his conflict with Satan in the wilderness, Christ was applying them to his own life and thereby demonstrating that he was under the authority of Scripture. His victory was accomplished through obedience to the Scriptures, as he used them as the ultimate authority for every area of his life. At another time, speaking of his relationship with his Father, Jesus said, 'I know him and keep his word' (*John* 8:55). From beginning to end, Christ's life and ministry were governed by the authority of Scripture.

As well as testifying to the truth of the Scriptures by submitting himself to their authority, Christ also declared their inspiration as he fulfilled in his life, death and resurrection the Messianic prophecies they contained. Over and over again he said, 'This is being done in order that that which is written might be fulfilled.' Christ's perfect fulfilment of the Old Testament Scriptures can be seen in any cursory examination of some of the more prominent Messianic prophecies:

Genesis 12:3, 21:22, 49:10; Numbers 24:17–19; 2 Samuel 7:12–13; 1 Chronicles 17:11–14—These Scriptures reveal the family lineage of the Messiah. He will be a descendant of Abraham, Isaac and Jacob from the tribe of Judah, the family line of Jesse and a direct descendant of King David.

Micah 5:2—His place of birth will be Bethlehem.

Isaiah 7:14—He will be born of a virgin.

Daniel 9:24–27—The time of his public ministry as the Messiah will be after the Jews' return from the Babylonian captivity and before the destruction of Jerusalem in 70 A.D.

Isaiah 9:6; Psalm 2:1–12—His nature will be both God and man, and he will be the Son of God.

Isaiah 35:5–6—He will perform miracles.

Psalm 41:9; Zechariah 11:11–13—He will be betrayed by a friend for thirty pieces of silver.

Zechariah 9:9—He will enter Jerusalem on the back of a donkey being proclaimed as the Messiah and King.

Isaiah 50:6, 52:14—He will be beaten, scourged and tortured by the Jews.

Isaiah 53:7—He will be silent before his accusers.

Psalm 22:6–8—He will be crucified.

Isaiah 53:8, 12—He will be killed.

Isaiah 53:4–6, 12—He will suffer and die for the sins of the world.

Isaiah 49:6—He will be a source of salvation to the Gentiles.

Isaiah 53:9—He will be buried in a rich man's tomb.

Psalm 16:10—He will be raised from the dead.

The Authority of Scripture

There is only one man in history who was a Jew; a direct descendant of King David; born in Bethlehem before 70 A.D.; claimed to be the Son of God and Messiah; performed miracles; entered Jerusalem on the back of a donkey being proclaimed as King; was betrayed by a friend for thirty pieces of silver; was scourged, beaten, spat upon and tortured by the Jews; was silent in his sufferings; suffered death by crucifixion; reportedly died for the sins of the world; was buried in a rich man's tomb and three days later was reported to be resurrected. His name is Jesus Christ.

The canonical Scriptures whose prophecies are thus fulfilled in Christ are God's inspired revelation to man. This is the testimony of the Bible to itself and the testimony of the Lord Jesus Christ. As such they must be authoritative in all matters of faith.

* * *

Given the authority of the canonical Scriptures, it is essential to ascertain what documents should be included within them. Here, too, there is an important disagreement between the Roman Catholic Church and the Protestant Church, because Rome includes the Apocrypha as part of the Old Testament canon. The term Apocrypha describes a group of fourteen or fifteen documents, written between the second century B.C. and the time of Christ. The Church of Rome has included twelve of these in the canon of the Old Testament. In particular those writings included by Rome are—The Wisdom of Solomon, Ecclesiasticus, Tobit, Judith, I and II Maccabees, Baruch, Letter of Jeremiah, Additions to Esther, Prayer of Azariah, Susanna, and Bel and the Dragon. The Roman Church has to hold on to the notion of the direct inspiration of the Apocrypha because, as we will see later, some of its distinctive doctrines, including the existence of purgatory, hang on particular interpretations of texts found only in the apocryphal books. If it can be shown that these books were not accepted by the early Church as part of the legitimate scriptural canon, then the legitimacy of these distinctive Roman doctrines is destroyed.

The first council in the history of the Western Church which officially defined the limits of the scriptural canon was the Roman Catholic Council of Trent, which met in the mid-sixteenth century after the beginning of the Reformation. It included the apocryphal writings of Baruch, Judith, Tobit, Wisdom, Ecclesiasticus, Bel and the Dragon, an addition to the Book of Esther, and First and Second Maccabees in the canon of Scripture. To support its view, Trent pointed to the North African provincial Councils of Hippo in 393 A.D. and Carthage in 397 A.D. under the leadership of Augustine, in which, it claimed, the 'Church' formally defined the content of the canon including the Apocrypha. However, this ignores the fact that there was an established, recognized canon in the Church long before these fourth-century councils took place. Origen (185-254 A.D.), for instance, stated that 'no one should use for the proof of doctrine books not included among the canonized Scriptures'.[3] Because these councils were geographically provincial, they could not speak for the Church as a whole. In addition, we shall see that the endorsement these councils gave to the Apocrypha was not of the kind that the Roman Catholic Church claims.

It is quite clear that the Hebrew Old Testament canon used by the Jews of Palestine at the time of Christ did not include the Apocrypha. All the evidence points to the fact that this Hebrew canon was comprised of the same thirty-nine books which exist in contemporary Protestant Bibles. Jesus refers to the Scriptures as comprising 'the Law of Moses, the Prophets and the Psalms' (*Luke* 24:44), which was a convenient summation of the traditional list of books and did not include the Apocrypha. Jesus and the New Testament authors *never* quote from the Apocrypha, though they quote prolifically from the vast majority of the Old Testament canonical books.

The first century Jewish historian, Josephus, tells us that the Hebrew canon consisted of twenty-two books and did not include the Apocrypha.[4] The difference between the thirty-nine books in Protestant Bibles and the twenty-two original books can be attributed to the fact that some books which are grouped together in the Hebrew canon were separated later. For example, the twelve minor prophets were originally considered to be one book. Josephus categorically rejects the Apocrypha as being truly inspired. The work of the first century Jew, Philo, seems to support Josephus, because although he wrote extensively on the Old Testament he never quoted from the Apocrypha. Even the Roman Catholic Church affirms the fact that the Jews did not accept the Apocrypha, in that it was not part of the Hebrew canon, and acknowledges that the Protestant Church follows the canon of the Jews. The *New Catholic Encyclopedia* states:

For the Old Testament, however, Protestants follow the Jewish canon; they have only the Old Testament books that are in the Hebrew Bible.[5]

Some scholars have suggested that the Septuagint, the Greek translation of the Hebrew Old Testament, included the Apocrypha as part of the canon and that therefore there were two canons: a Palestinian one which did not include the Apocrypha; and an Alexandrian (Greek) version which did. This argument rests on the fact that the earliest copies we possess of the Septuagint, which were produced by Christians in the fourth century, include the Apocrypha. But it is probable that when the Septuagint came into existence six hundred years earlier it did not include the Apocrypha. We note, for instance, that Athanasius (*c.* 296-373), who was bishop of Alexandria (the city where the Septuagint was produced) did not include the Apocrypha as part of the Old Testament canon. In addition to this, Cyril of Jerusalem, writing in the fourth century, catalogued the Old Testament books which were canonical and which, he said, were translated by the Septuagint translators, and he also did not include the writings of the Apocrypha.[6]

The first list of the books of the Old Testament canon given to us by a Christian writer is from the pen of Melito of Sardis. His list is preserved in the writings of Eusebius, the Church historian.[7] Melito tells us that he went to Palestine to ascertain the exact number of books which comprised the Hebrew canon, and he gives the names of the books and their number as twenty-two—a reaffirmation of the number given by Josephus. Origen[8] also names twenty-two books in his list of the Hebrew canon. Epiphanius,[9] Basil the Great,[10] Gregory of Nazianzen[11] and Hilary of Poitiers[12] all agree with Josephus and Origen, and omit the writings of the Apocrypha.

After listing the twenty-two Old Testament books and the twenty-seven authorized canonical books of the New Testament, Athanasius wrote: 'These are the fountains of salvation, that they who thirst may be satisfied with the living words they contain. In these *alone* is proclaimed the doctrine of godliness.'[13] He explicitly states that the canonical Scriptures alone were used for the determination of doctrine while the books of the Apocrypha held ecclesiastical sanction for reading only and were not considered part of the canon.[14] This distinction is further amplified by Rufinus at the beginning of the fifth century.[15] He is important as a witness to the exact nature of the canon of Scripture for he lived in Rome and wrote his comments on Scripture just a few years after the Councils of Hippo and Carthage under Augustine. He claims that the list he gives is that which the Fathers have handed down to the Church, and that these books alone are used to confirm doctrine and deduce proofs for the faith. He divides the writings circulating in the Church of his day into three broad categories. First, there is the canon of inspired Scripture of the Old and New Testaments which he enumerates. Secondly, there are what he calls 'ecclesiastical' writings which were read in the Church but were not authoritative for the defining of doctrine. He specifically mentions the Old Testament Apocrypha in this category. Then there was a third classification of writings which he designates as 'apocryphal', by which he means heretical writings which were not read in the Church.

Rufinus' view is also confirmed by Jerome. He excluded the Apocrypha from his Latin translations of the Old Testament because he said it was not included in the canon of the Hebrews. He also argued that the writings of the Apocrypha were useful for edification and for reading in the Church but were not authoritative for the establishment or confirmation of doctrine, and confirmed that the Church of his day did not grant canonical status to the writings of the

The Authority of Scripture

Apocrypha as they were not regarded as having been inspired by God. In commenting on the writings known as the Wisdom of Solomon and Ecclesiasticus, Jerome concluded that:

> As, then, the Church reads Judith, Tobit, and the books of Maccabees, but does not admit them among the canonical Scriptures, so let it also read these two volumes for the edification of the people, not to give authority to doctrines of the Church . . . I say this to show you how hard it is to master the book of Daniel, which in Hebrew contains neither the history of Susanna, nor the hymn of the three youths, nor the fables of Bel and the Dragon . . .[16]

Similarly, Gregory the Great affirmed the same view in relation to 1 Maccabees:

> With reference to which particular we are not acting irregularly, if from the books, though not Canonical, yet brought out for the edification of the Church, we bring forward testimony. Thus Eleazar in the battle smote and brought down an elephant, but fell under the very beast that he killed (*1 Macc.* 6.46).[17]

In the Greek Church, the leading Fathers all followed in the footsteps of Athanasius, Epiphanius and Cyril of Jerusalem in rejecting the Apocrypha as part of the canon. For example, Anastasius, the patriarch of Antioch (560 A.D.) and Leontius of Byzantium (580 A.D.) both taught that the Old Testament canon consisted of twenty-two books, as did John of Damascus, writing two centuries later.

Rufinus, Jerome, Anastasius, Leontius, Gregory the Great, and John of Damascus all wrote after the provincial Councils of Carthage and Hippo under Augustine. Therefore, to say that these councils somehow authoritatively established the canon of Scripture is not true. John Cosin, in his work *The Scholastical History of the Canon*, cites fifty-two major ecclesiastical writers from the eighth to the sixteenth centuries who affirmed the view of Jerome. Cardinal Cajetan, the great opponent of Luther in the sixteenth century, in his *Commentary on all the Authentic Historical Books of the Old Testament* which was dedicated to Pope Clement VII, fully supported Jerome's teaching in separating the Apocrypha from the Hebrew canon. Cajetan's analysis helps us to understand the meaning of the word 'canon' as employed by Augustine and the Council of Carthage:

> Here we close our commentaries on the historical books of the Old Testament. For the rest (that is, Judith, Tobit, and the books of Maccabees) are counted by St Jerome out of the canonical books, and are placed amongst the Apocrypha, along with Wisdom and Ecclesiasticus, as is plain from the *Prologus Galeatus*. Nor be thou disturbed, like a raw scholar, if thou shouldest find anywhere, either in the sacred councils or the sacred doctors, these books reckoned as canonical. For the words as well of councils as of doctors are to be reduced to the correction of Jerome. Now, according to his judgment, in the epistle to the bishops Chromatius and Heliodorus, these books (and any other like books in the canon of the Bible) are not canonical, that is, not in the nature of a rule for confirming matters of faith. Yet, they may be called canonical, that is, in the nature of a rule for the edification of the faithful, as being received and authorised in the canon of the Bible for that purpose. By the help of this distinction thou mayest see thy way clearly through that which Augustine says, and what is written in the provincial council of Carthage.[18]

The word 'canon', then, came to have two meanings—one broad and the other narrow. The books that were considered inspired and authoritative for the establishing of doctrine held a proto-canonical status. The apocryphal or ecclesiastical books, on the other hand, while not authoritative in defining doctrine were nonetheless valuable for the purpose of edification and held a secondary or deutero-canonical status. It is in this way that the Church historically has generally understood Augustine and the Council of Carthage.

In his writings Augustine lists the Apocrypha as part of the general canon.[19] However, he also clearly affirms the fact that it was not accepted by the Jews as part of the canon of the Old Testament and it is clear from statements that he makes on other occasions that he held to the broad interpretation of the word 'canon' as described above:

> During the same time also those things were done which are written in the book of Judith, which, indeed, the Jews are said not to have received into the canon of the scriptures . . . And the reckoning of their dates is found, not in the Holy Scriptures which are called canonical, but in others, among which are also the books of the

The Authority of Scripture

Maccabees. These are held as canonical, not by the Jews, but by the Church, on account of the extreme and wonderful sufferings of certain martyrs.[20]

The Jews do not have this Scripture which is called Maccabees, as they do the law and the prophets, to which the Lord bears testimony as to his witnesses. But it is received by the Church not without advantage, if it be read and heard soberly, especially for the sake of the history of the Maccabees, who suffered so much from the hand of persecutors for the sake of the law of God.[21]

Clearly, Augustine believed that the Church held the Apocrypha to be canonical in the broad sense that these writings provided a good example and an inspiration to perseverance in the faith.

The above quotations clearly demonstrate that the Councils of Hippo and Carthage did not establish the canon of the Scriptures, for their decrees on the Old Testament were unsupported by the Church's earlier testimony and were not accepted afterwards. Right down to the time of the Reformation the clear testimony of the authorities in the Church as a whole affirms the view of Jerome, and it prevailed until the Council of Trent. Not until the mid-sixteenth century at Trent did the Roman Catholic Church approve the Apocrypha as part of the Old Testament canon. That such approval did *not* take place at Hippo or Carthage is affirmed in these comments by the *New Catholic Encyclopedia*:

St Jerome distinguished between canonical books and ecclesiastical books. The latter he judged were circulated by the Church as good spiritual reading but were not recognized as authoritative Scripture . . . The situation remained unclear in the ensuing centuries . . . According to Catholic doctrine, the proximate criterion of the biblical canon is the infallible decision of the Church. This decision was not given until rather late in the history of the Church at the Council of Trent . . . The Council of Trent definitively settled the matter of the Old Testament Canon. That this had not been done previously is apparent from the uncertainty that persisted up to the time of Trent.[22]

Here is an authoritative Roman Catholic source affirming the fact that it was not until the sixteenth century that the Roman Catholic Church established the canon of the Old

Testament. The Encyclopedia's use of the word 'uncertainty' relative to the Church's view on the Apocrypha down to the time of the Council of Trent is very misleading however. There was absolutely no doubt or uncertainty about the matter. The Apocrypha was not considered to be part of the Old Testament canon. But at least it is honest enough to give an accurate picture of when the Old Testament canon was truly and authoritatively determined by the Roman Church.

Our analysis has shown that the vast weight of historical evidence falls on the side of excluding the Apocrypha from the category of canonical Scripture. It is interesting to note that the only two Fathers of the early Church who are considered to be true biblical scholars, Jerome and Origen (and who both spent time in the area of Palestine and were therefore familiar with the Hebrew canon), rejected the Apocrypha. And the near unanimous opinion of the Church followed this view. And coupled with this historical evidence is the fact that these writings have serious internal difficulties in that they are characterized by heresies, inconsistencies and historical inaccuracies which invalidate their being given the status of Scripture.

What we have considered is highly significant. The Protestant Church is continually charged with upholding dogmas which first appeared very late in the history of the Church. The Reformers' teaching on *sola scriptura*, the Roman Church claims, was unknown before the sixteenth century. But as the *New Catholic Encyclopedia* itself acknowledges, the truth is that it is the Roman Catholic Church which has introduced dogmas which are very late in the history of the Church, for this ruling on the canon comes in the middle of the sixteenth century! As we have seen, it is a ruling contrary to the testimony of the Jews to the canon of Scripture, to the general patristic witness of the Church and to the overall consensus of the Church right down to the time of the Reformation. What right does any council or individual have to change the canon received by the Jews, to whom according to the New Testament had been committed the very *oracles of God*?

2

Scripture and Tradition

The Greek word for tradition is *paradosis*. The primary meaning of the verb from which it comes is 'to give up' or 'to give over'. In the New Testament the word denotes the idea of teaching which is communicated, given over, either orally or in written form[1] and it is translated 'traditions' in our versions when Paul says, 'So then, brethren, stand firm and hold to the traditions which you were taught, whether by word of mouth or by letter from us' (*2 Thess.* 2:15). In the same epistle he says: 'Now we command you, brethren, in the name of our Lord Jesus Christ, that you keep aloof from every brother who leads an unruly life and not according to the tradition you received from us' (*2 Thess.* 3:6).

The Roman Catholic Church claims that what Paul is referring to here is a body of truth which is independent of Scripture and which was handed down orally in the churches and continued through the succession of bishops. It supposes that Paul's use of the word 'tradition' in his letter to the Thessalonians is an endorsement of the same kind of tradition to which it adheres. Karl Keating, a leading contemporary Roman Catholic apologist, asserts that the oral preaching and teaching of the apostles were somehow independent of Scripture and he draws on Paul's writings to bolster his point: 'Paul illustrated what Tradition is: "The chief message I handed on to you, as it was handed on to me, was that Christ, as the Scriptures foretold, died for our sins . . . That is our preaching, mine or theirs as you will; that is the faith that has come to you" (*1 Cor.* 15:3,11).'[2]

However, the text which Keating quotes undermines his

[15]

whole position. The truths which Paul says he received from Christ and handed on and preached orally were the same as those which could be verified from the Scriptures. His preaching and teaching were simply the declaration and interpretation of the inspired Word of God. In this text, as elsewhere, Paul's concern was to demonstrate that the gospel he preached could be validated by the Old Testament Scriptures.[3]

The truths Paul first communicated to the churches in an oral fashion, especially the content of the gospel, he later committed to writing—and he explicitly warned believers in Colossae to 'beware of philosophy and empty deception, which is according to the traditions of men, the elementary principles of the world, rather than according to Christ' (*Col.* 2:8). Paul's test to expose the teachings of errorists is to see whether they contradict the divine truth of the gospel by adding to the work of Christ and ultimately centring salvation in man rather than in Christ. This is the definitive New Testament model for ascertaining truth. The Bereans, we are told in Acts 17:11, compared Paul's oral message with the Word of God to make certain that it conformed to the inspired Scriptures. Only then would they accept it. If this was done with the teaching and preaching of an apostle, it is even more necessary for the teachings of those who are not apostles. Thus, where any teaching or tradition conforms to Scripture, it is to be received; and where it does not conform to Scripture, it is to be rejected.

This is exactly the attitude that Jesus adopted towards the issue. Tradition, in his view, was never an authority in and of itself but was to be judged by the Word of God, and where it was found wanting, to be rejected. For example, Matthew 15:1-9 recounts how Jesus confronted the Pharisees about their tradition and its relationship to the Scriptures. These religious leaders had become indignant with the disciples of Christ because they seemed to disregard the tradition of the elders. This was a body of teaching which had developed over time from the interpretations of the law given by the leading teachers in Judaism. Eventually this body of teaching developed to the point of being equal in authority with the Word of God, and it was for this reason that the Pharisees drew

Jesus' attention to it. They felt that to disobey the tradition was to disobey God. Instead of acceding to the authority of this tradition, however, Jesus denounced the Pharisees because their observance of it actually violated God's Word. His denunciation can be summed up in the following points:

1. You teach as doctrines the precepts of men. That is, you teach that your interpretations and rules are equal to Scripture.

2. Neglecting the commandment of God you hold to your tradition.

3. You set aside the commandment of God in order to keep your commandment.

4. You invalidate the Word of God by your tradition which you have handed down.

Jesus did not condemn all tradition, only that which had been elevated in authority to a position of equality with the Word of God and which invalidated Scripture. Here is a very important principle: *what Jesus is saying is that tradition is not inspired and therefore not inherently authoritative.* The ultimate standard for determining the rightness or wrongness of any teaching or tradition is the Word of God. According to the incarnate Son of God, any teaching which violates Scripture is utterly condemned by his Father. For when this takes place, as it did with the Pharisees, the teaching of men displaces the Word of God, and the authority of men displaces the authority of God. Thus, according to Christ, Scripture is the final arbiter in all matters of faith and practice, since Scripture is the judge of tradition.

A large portion of the Sermon on the Mount is a correction by Jesus of some of the fundamentally false teachings and misinterpretations of Scripture that made up the Jewish tradition. Repeatedly, he said to his hearers: 'You have heard it said, but I say to you'; or, 'You have heard that the ancients were told, but I say to you.' He was rebuking the Jewish leadership for upholding their traditional interpretations of

Scripture which invalidated or contradicted the Word of God. This is always the danger with tradition. It can distort, pervert and annul the Scriptures through misinterpretation and misapplication. Jesus used Scripture to correct those traditions and teachings which had become corrupted, and he set us the example of how we are to judge them. To be acceptable to God, both tradition and the teachings which undergird it must at all times conform and be subordinate to his inspired Word. Thus we see that the principle of *sola scriptura* is a biblical teaching and principle.

This is why the apostles were so careful to guard the truths of the 'good news' of the salvation available to men through faith in Jesus Christ and to attack any incidence of false teaching within the early Church. They preached a message which had a very specific content and which they had received from the Lord Jesus Christ. Any teaching which contradicted that of Jesus was anathematized by the apostles, as we can see in their writings which were recognized by the early Church as the Word of God. For instance, in his letter to the Galatian churches Paul lamented the fact that the believers there 'are so quickly deserting Him who called you by the grace of Christ, for a different gospel; which is really not another; only there are some who are disturbing you, and want to distort the gospel of Christ. But even though we, or an angel from heaven, should preach to you a gospel contrary to that which we have preached to you, let him be accursed. As we have said before, so I say again now, if any man is preaching to you a gospel contrary to that which you received, let him be accursed' (*Gal.* 1:6-9).

Paul wrote to oppose the teachings of certain men who had come to these churches claiming that the gospel the apostle preached to them was deficient and that they had the true gospel. But Paul attacked their teachings as a distortion or perversion of the gospel because they contradicted the truth as God had given it through his own Son. What this demonstrates is that the gospel in Paul's time was a completed message which would not be subject to 'development' over time, in the sense that there could be dogmas added to the truth of the faith which were not clearly taught by the apostles. It was a body of truth whose contents were defended by the apostles and which were preserved in the New Testament epistles. This truth is reiterated in Jude 3 where we read that we are to contend for 'the faith once for all delivered to the saints'. The Church of Rome, of course, partly defends its tradition under the notion of the 'development of doctrine'. That is, that the apostles left truth in germ in the Scriptures which took centuries to develop fully. Teachings, implicitly recorded in Scripture, are slowly over time more fully revealed by the Spirit of God as he gives deeper understanding. This is a clever theory. No-one denies that there can be a development in understanding the deep truths of Scripture over time, but the theory now under consideration cannot legitimize Roman Catholic tradition for it fails in two very important tests—the test of Scripture and the test of history. If any doctrine is claimed as a true development it must be consistent with the truth of Scripture (its alleged source) and it should be supported by the testimony of the Church to the manner in which it has been increasingly understood in the course of history. But as we will see, the tradition of Roman Catholicism, in much of its teaching, is not a fuller development of the truth of the Word of God but a direct contradiction of it. And further, instead of there being a consistent development in understanding, there is much in the tradition which contradicts the express teaching of the Fathers of the early Church. The tragic result of the development of this tradition is that the Roman Catholic Church has embraced and is responsible for promoting teachings which are a departure from the truth of the gospel so clearly revealed in the Word of God.

What was this gospel proclaimed orally by the Lord and the apostles and handed down as a body of doctrine to the Church? It is fully revealed in the New Testament. Paul's argument in his second letter to Timothy, as it is to us, is that the message of the gospel is clear and complete—it does not need to be *supplemented* by tradition. What Christ has done as Saviour is to fulfil the demands of the law of God on our behalf. As God's creation we are all required to obey his law perfectly. If we transgress his law in any way we commit sin, incur guilt before him and come under the judgment and condemnation of the law. Since the law reveals to us that we are all sinners by nature and by practice, we will all be eternally condemned unless God saves us. Man cannot save himself because God demands perfect obedience, and the penalty of death if we sin. Our only hope is in Christ, because Jesus kept the law perfectly for us in living as a man and then going to the cross to bear our sins. He suffered the condemnation our sins deserved by dying our death; he bore the wrath of God for us on the cross and made a perfect atonement. Then he was raised from the grave and ascended to heaven to be the living Saviour and Lord to all who come to him by repentance and faith. To them he will impute his own perfect righteousness, the merits of his death, and give eternal life and the forgiveness of sins. It is a complete and 'great salvation'.

What does it mean to come to Christ by repentance and faith? It means that an individual realizes that the work Christ has done is perfect and that no human work can be added to it for our acceptance with God. There must be a forsaking of all human merit and a turning to Christ alone as the source of salvation. The Scriptures constantly tell us that salvation is not by works.[4] In fact, human attempts to *earn* salvation actually pervert the gospel.[5] The attempt to add man's works to the work of Christ was precisely the teaching that Paul's letter to the Galatians condemned in such forceful terms. The new teachers claimed that Christ's work was not sufficient, and they were attempting to add their merit to the merit of Jesus. This is a false gospel, Paul warned the Galatians: men are saved by forsaking themselves and coming in repentant faith to Christ as Lord and Saviour. There is a turning from the world, sin and self, and a submission to him as Lord; and there is a rejection of all trust in human merit to accept him as Saviour and receive the free gift of his righteousness. Salvation is a gift. Believers are reckoned righteous—'justified'—on account of Christ alone.

But the justification which belongs to believers in Christ will always produce a life of sanctification or good works. Though salvation is not earned by human merit, a truly saved person will pursue a holy life. This is the main point which James deals with in his epistle. James appears to contradict texts we have quoted when he states that 'faith, if it has no works, is dead, being by itself . . . You see that a man is justified by works, and not by faith alone' (*James* 2:17, 24). This apparent contradiction is cleared up when we realize that Paul and James are dealing with two different aspects of salvation. Paul is dealing with the nature of justification, while James is dealing with the nature of the faith which belongs to the justified. James is not writing to people such as those at Galatia, who were trying to set up a different gospel by adding to faith in Christ's atoning work, but to those influenced by a different kind of false teaching—that the faith which justifies does not necessarily result in changes in a person's moral life. He therefore distinguishes between dead, false faith and living, true faith and he shows that authentic faith is seen in good works. In other words, if a man says that he is justified by the grace of God, that grace will be evidenced in his life. A life of holiness naturally flows from a justified life. Where this is not evident, James says, the faith is empty and useless.

Paul actually teaches the same thing as James. He constantly emphasizes that salvation results in radical changes in the moral life of an individual and where these changes are not observed, that person has never entered the kingdom of God.[6] In Ephesians 2:8-9, Paul makes it absolutely clear that salvation is not by works and then in verse 10 he says, 'For we are His workmanship, created in Christ Jesus for good works, which God prepared beforehand, that we should walk in them.' The result of regeneration and salvation through union with Christ is always a life of good works. Justification is by faith alone apart from works. But the faith that justifies always *works*.

3

Tradition and Roman Catholicism

As we have seen, the Roman Catholic Church teaches that there are two sources of divine revelation, the Scriptures and the oral tradition. The latter it alleges can be traced back to the apostles through the succession of the bishops of Rome. It does not simply claim the illumination of the Holy Spirit for its historic teaching, but inspiration on a level equal to that of the Old and New Testaments. As we examine this claim more closely, we will focus on the two issues which lie at the heart of the matter. In this chapter we will explore whether it can it be shown historically that the general claims the Roman Catholic Church makes for tradition are valid; then, in the remaining chapters, we will examine the more important question of whether the teachings of the Church's tradition conform to or contradict the teaching of Scripture. This is, after all, the test Jesus gave us to be applied to any tradition to ascertain its validity. This is the test he applied to the Church of his own day and it is the test the Bereans applied to the teaching of Paul, who was an apostle.

* * *

One of the vital elements in the claims of the Roman Catholics for their tradition is that its basic teachings have been handed down from the apostles without distortion or corruption. Yet when we investigate the historicity even of the concept of tradition itself, we find that there has been tremendous change through the centuries. To the early

[22]

Tradition and Roman Catholicism

Fathers, the Scriptures were the only source of revelation and the ultimate standard of authority or rule of faith. Tradition was viewed primarily as the oral presentation of scriptural truth, or the codifying of biblical truth into creedal expression. But at every point the foundation for that tradition was Scripture, and not a separate revelation via oral tradition.

From the first writings of the Apostolic Fathers onwards we find the Old and New Testaments quoted extensively and appealed to as the authoritative standard of divine revelation. As J. N. D. Kelly has pointed out:

> The clearest token of the prestige enjoyed by the latter [Scripture] is the fact that almost the entire theological effort of the Fathers, whether their aims were polemical or constructive, was expended upon what amounted to the exposition of the Bible. Further, it was everywhere taken for granted that, for any doctrine to win acceptance, it had first to establish its scriptural basis.[1]

While all of the Fathers constantly referred to Scripture, some of them, in particular the second- and third-century apologists Irenaeus and Tertullian, also appealed to an apostolic tradition handed down to the churches. But we need to understand clearly what these Fathers meant when they used the term. In the early history of the Church, the word 'tradition' came to embody three major categories in its meaning:

> It first of all meant the rule of faith, or apostolic doctrine handed down from the apostles.

> Secondly, it referred to ecclesiastical customs or practices which had a long history of use in the Church.

> Thirdly, it embodied the consensus of patristic interpretation.

We will examine each of these briefly:

1. In the references which Irenaeus and Tertullian make to the oral tradition or rule of faith, they leave us in no doubt as to the exact nature of what they mean by tradition and its

relationship to Scripture. Irenaeus, for example, says:

> We have learned from none others the plan of our salvation, than from those through whom the gospel has come down to us, which they did at one time proclaim in public, and, at a later period, by the will of God, handed down to us in the Scriptures, to be the ground and pillar of our faith ...[2]

Irenaeus here states that what had been originally proclaimed and taught orally by the apostles was at a later time, by the will of God, handed down to them—not orally—but in the Scriptures. How did he know what the apostles had preached orally? He has a record of it in the written Scriptures. And Irenaeus makes it clear, as does Tertullian, that there was no truth left dependent upon oral transmission. The entirety of the message of the faith was committed to writing by the apostles. Now, in order to understand why Irenaeus is writing the treatise from which we have quoted, and speaking on the subject of oral tradition and Scripture in the way that he does, we need to understand the circumstance with which he was faced. His use of the word tradition has a very specific content and context, and unless we understand that content and context we will misinterpret what he means.

Irenaeus wrote *Against Heresies* to counter the heretical teachings of the Gnostics. These were men who did not dispute the authority of Scripture but they supplemented its message with another. They claimed to have access to an oral tradition, independent of Scripture, handed down by the apostles, of which they alone were the recipients. In this way they sought to blunt the *ultimate* and *final* authority of Scripture by saying that not everything the apostles had taught was in Scripture. The gnostics professed to possess additional revelation which had been handed down to them orally from the apostles. Irenaeus maintained, on the contrary, that what the apostles had at one time proclaimed orally they then committed to writing and handed down in the Scriptures, which thus became the authoritative standard of truth to which all teachings must conform. They are 'the ground and pillar of our faith'. A secret oral tradition independent of Scripture, and which does not conform to the teaching of Scripture, is therefore, in his view, a gnostic heresy. To Irenaeus, tradition is simply another term for the oral proclamation of the truth of Scripture in preaching, teaching or creedal statements. It is not an independent source of revelation but a verbal presentation of the one authoritative revelation of God—the Holy Scriptures. Tradition is equal to the apostolic doctrine which is equal to the Scriptures. In other words, the foundation of tradition is always the Word of God.[3]

Irenaeus and Tertullian also define in their writings in explicit terms the *content* of the apostolic tradition which had been handed down to them.[4] What their writings show is simply a summation of the major teachings of the Old and New Testaments. And what we shall find as we compare the distinctive teachings of Roman Catholicism to what these early Fathers define as apostolic tradition is that the Roman Catholic Church has added to the rule of faith teachings which were not part of the teaching of the early Church.

The *concept* of tradition promoted by the Roman Catholic Church is not that of the early Church for the Church of Rome has embraced the very concept promoted by the gnostics and rejected by the Fathers as heresy. The early Fathers knew nothing of an oral tradition independent of Scripture as a source of revelation, and which was equally as authoritative as Scripture. For them, Scripture was the ultimate and final authority. This is affirmed by the writings of the Fathers themselves. Augustine, for example, writes:

What more shall I teach you than what we read in the apostle? For Holy Scripture fixes the rule for our doctrine, lest we dare be wiser than we ought. Therefore I should not teach you anything else except to expound to you the words of the Teacher.[5]

It [the city of God] believes also the Holy Scriptures, old and new which we call canonical, and which are the source of the faith by which the just lives and by which we walk without doubting whilst we are absent from the Lord.[6]

From among the things that are plainly laid down in Scripture are to be found all matters that concern faith and the manner of life.[7]

I am not bound by the authority of this epistle because I do not hold the writings of Cyprian as canonical, and I accept whatever in them agrees with the authority of the divine Scriptures with his approval, but what does not agree I reject with his permission.[8]

This position is echoed in the writings of Cyril of Jerusalem (fourth century). He states that all that he teaches must be verified by Scripture and nothing is to be accepted without it:

... concerning the divine and sacred Mysteries of the Faith, we ought not to deliver even the most casual remark without the Holy Scriptures: nor be drawn aside by mere probabilities and the artifices of argument. Do not then believe me because I tell thee these things, unless thou receive from the Holy Scriptures the proof of what is set forth: for this salvation, which is of our faith, is not by ingenious reasonings, but by proof from the Holy Scriptures.[9]

There could be no clearer statement of the principle of *sola scriptura* than these statements. Cyril says that he is handing on to these initiates in the faith the tradition which had been faithfully handed down from the apostles and he *explicitly* states that this tradition or teaching, in every aspect, was contained in and could be verified from Scripture. He does not say one word about an oral tradition independent of Scripture. In fact, it is clear from his statements that there was no oral tradition. His statements are particularly significant for he was responsible for instructing catechumens in the basics of the faith and his *Catechetical Lectures* from which the above quotes are taken were written for that purpose. He was a bishop of one of the most important and prestigious sees in the early Church and from a Roman Catholic perspective part of the infallible-teaching *magisterium* (teaching authority). And Cyril is simply representative of the teaching of the Fathers as a whole.

The concept of tradition as being oral in nature and a separate source of revelation independent of Scripture was clearly not the view of the early Church nor that of the Church for centuries after the patristic age. To as late as the fourteenth century the Church viewed the Scriptures as the only source of revelation and the ultimate authority in all matters related to faith and morals. But late in the Middle Ages the concept of oral tradition being itself a source of revelation developed.[10] This was adopted by the Council of Trent in the sixteenth century as the authoritative position of the Roman Catholic Church. According to this new belief, the Church's interpretation of Scripture is equally as authoritative as Scripture, so there are two sources of revelation, the Holy Scriptures and oral tradition.[11] In contrast with the patristic and early medieval churches, Trent committed the Church of Rome to the teaching that Scripture is not the final rule of faith. Scripture and tradition are considered to be equally inspired.

But someone may object, Did not the Fathers refer to unwritten tradition which was separate from Scripture in authority? And the answer is yes. For example, Tertullian states:

> For wherever it shall be manifest that the true Christian rule and faith shall be, there will likewise be the true Scriptures and expositions thereof, and all the Christian traditions.[12]

But many misunderstand the language of the Fathers at this point for such appeals were not a reference to doctrine or dogmas of the faith but to ecclesiastical customs and practices which had a long history of use in the Church. All appeals in the Fathers to unwritten tradition are of this nature. They *never* refer to the essentials of the faith. And this brings us to a consideration of our next major category of tradition—ecclesiastical customs.

2. The seeds of the Roman doctrine on tradition can be traced back to Basil the Great's fourth-century work, *On the Holy Spirit*, in which Basil formulated a novel concept of tradition.[13] He propounded the view that the Church had received both unwritten as well as written traditions from the apostles and that these oral traditions were equally as binding on Christians as those which were written in Scripture. But what he is referring to in his reference to oral apostolic traditions are ecclesiastical customs and if we study Basil's work carefully we can see that the later application of the Church of his teaching about oral tradition as being a second source of revelation was a distortion of his true intention.

In his treatise *On the Holy Spirit,* Basil explicitly promotes the idea that the tradition includes practices in the Church which are not recorded in Scripture, but are nonetheless apostolic in origin and therefore apostolic in authority since they were orally handed down. But he is very careful to make a distinction between apostolic doctrine (or the rule of faith), which *is* recorded in Scripture, and common practices which have been in use in the Church for centuries. These include customs such as looking to the east in prayer, standing in prayer on the first day of the week, and trine immersion in baptism (separate immersions for the Father, Son and Holy Spirit). Though he affirms the authority of these unwritten traditions he also maintains that all customs and teachings in the Church must be validated by the authority of Scripture, by which he means that it must be shown that these customs in no way contradict Scripture:

It remains for me to trace the origin of the word 'with', to explain what force it has, and to shew that it is in harmony with Scripture.[14] Therefore let God-inspired Scripture decide between us; and on whichever side be found doctrines in harmony with the Word of God, in favour of that side will be cast the vote of truth.[15]

For Basil, as for the Fathers of the early Church, Scripture was the final authority

3. As time went on, tradition began to take on an added dimension. Because of the various heresies with which the Church had to contend and the diversity of meaning that could be attributed to Scripture depending upon the method of interpretation employed, tradition was turned into a source of authoritative interpretation. From the middle of the fifth century we begin to see the emergence of a body of recognized Church Fathers as interpreters of Scripture, whose interpretations would eventually be accorded the status of authoritative 'tradition'. The basis of final authority was still the Word of God and tradition was still subordinate to it, but the authority of the Scriptures became identified with their (supposedly correct) interpretation. Vincent of Lérins was one of the first to propound this principle of tradition which embraced the concept of an authoritative

Tradition and Roman Catholicism

consensus of interpretation and became known as *the universal consent of the Fathers*:

> Whether I or any one else should wish to detect the frauds and avoid the snares of heretics as they rise, and to continue sound and complete in the Catholic faith, we must, the Lord helping, fortify our own belief in two ways: first, by the authority of the Divine Law, and then, by the tradition of the Catholic Church.
>
> But here some one perhaps will ask, Since the canon of Scripture is complete, and sufficient of itself for everything, what need is there to join with it the authority of the Church's interpretation? For this reason—because, owing to the depth of Holy Scripture, all do not accept it in one and the same sense, but one understands its words in one way, another in another; so that it seems to be capable of as many interpretations as there are interpreters ... Moreover, in the Catholic Church itself, all possible care must be taken, that we hold that faith which has been believed everywhere, always, by all. For that is truly and in the strict sense Catholic, which, as the name itself and the reason of the thing declare, comprehends all universally. This rule we shall observe if we follow universality, antiquity, consent. We shall follow universality if we confess that one faith to be true, which the whole Church throughout the world confesses; antiquity, if we in no wise depart from those interpretations which it is manifest were notoriously held by our holy ancestors and Fathers; consent, in like manner, if in antiquity itself we adhere to the consentient definitions and determinations of all, or at the least of almost all priests and doctors.[16]

It is important to note how Vincent defines the term tradition. It is not a body of doctrine handed down orally from the apostles independent of Scripture, but is the Church's *interpretation* of Scripture. Vincent emphasizes the importance of universality, antiquity and consent in the Church's tradition. He is, in effect, reiterating a concept which was implicitly taught by Irenaeus[17] and he formulates it into a working principle. He is saying that the true test for determining whether or not a teaching is truly apostolic and Catholic is to subject it to the test of the unanimous consent of the Fathers. Can a particular teaching claim universality, antiquity and consent? If it cannot, this means that it is novel and is to be rejected.

This concept of universal consent is a principle which took

root in the Church and influenced all the theological debates which followed throughout the ensuing centuries and was, many centuries later, officially adopted by the Roman Catholic Church at the Council of Trent:

> Furthermore, to check unbridled spirits, it decrees that no one relying on his own judgment shall, in matters of faith and morals pertaining to the edification of Christian doctrine, distorting the Holy Scriptures in accordance with his own conceptions, presume to interpret them contrary to that sense which holy mother Church, to whom it belongs to judge of their true sense and interpretation, has held and holds, or even contrary to the unanimous consent of the Fathers, even though such interpretations should never at any time be published.[18]

A little over three hundred years later, Rome reaffirmed these decrees at the First Vatican Council in 1869-70 in almost identical terms:

> And as the things which the holy Synod of Trent decreed for the good of souls concerning the interpretation of Divine Scripture, in order to curb rebellious spirits, have been wrongly explained by some, we, renewing the said decree, declare this to be their sense, that, in matters of faith and morals, appertaining to the building up of Christian doctrine, that is to be held as the true sense of Holy Scripture which our holy Mother Church hath held and holds, to whom it belongs to judge of the true sense and interpretation of the Holy Scripture; and therefore that it is permitted to no one to interpret the Sacred Scripture contrary to this sense, nor, likewise, contrary to the unanimous consent of the Fathers.[19]

Two major things were affirmed in these decrees. First, that the Roman Catholic Church alone has the authority to interpret Scripture correctly. And secondly, that no one, the Church included, is to hold an interpretation of Scripture which is contrary to the unanimous consent of the Fathers. Thus, the Roman Catholic Church has officially committed and bound itself, through two ecumenical Roman Councils, to the principle of unanimous consent relative to its teachings and to its interpretation of Scripture. This is an authoritative test by which the Roman Church itself can be judged.

Tradition and Roman Catholicism

This is a real problem for the Church of Rome for what becomes evident, as one applies the test of unanimous consent to the specific teachings of Roman tradition, is that *this 'unanimous consent of the Fathers' on which the Roman Catholic Church's authority rests is a complete illusion, because such a consent is historically non-existent.* The very test by which the Church of Rome says that its teachings can be validated undermines the authority of its tradition for none of the distinctive teachings which embody the content of the tradition can be upheld by the unanimous consent of the Fathers. Unanimous consent on the major doctrines of the Christian creed does exist. But unanimous consent for the teachings of the Roman Catholic tradition does *not* exist.

Even Roman Catholic writers such as Boniface Ramsey have been forced to admit that, historically, this is true:

> Sometimes, then, the Fathers speak and write in a way that would eventually be seen as unorthodox. But this is not the only difficulty with respect to the criterion of orthodoxy. The other great one is that we look in vain in many of the Fathers for references to things that many Christians might believe in today. We do not find, for instance, some teachings on Mary or on the papacy that were developed in medieval and modern times.[20]

As this chapter has shown, the Church cannot even claim unanimous consent from the early Fathers onwards for its current teaching on the nature of tradition itself, much less for a comprehensive body of doctrine with the exception of the broad biblical doctrines such as the existence of one God; the inspiration of Scripture; the recognition of Jesus Christ as Saviour and Lord; and baptism.

In summarising our study thus far of Scripture and tradition, we have seen that there are two tests by which we can legitimately judge the tradition of the Roman Catholic Church. The test of history—of unanimous consent—and the test given by Jesus—the test of Scripture. Does the teaching conform to or invalidate Scripture? In applying these tests to the Roman Catholic tradition what do we conclude?

As to the test of history, any objective historical analysis must come to the following conclusions regarding the teaching of the early Church on tradition:

First: there is no such thing as an oral tradition which has been handed down from the apostles in an unbroken succession which is independent of Scripture in content and equal in authority to the Word of God. We therefore conclude, that based on the meaning of tradition employed by the early Church, the early Church did indeed explicitly treat and adhere to the principle of *sola scriptura*. Not only is this Protestant teaching biblical, but contrary to Roman Catholic assertions, it is historical. It is the Roman Catholic Church's teaching on tradition which is both unbiblical and unhistorical.

The conclusion has to be that the Roman Catholic Church has promoted and embraced a concept of tradition which undermines the biblical teaching of *sola scriptura* by dogmatically asserting that its tradition is a source of revelation.

Second: there is no such thing as the unanimous consent of the Fathers regarding the content of the teaching of the Roman Church's tradition. In the content of its tradition, the Roman Catholic Church has added to the original deposit of the faith and has introduced teachings which it says are necessary for salvation but which were non-existent in the early Church.

As to the test of Scripture we will find that the distinctive teachings of the Roman Catholic tradition are not only teachings which in many cases cannot be found in Scripture but are actually contradictory to it. We have already seen this in regard to the teaching of the Roman Church on the nature of tradition itself. Roman Catholic belief undermines Scripture's own teaching on its sufficiency and finality. The Roman Catholic Church is open to the same charge brought by Jesus against the Jews of his day relative to their tradition. It adheres to traditions which invalidate the Word of God.

Both in the *concept* and in the *content* of tradition, the Roman Catholic Church has departed from the teaching of the early Church, with the result that it has departed from the *practice* of the early Church regarding the authority of Scripture. The Roman Catholic Church has repudiated the principle of *sola scriptura* in order to elevate its tradition to a position of authority equal to the Scriptures. In so doing it has embraced the heresy of Gnosticism condemned by Irenaeus and Tertullian as well as that of the Jews which was condemned by Jesus.

Unless we also would deny Scripture, we must affirm that the Roman Catholic Church in its teaching on tradition is no longer truly Catholic, it is *Roman*. This will become more and more evident as we examine the specific teachings which make up the content of that tradition.

4

The Papacy and the 'Rock' of Matthew 16

Having looked at the subject of Roman Catholic tradition in a general sense, we now turn to specific areas of teaching which make up the content of that tradition. This is important because, as we have already noted, the ultimate issue at stake in the debate concerning Scripture and tradition is that of authority. The Roman Catholic Church claims to be sanctioned with an ultimate ruling and infallible teaching authority over the entire Church of Jesus Christ through the unbroken succession of popes and bishops from Peter. Vatican I, which met in 1869-1870, essentially set out the following propositions on the right of papal rule and infallibility:[1]

1. Christ gave Peter the primacy of jurisdiction over the entire Church as well as the entire world.
2. Inherent in the primacy of jurisdiction is also an infallible teaching authority over the entire Church.
3. This right of jurisdiction is passed down to Peter's successors, the bishops of Rome, for all time.
4. When speaking *ex cathedra*, that is, when speaking in his official capacity as pope, and defining a doctrine on a matter of faith or morals, the Roman pontiff teaches infallibly.
5. The Roman pontiff has absolute authority in himself; possesses authority over all councils; his judgment cannot be questioned; he, himself, can be judged by no human tribunal.

6. The Roman Church has ever remained free from all blemish of error and the doctrines of the Catholic faith have always been kept undefiled by her.

7. If any questions of faith arise within the Church universal they must be defined by the judgment of the Roman pontiff.

8. It has at all times in the history of the Church been necessary that every Church throughout the world should agree with the Roman Church.

9. These teachings have always been held by the entire Church through all ages and can be validated by the Scriptures, the canons of general councils and the unanimous consent of the Fathers.

10. It is necessary for salvation that everyone who professes to be a Christian must be submitted to the authority of the Roman pontiff in all areas of faith, morals and discipline, and if anyone disagrees with these teachings of Vatican I they are anathematized.

This is the cornerstone of the doctrine of the Roman Catholic Church's tradition. According to Vatican I, papal rule and infallibility rest on two foundations: the Scriptures and the facts of history. In this and the next chapter we want to analyze the scriptural and historical claims for these papal teachings.

The scriptural foundation is Rome's exegesis of Matthew 16:18-19, John 21:15-17 and Luke 22:32. Our examination of these crucial issues must therefore begin with Jesus' words to Peter in these passages. In this chapter we will see how Roman Catholic theologians have interpreted them and consider whether they can be interpreted in a different and more accurate way, and how the early Church and the Church Fathers interpreted them. Does their interpretation support the Roman Catholic claim for papal authority and infallibility? We take first the words of Christ in Matthew 16:18-19:

And I also say to you that you are Peter, and upon this rock I will build My church; and the gates of Hades shall not overpower it. I will give you the keys of the kingdom of heaven; and whatever you bind on earth shall be bound in heaven, and whatever you shall loose on earth shall be loosed in heaven.

As is well-known, 'this rock' is interpreted by Rome to mean the person of Peter himself. The exegesis is that Christ changes the apostle's name from Simon to Peter, and then tells Peter that he is going to build his Church on him personally. That this is the meaning Christ intends is placed beyond all doubt, it is claimed, by his words which immediately follow. He promises to give to Peter the keys of the kingdom of heaven with authority to bind and loose. Roman Catholic apologists point out that since keys represent authority in Scripture, Peter is given supreme authority over the entire Church and this is passed on to the Roman bishops who are his successors. But it is not only authority over the Church which is handed down. Rome teaches that the gift of infallibility is *implied* in Christ's promise that the gates of Hades will not prevail against the Church, and that the promises of Christ to be with the Church by his Spirit (*Matt.* 28:20, *John* 14:16-17, 26) and Christ's words to Peter in John 21 and Luke 22 likewise presuppose infallibility.

The Protestant Church, on the other hand, generally asserts that this exegesis is incorrect. It maintains that when Christ states he will build his Church on a rock, he is not referring to Peter personally but to Peter's confession that Christ is the Son of God, and therefore to Jesus as the rock. This point of view is validated by a number of lines of reasoning without having to repeat the worn-out arguments on the differences between the Greek terms *petros* and *petra* in Matthew 16. In particular, these supporting evidences are Peter's own interpretation of the rock of the Church; the larger contextual meaning of the word rock as it is used in both the Old and New Testaments; the contextual interpretation of the entire Matthew 16 passage, beginning with verse 13 and going through verse 19; and finally the overall patristic interpretation of Matthew 16. We will look at each of these evidences in turn. If there is one person who should have known what Christ meant by the words he spoke as recorded in Matthew 16:18 it was Peter himself. Did Peter

The Papacy and the 'Rock' of Matthew 16

consider himself to be the first pope and the rock on which the Church would be built? Peter himself gives us the answer in 1 Peter 2:4-8, where he says:

And coming to Him as to a living stone, rejected by men, but choice and precious in the sight of God, you also, as living stones, are being built up as a spiritual house for a holy priesthood, to offer up spiritual sacrifices acceptable to God through Jesus Christ. For this is contained in Scripture: 'Behold I lay in Zion a choice stone, a precious corner stone, and he who believes in Him shall not be disappointed.' This precious value, then, is for you who believe. But for those who disbelieve, 'The stone which the builders rejected, this became the very corner stone,' and 'A stone of stumbling and a rock of offence.'

The precious stone and cornerstone, the rock upon which the Church will be built, according to Peter, is not himself, but the Lord Jesus Christ. Nor does Peter view himself as being vested with authority over the other apostles. In 1 Peter 5:1-4 he states:

Therefore, I exhort the elders among you, as your fellow elder and witness of the sufferings of Christ, and a partaker also of the glory that is to be revealed, shepherd the flock of God among you, exercising oversight not under compulsion, but voluntarily, according to the will of God; and not for sordid gain, but with eagerness; nor yet as lording it over those allotted to your charge, but proving to be examples to the flock. And when the Chief Shepherd appears, you will receive the unfading crown of glory.

Peter refers to himself simply as a fellow elder with the other elders of the Church, all of whom are under the ultimate authority of the Chief Shepherd, the Lord Jesus Christ. Peter does not think of himself as the vicar of Christ or the visible head of the Church. He is an apostle among other apostles of equal standing and a fellow elder with other elders. There is only one head and one ruler of the Church and that is Jesus Christ. This exegesis of the rock as being Christ who is the foundation of the Church as the One upon whom the Church would be built finds support from both the Old and New Testaments. In the Old Testament we find the Lord himself described as the rock, the one sure foundation of security and salvation. For example:

Psa. 62:5–6: My soul, wait in silence for God only, For my hope is from Him. He only is my rock and my salvation, My stronghold; I shall not be shaken.

Psa. 18:1–2: I love Thee, O LORD, my strength. The LORD is my rock and my fortress and my deliverer, My God, my rock, in whom I take refuge.

Psa. 89:26: He will cry to Me, 'Thou art my Father, My God, and the rock of my salvation.'

Over and over again in the Old Testament it is God himself who is referred to as the rock—as *the* one and only source and foundation and refuge for salvation and deliverance.

In the familiar prophecy in Daniel 2:31-44 we read of the stone which strikes the kingdoms of the world and then itself stands for ever. The Jews saw the stone as the person of the Messiah. Obviously it represents that which is divine for it is described as a stone 'cut out without hands'.

The word 'foundation' is another important word, parallel with the word rock, and it is also used in reference to the person of the Lord himself. In the Old Testament, the word in a literal sense refers to the foundation upon which a building rests. For example in Ezra 3:10 it says, 'Now when the builders had laid the foundation of the temple of the Lord the priests stood in their apparel with trumpets . . . to praise the Lord.' This word is important for it is used in a key passage in the Old Testament that is appropriated by the New Testament apostles as speaking of the Lord Jesus Christ. In Isaiah 28:16 we read:

Therefore thus says the Lord God, 'Behold, I am laying in Zion, a stone, a tested stone, a costly cornerstone for the foundation, firmly placed. He who believes in it will not be disturbed.'

Notice the threefold description here. The stone or rock is not only a cornerstone, but a foundation. And this is the very passage which we have seen Peter use with reference to the Lord Jesus Christ. Peter also, along with Paul, applies to Christ the descriptions of the Messiah in Isaiah 8:13 and Psalm 118:22 as the rejected stone, the stone of stumbling and rock of offence. In Acts 4:11-12 he says:

> He is the stone which was rejected by you, the builders, but which became the very cornerstone. And there is salvation in no-one else, for there is no other name under heaven that has been given among men, by which we must be saved.

So here we see the terms stone and cornerstone being identified with the salvation which is in Jesus Christ alone. Paul re-emphasizes this in three other passages. In Ephesians 2:20 he states that the Church is built upon the foundation of Christ as the cornerstone, and in 1 Corinthians 10:4 he states specifically that the rock is Christ. In 1 Corinthians 3:11 he says, 'For no man can lay a foundation other than the one which is laid—which is Jesus Christ.'

To whom then do the Scriptures, both Old Testament and New Testament, consistently point as the rock, the stone, the cornerstone and the foundation upon which the Church would be built? Jesus Christ the Lord, the Son of the living God, he alone is the rock of our salvation.

These facts then give the broader context in which to interpret Christ's words to Peter in Matthew 16. Peter does not refer to himself as the rock, but to Christ, and the broader context of the scriptural teaching on the rock justifies our interpreting the rock of Matthew 16 as referring to the person of the Lord Jesus Christ as opposed to Peter. But, in addition to this, there are other considerations in Matthew 16 which do not support the Roman Catholic interpretation. There is absolutely nothing in this passage which speaks of successors to Peter and the passing on of his personal prerogatives to them. The keys, rather than signifying the establishment of the institution of the papacy and supreme authority to rule the Church and the world, are representative of the authority to exercise discipline in the Church and to proclaim the gospel, declaring the free forgiveness of sins in the Lord Jesus Christ. Such a declaration opens the kingdom of God to men or, if they reject the message, closes it to them. The keys are not the possession of a single individual, for exactly the same authority which Christ promises to Peter he also grants to the other apostles in Matthew 18:18 and John 20:22-23. They are all given authority to bind or loose by declaring the forgiveness of sins through Christ. They are all equals under the authority of one head, the Lord Jesus. The authority they are given is a delegated, declarative authority, which is in Christ's name and comes from him who alone possesses the supreme authority to rule the Church.

To justify such an interpretation, we must make a careful investigation of Matthew 16:13-19 and the passages related to it. Jesus tells his disciples that he will build his Church and that the gates of Hades will not prevail against it. He reveals that there are two kingdoms on this earth: the kingdom of God or of heaven, and all who are part of the true Church are part of this kingdom; and the kingdom of Satan as represented by the gates of Hades. The two are obviously in conflict with one another. Gates are defensive, enclosing Satan and the men and women whom he would lead to eternal destruction. When Jesus says that he will build his Church, he is saying that he is going to invade Satan's kingdom and his defences will not be able to withstand the attack. The Church will be built, the kingdom of God will be advanced. But how are the prisoners within Satan's kingdom set free into the kingdom of God, so that the Church is built? The answer is through the proclamation of the gospel which declares the forgiveness of sins, deliverance from Satan and eternal judgment, and the certain gift of eternal life—all based on the person and atoning work of Jesus Christ.

Men enter the kingdom when they are born again and redeemed by the blood of Christ, and it is this to which the terms 'binding' and 'loosing' in Matthew 16:19 refer. The Greek word for 'loose' is *luo*. It means to destroy; to set free one who is bound; to loosen; to release; to dissolve. It is used in 1 John 3:8 where the apostle writes: 'The one who practices sin is of the devil; for the devil has sinned from the beginning. The Son of God appeared for this purpose, that He might destroy the works of the devil.' The word 'destroy' here is *luo* and it has direct reference to Satan and sin. This emphasis is brought out even more emphatically by

The Papacy and the 'Rock' of Matthew 16

Revelation 1:5: 'To Him who loves us, and released [*luo*] us from our sins by His blood' which could just as accurately be translated, 'who [loosed] us from our sins by His blood.' This is the basic idea behind loosing. It speaks of deliverance from Satan and coming under the dominion of God, and therefore entering into his kingdom and receiving forgiveness of sins through faith in Christ.[2]

The Greek word Jesus uses in Matthew 16:19 for 'binding' is *deo*, which simply means to be bound; to be in bonds; to be a captive. So 'binding' and 'loosing' have to do with the proclamation of the gospel and the certainty of forgiveness and deliverance in Jesus Christ for those who repent and believe. Men and women who receive the message and come to Christ will be loosed from their sins, and will enter into the kingdom of God.

It is significant that in the thematically parallel passage in John 20, just before Jesus commissioned his disciples and vested them with the authority of the keys on the night before he was crucified, he told them: 'As the Father has sent Me, I also send you' (*John* 20:21). He then granted them authority to continue to do what the Father had sent him to do. The Father sent Jesus with authority to preach the gospel, and in giving the disciples authority to forgive and retain sins he is simply authorizing them to preach the gospel also. The authority they receive is a delegated authority, as is clear from Matthew 28:18-19 where Jesus says, 'All authority has been given to Me in heaven and on earth. Go therefore and make disciples of all the nations.' This delegated authority was not jurisdictional, it was declarative—to proclaim the message of the gospel, which is clear from the recorded history of the activity of the disciples after the ascension of Christ and of the amplification of Christ's commission given in Luke 24:46-49:

> Thus it is written, that the Christ should suffer and rise again from the dead the third day; and that repentance for forgiveness of sins should be proclaimed in His name to all the nations, beginning from Jerusalem. You are witnesses of these things. And behold I am sending forth the promise of My Father upon you; but you are to stay in the city until you are clothed with power from on high.

Following the anointing of all the disciples at Pentecost, the book of Acts relates how they exercised the function of the keys in proclaiming the gospel they were commanded to preach. They faithfully testified to the person and work of Christ and the urgent need for repentance and faith, assuring men that they could be loosed, but warning them that if they rejected the message they would be bound (*Acts* 2:14-40; 3:11-26; 5:29-32; 8:25-37; 10:34-48; 13:17-52; 14:14-18; 16:30-31; 17:1-4, 22-34; 19:20-21; 24:10-27; 26:1-29; 28:23-31). This is the meaning of binding and loosing as Jesus describes it in Matthew 16:19. It is authority to declare the gospel and offer men the kingdom of God and free forgiveness of sins. As Christ is preached and men respond, the kingdom of God will be extended and the Church will be built.

In an attempt to find some biblical sanction for the Roman Catholic teaching that the 'rock' of Matthew 16 refers to Peter, his successors and the establishing of a papal office, some contemporary Roman Catholic apologists appeal to the key of David mentioned in Isaiah 22:20-22:

> Then it will come about in that day, that I will summon My servant Eliakim the son of Hilkiah and I will clothe him with your tunic, and tie your sash securely about him, I will entrust him with your authority, and he will become a father to the inhabitants of Jerusalem and to the house of Judah. Then I will set the key of the house of David on his shoulder, when he opens no one will shut, when he shuts no one will open.

Roman apologists assert the following: First, the position Eliakim was put into was a dynastic position, i.e., one that had successors. Second, usage of the term 'key' connects this passage with Jesus' statement in Matthew 16:19, and Jesus may even be quoting Isaiah 22:22. They then parallel the 'opening and shutting' of Isaiah 22 with the 'binding and loosing' of Matthew 16. Peter, they assert, is the 'prime minister' of the Church. There is no tension or 'tug-of-war' between Peter and Jesus, just as there was none between the king and prime minister in the Old Testament. Since the passage in Isaiah refers to an office that has successors, then Jesus must mean Peter to have successors as the 'prime minister' of the Church.

The Papacy and the 'Rock' of Matthew 16

But the Lord Jesus Christ has already given the correct interpretation and application of the Isaiah 22 passage: in Revelation 3:7 Jesus quotes from Isaiah 22:22 and applies it to himself! 'And to the angel of the church of Philadelphia write: He who is holy, who is true, who has the key of David, who opens and no one will shut, and who shuts and no one opens, says this . . .' Who is the one who holds the key? (note the present tense—since this is spoken after the resurrection, and, it would seem probable, after the death of Peter). The Lord Jesus Christ, and nobody else.[3]

Scripture teaches that the Lord Jesus Christ is the only head of the Church (*Col.* 1:18) and that the Holy Spirit is his vicar on earth. In John 14:16 Jesus promises to send the Holy Spirit to his Church permanently to indwell believers. He says, 'And I will ask the Father, and He will give you another Helper, that He may be with you forever; that is the Spirit of truth.' Note that he refers to the Holy Spirit as 'another' Helper. The word 'another' here obviously implies that just as Jesus had been the Helper to the disciples during his ministry on earth, so the Holy Spirit would take his place when he ascended into heaven. The Holy Spirit will rule the Church and direct it in Christ's bodily absence—Jesus did not appoint a human head and ruler of his Church, but told us that the Holy Spirit will fulfil that function.

* * *

As convincing as these exegetical arguments are, there is an additional reason for believing that this interpretation of Matthew 16 is the correct one. It is that this exegesis of Jesus' words to Peter best fits the history of the New Testament Church as well as the history of the Church in the centuries following the apostolic age. The First Vatican Council (1869-70) convened by Pope Pius IX, affirmed that it could validate its claims and its interpretation of Matthew 16:18-19 by the practice of the Church throughout the ages, as well as through the universal consent of the Fathers.

But if the Roman Catholic interpretation were correct, after the resurrection and ascension of Christ, and the outpouring of the Holy Spirit, we would expect to see Peter as the undisputed head and ruler of the Church, acknowledged as such by the apostles and the Church in general. We would expect to see Peter playing the dominant role in the building of the Church, and we would expect to see a clear and unanimous testimony of the early Church—in its teaching and its practice, and in the writings of the Fathers—to the Roman Catholic interpretation of Matthew 16:18-19.

We would also expect to find an acknowledgement of the bishop of Rome as the successor of Peter and supreme ruler of the entire Church with ultimate authority in all matters related to faith, morals and discipline, and a submission to him in that rule. After all, Vatican I explicitly says that it has at all times been necessary for all Christians to be in agreement with the Bishop of Rome and that this has, in fact, been the perpetual practice of the Church from the very beginning. Finally, we would expect to find the popes exercising their special prerogatives in leading and guiding the Church in positively proclaiming the truth and protecting it from heresy. These are what we would expect—but what do the historical facts tell us?

There is no doubt that Peter plays a dominant role in the New Testament history prior to the crucifixion and resurrection of Jesus. When the apostles are named in Scripture, Peter is almost always mentioned first; Peter was the one who generally spoke for the other apostles and he is the most fully-drawn figure of them all in the Gospel accounts of the ministry of Jesus. But do we see Peter as the dominant figure, the supreme ruler and teacher in the Church after the resurrection of Christ? No. Peter is the first to preach the gospel to the crowds at Pentecost and is also the first to open the kingdom to the Gentiles by preaching to Cornelius—pioneering actions which are certainly a fulfilment of Christ's promise to him. However, the biblical accounts present powerful evidence that Peter was not accorded greater authority than the other apostles and was certainly not seen as the head of the new Church.

The book of Acts records that the Jerusalem Council was presided over not by Peter, but by Jesus' brother James. Peter was *sent* by the Church along with John on a mission to Syria, an unlikely event if Peter was the *de facto* leader; while in one of the most dramatic events of the apostolic era, Paul actually rebuked Peter at Antioch for behaviour which was compromising the truth of the gospel (*Gal.* 2:11-14). Paul was responsible for establishing churches and setting up their ruling organizations across Europe and Asia-Minor, but he says absolutely nothing in any of his epistles about the need to be in submission to Peter as the supreme head of the Church. In fact, Paul regarded himself as personally responsible for overseeing, guiding and protecting these fledgling believers. He considered himself to be on an equal plane with all the other apostles (*2 Cor.* 12:11)—he was the apostle to the Gentiles while Peter was the apostle to the Jews. Paul operated independently and on his own authority, as opposed to being under the authority of Peter.

While there is some historical evidence that Peter may have been in Rome and was martyred there, there is absolutely no evidence to suggest that he was ever bishop of Rome.[4] There are a number of writings from the first to the fifth centuries which speak of the fact that both Peter and Paul founded the church at Rome and that both were martyred there. But these records say nothing about Peter staying in Rome and exercising a ministry as a bishop. In fact, Irenaeus specifically says that Peter and Paul both left Rome after founding the church there.

The *Catalogus Liberianus* (354 A.D.) reports that Peter went to Rome and spent twenty-five years in the city as bishop until his martyrdom. But this statement is contradicted by the facts of history. Peter was an apostle and apostles did not function as bishops over local churches. They ordained presbyters who became overseers, and it was these men who were, in turn, responsible to the apostles. To speak of anyone being a bishop over the church as early as the first century is anachronistic, for the episcopate was a later development.

Further, when Paul wrote his epistle to the Romans and his various epistles from prison in Rome there is absolutely no mention of Peter. Paul also wrote to the Romans expressing the wish to come to them to impart some spiritual gift, in order that they might be established. He would scarcely have done so if Peter were already in Rome. And we know from other scriptures that it was Paul, not Peter, who was called to lead in the evangelization of the Gentiles (*Gal.* 2:8).

It has also been claimed that Peter established his line of successors by ordaining Linus to take over the bishopric at his death. But in his major work, *Against Heresies*, Irenaeus tells us that when Peter and Paul had founded the church at Rome and built it up, they both committed its oversight to Linus then left the city. Anacletus followed Linus, and he was followed by Clement. It is obvious that Peter, according to Irenaeus, was not the bishop of Rome and Linus was not the second pope for he exercised his ministry in Rome while Peter was still alive. From a Roman Catholic perspective this presents the problem of having two popes reigning at the same time.

The fact is, we know very little about the activities and whereabouts of the Apostle Peter after the resurrection of Christ. We know that he was in Jerusalem and Antioch, but his life and ministry are very much eclipsed by the Apostle Paul. Given that Peter was certainly in Antioch, it would seem that the bishop of Antioch has more of an historical right to claim the supposed supremacy of Peter than the bishop of Rome, if the right rests on the actual place where Peter exercised his ministry.

There has been a strong tradition that Peter was martyred at Rome, but whereas we do know that Paul was in Rome and had a direct influence on the church there, we do not know that for certain about Peter. In the light of these facts, the Roman Catholic historian Richard McBrien concludes: 'The question to be posed, therefore, on the basis of an investigation of the New Testament is not whether Peter was the first pope, but whether the subsequent, post-biblical development of the Petrine office is, in fact, consistent with the thrust of the New Testament.'[5]

Vatican I claims that the Roman Catholic interpretation of Matthew 16:18-19 has been held universally throughout the Church and that it can appeal to the unanimous consent of the Fathers. Yet the early Fathers are quite varied in their opinions and interpretations of Matthew 16:18-19. Some speak of the 'rock' to mean Christ, some to mean Peter and others to mean Peter's confession of Christ. No Fathers of the first two centuries can be cited as supporters of the

Roman Catholic interpretation of Matthew 16:18. They are silent on the interpretation of the 'rock', and the overwhelming majority of the Fathers through the entire patristic age (Augustine, Tertullian, Cyprian, Chrysostom, Ambrose, Jerome, Basil the Great, Hilary of Poitiers, Cyril of Alexandria, Athanasius, Ambrosiaster, Pacian, Epiphanius, Aphraates, Ephraim, John Cassian, Theodoret, Eusebius, Gregory the Great, Isidore of Seville, John of Damascus, and many others) all disagree with the Roman Church's interpretation of Matthew 16:18.[6] The vast majority of the Fathers do not recognize the personal prerogatives of Peter as being transferred in a personal way to the bishop of Rome, thereby making him the head of the Church.[7]

Roman Catholic apologists are quick to protest against such a statement by referring to the many adulations given by the Fathers to the apostle Peter. What they say is partially true. Many of the Fathers speak in very exalted terms of Peter referring to him as 'coryphaeus', leader of the apostles, first of the disciples, foundation of the Church and teacher of the world. But such praise of Peter does not support the Roman Catholic claims. First of all, many of the terms such as 'coryphaeus', teacher of the world and foundation of the Church were applied by the Fathers not only to Peter but to the other apostles as well, especially Paul and John. Secondly, Roman Catholic apologists make the common error of assuming that because a particular Father speaks of Peter in a certain way, his comments likewise refer to the bishop of Rome as Peter's successor. But this is simply not the case. Their words about Peter are unique to Peter, or they apply to the other apostles as well. But they have no reference to the bishops of Rome at all, because the Fathers make no such application. This is a classic case of a much-later generation reading a preconceived theology into earlier writings. An examination of patristic literature on Matthew 16:18-19 will prove this point. We will find a unanimity of interpretation of Matthew 16:18-19, but it is one of near unanimous opposition to the Roman Catholic interpretation as articulated by Vatican I.

Augustine is fairly representative of the opinion of the Fathers in these comments on Matthew 16:

But whom say ye that I am? Peter answered, 'Thou art the Christ, the Son of the living God.' One for many gave the answer, Unity in many. Then said the Lord to him, 'Blessed art thou, Simon Barjonas: for flesh and blood hath not revealed it unto thee, but My Father which is in heaven.' Then He added, 'and I say unto thee.' As if He had said, 'Because thou hast said unto Me, "Thou art the Christ the Son of the living God," I also say unto thee, "Thou art Peter."' For before he was called Simon. Now this name of Peter was given him by the Lord, and in a figure, that he should signify the Church. For seeing that Christ is the rock (*petra*), Peter is the Christian people. For the rock (*petra*) is the original name. Therefore Peter is so called from the rock; not the rock from Peter; as Christ is not called Christ from the Christian, but the Christian from Christ. 'Therefore,' he saith, 'Thou art Peter; and upon this Rock' which thou hast confessed, upon this rock which thou hast acknowledged, saying, 'Thou art the Christ, the Son of the living God, will I build My Church;' that is upon Myself, the Son of the Living God, 'will I build My Church.' I will build thee upon Myself, not Myself upon Thee.

For men who wished to be built upon men, said, "I am of Paul; and I of Apollos; and I of Cephas," who is Peter. But others who did not wish to build upon Peter, but upon the Rock, said, "But I am of Christ." And when the Apostle Paul ascertained that he was chosen, and Christ despised, he said, "Is Christ divided? was Paul crucified for you? or were ye baptized in the name of Paul?" And, as not in the name of Paul, so neither in the name of Peter; but in the name of Christ: that Peter might be built upon the Rock, not the Rock upon Peter.[8]

These comments by Augustine are highly significant. Here we have the man claimed by Rome as their most renowned theologian of the patristic age, the pre-eminent member of the 'infallible' *magisterium*, and yet he gives an interpretation of the most important passage in all the Bible for the claims of the Roman Catholic Church and its authority, which is diametrically opposed to the Roman interpretation. How does one explain this? If there were truly, as Vatican I states, a unanimous consensus of interpretation of the Roman meaning of this passage, why do we find Augustine deliberately going against such a consensus? The answer, quite simply, is that there never was such a consensus.

Tertullian, at the beginning of the third century, was the first to identify the 'rock' of Matthew 16:18 with Peter in his treatise *On Modesty*. But what he means by this identification is not that Peter is the rock in the sense that the Church is built on him, but that it is built through him as he preaches the gospel. And the keys are the declarative authority to proclaim the forgiveness or loosing of sins in Jesus Christ.[9]

Cyprian, like Tertullian, states in his work *On the Unity of the Church* that the rock of Matthew 16 is the person of Peter. But he also did not mean this in the sense of the Roman Catholic interpretation. His view is similar to that of Augustine in maintaining that Peter is a symbol of the principle of unity. The entire episcopate, according to Cyprian, is the foundation of the Church, though Christ himself is the true rock. All of the bishops constitute the Church and rule over their individual areas of responsibility as co-equals:

> Certainly the other Apostles also were what Peter was, endued with an equal fellowship both of honour and power; but a commencement is made from unity, that the Church may be set before us as one; which one Church, in the Song of Songs, doth the Holy Spirit design and name in the Person of our Lord.[10]

The Roman Catholic historian, Michael Winter, acknowledges that though Cyprian does describe the rock as referring to Peter, he does not mean this in a pro-Roman sense:

> Cyprian used the Petrine text of Matthew to defend episcopal authority, but many later theologians, influenced by the papal connections of the text, have interpreted Cyprian in a pro-papal sense which was alien to his thought . . . Cyprian would have used Matthew 16 to defend the authority of any bishop, but since he happened to employ it for the sake of the Bishop of Rome, it created the impression that he understood it as referring to papal authority . . . Catholics as well as Protestants are now generally agreed that Cyprian did not attribute a superior authority to Peter.[11]

Many have also misunderstood Cyprian's use of the term the 'chair of Peter'. Cyprian states: 'There is One God, and One Christ, and One Church, and one chair founded by the word of the Lord on the Rock (Peter). Another altar cannot be set up, nor a new priesthood made, besides the one altar and one priesthood.'¹² The confusion arises from assuming that Cyprian's use of the term has reference in an exclusive sense to the See of Rome. But this was not the meaning Cyprian intended to communicate. The 'chair of Peter' was a term that applied to all bishops no matter what see they were in and all were the successors of Peter. As Roman Catholic historian Robert Eno states: 'The Chair of Peter . . . belongs to each lawful bishop in his own see. Cyprian holds the Chair of Peter in Carthage and Cornelius in Rome. . .You must hold to this unity if you are to remain in the Church.'¹³

For Cyprian, the bishop of Rome holds a primacy of honour but he does not possess universal jurisdiction over the Church. Cyprian did not view the bishop of Rome to be his superior.

Another Latin Father who is often cited in support of the Roman interpretation of Matthew 16:18 is Ambrose. It is not uncommon in polemical literature to read the following quotation from his writings: 'It is to Peter himself that He says: "You are Peter, and upon this rock I will build My Church." Where Peter is, there is the Church.'¹⁴

The interpretation often given to these words is that the rock is Peter and that the bishops of Rome, as his successors, are the rocks of the Church. Therefore the Church is founded upon the universal rule of the bishops of Rome, for where Peter is, there is the Church. However, Ambrose has made other comments on Peter and Matthew 16 and has explained exactly what he means when he says that Peter is the rock.¹⁵ He means it in the sense that he was the first to openly confess faith in Christ as the Messiah and Son of God. The rock, then, is not Peter himself, but Peter's confession of faith. It is this faith which is the foundation of the Church. Peter possesses a primacy but, as Ambrose explains, it is one of confession and faith, not of honour or rank in the sense of ruling over the other apostles. So when Ambrose states that 'Where Peter is, there is the Church', he means where Peter's *confession* is, there is the Church. He does not mean the bishops of Rome at all.

What has been said of the Latin Fathers can be said equally of those from the East. For example, Chrysostom is typical when he refers to Peter as the 'leader of the apostles' (*On the*

Inscription of the Acts, II) and 'head of the choir' (*Homily 88 on John*) and yet he does not interpret the rock of Matthew 16:18 in the Roman Catholic sense.[16] Chrysostom argues that the rock is not the person of Peter, but Peter's confession of faith in Christ to be the Son of God. And, like Ambrose, he says that where Peter is, there is the Church in the sense of Peter's confession: 'Though we do not retain the body of Peter, we do retain the faith of Peter, and retaining the faith of Peter we have Peter.'[17]

Chrysostom followed the teaching of Origen that the rock is to be interpreted as Peter's confession of faith and this exegesis became standard for the Eastern Church as a whole throughout the centuries. On the one hand the Eastern Fathers and theologians held very high views of the status of the apostle Peter but they did not transfer that status to the bishops of Rome. In their thinking, Rome was not the only see founded by Peter and, as with Cyprian, all bishops are the successors of Peter. The great twelfth-century Orthodox theologian, Theophylact of Bulgaria, in his comments on Matthew 16:18, follows the patristic tradition and reveals how the East could speak of the Church being founded on Peter and yet interpret this in a completely non-Roman sense:

> The Lord favours Peter, giving him a great reward, because he built the church upon him. For since Peter had confessed Jesus son of God, Jesus said that this confession which Peter uttered would be the foundation of future believers, just as every man should be about to raise up the house of faith and should be about to lay this foundation. For even if we put together innumerable virtues, we, however, may not have the foundation—a proper confession, and we build in vain. Moreover since Jesus said my church, he showed himself to be the lord of creation: for all realities serve God ...Therefore if we shall have been confirmed in the confession of Christ, the gates of hell, that is, sins, will not prevail against us.[18]

Orthodox theologian John Meyendorff sums up the Orthodox point of view throughout the Middle Ages in these comments:

> Orthodox ecclesiastical writers were never ashamed of praising the 'coryphaeus' and of recognizing his pre-eminent function in the very foundation of the Church. They simply did not consider this

praise and recognition as relevant in any way to the papal claims, since any bishop, and not only the pope, derives his ministry from the ministry of Peter . . . It belongs to the essence of Orthodox ecclesiology to consider any local bishop to be the teacher of his flock and therefore to fulfil sacramentally, through the apostolic succession, the office of the first true believer, Peter.[19]

What all this reveals is that there is no patristic theological consensus to support the papal interpretation of Matthew 16:18-19 which equates the rock with the person of Peter and through him exclusively to the bishops of Rome thereby assigning them pre-eminence in the Church through the authority of the keys. The Roman Catholic Church cannot appeal to the 'universal consent of the Fathers' to support its exegesis of Matthew 16 because such a consensus does not exist. Appendix 5 documents the comments of twenty Fathers from the third to the eighth centuries on the meaning of Matthew 16, demonstrating that the overwhelming view of the Church has not been that set forth by the Roman Catholic Church.

This is not to say there was no pro-papal interpretation given in the history of the Church. From the fifth century there is the beginning of a clear and consistent papal interpretation, with Leo I being the first to combine the three Petrine passages of Matthew 16:18-19, Luke 22:32 and John 21:15-17 to promote papal claims. But this exegesis was never accepted by the Fathers of the patristic age or the leading theologians and doctors of the Eastern and Western Church for centuries afterwards. The medieval scholar and theologian, Karlfried Froehlich, affirms these facts when he says:

Three biblical texts have traditionally been cited as the religious foundation of papal primacy: Matt. 16:18-19; Luke 22:32; and John 21:15-17 . . .The combination of the three passages in support of the primatial argument reaches far back in the history of the Roman papacy. Leo I and Gelasius I seem to have been the first to use it . . . However, it would be a mistake to assume that the papal interpretation was the standard exegesis everywhere . . . Quite on the contrary, the understanding of these Petrine texts by biblical exegetes in the mainstream of the tradition was universally non-primatial before Innocent III, and that it was the innovative exegetical argumentation of this imposing pope which began to change the picture.[20]

The facts reveal that, apart from the popes themselves, the Roman Catholic interpretation of Matthew 16:18-19 has historically been universally rejected by the Church, in both the East and West. John Bigane has demonstrated that the predominant historical exegesis of Matthew 16:18 by the major theologians and doctors of the Church throughout the Middle Ages and to the mid-sixteenth century did not equate the rock with Peter but followed the patristic tradition in equating it with Christ or faith.[21] Roman apologists often claim that the Protestant exegesis of the Matthew 16 passage grew out of the Reformers' need to legitimize their opposition to the papacy and consequently they invented a novel exegesis which contradicted the traditional view of the Church as a whole. But such is not the case. The Protestant exegesis is confirmed by the universal testimony of the Church Fathers, as Oscar Cullmann observes: 'We thus see that the exegesis that the Reformers gave . . . was not first invented for their struggle against the papacy; it rests upon an older patristic tradition.'[22]

* * *

We have looked in detail at the historical exegesis of Matthew 16 with reference to the subject of papal primacy and we have seen that, relative to the issue of the meaning of the rock and keys, the Fathers unanimously reject the Roman Catholic interpretation. The same is true regarding the interpretation of Matthew 16 with respect to papal infallibility. None of the Fathers have interpreted the phrase—the gates of hell shall not prevail against the Church—as meaning that a personal infallibility had been conveyed to Peter and through him to the bishops of Rome as his successors. Such an interpretation is non-existent in the patristic literature. There is not one Father in the entire history of the Church who has interpreted the passage in that way. And when we investigate the interpretation of Luke 22 and John 21 we find exactly the same thing. There is not the slightest hint of a belief in papal infallibility in the Fathers who interpreted these passages.

The patristic exegesis of Luke 22:32 sees Christ's prayer for Peter as a guarantee that Peter's faith will not ultimately fail—not that he would be infallible. And it also saw Peter as representative of the Church as a whole, assuring us that Christ will not allow the Church ultimately to fall away.

And the situation is similar when we turn to the interpretation of John 21 where Jesus questions Peter about his love and commands him to feed his sheep. As for Luke 22, this verse had two meanings for the Fathers. The verse could first of all apply to Peter personally, in which case it had to do with the meaning of personal discipleship, or it applied to the Church as a whole in Peter who was representative of all who would hold positions of pastors within the Church. For the Fathers of the patristic age, this verse had nothing to do with papal primacy or with an exclusive teaching authority over the entire Church which implied a gift of infallibility. These views are those expressed by Augustine and Jerome and they became normative for the Church of the Middle Ages.

In his book *Origins of Papal Infallibility*, Brian Tierney has documented that in this time frame Luke 22 and John 21 were never applied exclusively to Peter and through him to the bishops of Rome. The theologians and exegetes of the eighth through the fourteenth centuries followed Augustine's interpretation and applied the verses to Peter personally and then to Peter as representative of the Church as a whole. All the theologians, doctors and canonists of the Church followed the patristic interpretation.

They did not view Luke 22 as granting a personal infallibility to Peter, much less to the bishops of Rome. According to them, Christ did not promise to Peter personal immunity from error in his leadership but the grace of final perseverance. Christ's promise to Peter was taken to mean simply that the Church would always survive, that the true faith would always live on. This was the common doctrine of the Church. It was the view of the universally recognized and authoritative *Glossa Ordinaria* of Johannes Teutonicus. So the whole view of the Church in interpreting Luke 22, whether it was to Peter personally or to the Church as represented in Peter, was one of indefectibility as opposed to infallibility.

The medieval theologians and canonists never taught that the popes were infallible. In fact, just the opposite. It was universally believed that popes could err. It was not until the fourteenth century that one begins to see a reinterpretation of the primary texts of Matthew 16, Luke 22 and John 21 to reflect a theory of papal infallibility.

Brian Tierney makes the interesting observation that Vatican I mentions the formula of Hormisdas—that in the Roman Church or the Apostolic See, the faith has always been kept undefiled—as proof of papal infallibility. However, as he points out, the Church for centuries did not interpret this statement as meaning a personal infallibility in the bishop of Rome but that the Church of Rome as a whole had always maintained the true faith, even though individual popes had erred. This is clear from the fact that the same ecumenical council of 680 A.D.—the sixth ecumenical council—which approved this statement, also condemned a pope as a heretic for teaching heresy.

Thus, as with the interpretation of Matthew 16, we find the Roman Catholic Church interpreting Scripture completely contrary to the unanimous consent of the Fathers and the overall church throughout the centuries. Vatican I teaches that this was the view of the Church from the very beginning. If so, we would find this view expressed in the patristic interpretation of Matthew 16, Luke 22 and John 21. And yet we do not find such a view. Prior to the fourteenth century there is not one word from a Father, doctor, theologian or canonist in the interpretation of these foundational passages of Scripture, which supports the teaching of papal infallibility.

∽ 5 ∽

Papal Authority and Infallibility: The Test of History

Having investigated the spurious scriptural foundation on which the Roman claims for papal primacy and infallibility are based, we now want to turn our attention to the second test the Roman Catholic Church appeals to as support for its teachings: the test of history. We want to explore whether, according to Vatican I, these teachings 'have been held by the entire Church through all ages', and can be validated by 'the canons of the general councils and the unanimous consent of the Fathers'.

* * *

When we look at the historical evidence we find that, just as in the area of theology, the Fathers and the early Church do not conform in practice to the Roman Catholic standard as defined by Vatican I.

There are two major writings of the first three centuries which Roman apologists enlist as historical evidence for a Roman primacy. The first is Clement's First Epistle, written to the Corinthian church around the year 96 A.D. The letter was written in response to division and rebellion in the congregation at Corinth in which presbyters of that church had been deposed. Clement rebuked the Corinthians and called for a restoration of the presbyters to their rightful position.

Is such a letter proof that the church at Rome, and in particular the bishop, had jurisdictional authority over the church at Corinth? The evidence does not suggest this. First of all, there seems to have been no single bishop of Rome at this point in history. Apparently, the leadership of the church was exercised collectively by a number of elders or presbyters as at Corinth. The letter of Clement itself does not identify him as the author. It seems that it was written by the church at Rome as a whole to the church at Corinth. Secondly, the writing of such a letter does not, in and of itself, suggest that there is any issue of primacy involved. Ignatius of Antioch, who died between 112 and 116 A.D., also wrote letters to different churches, including the church at Rome, rebuking, exhorting and giving instruction. Does this mean that Ignatius had a right of jurisdiction over these churches? Surely not, for that would mean that he had a right of jurisdiction over the church at Rome itself. There are other similar examples of bishops writing letters to churches in the history of the early Church. The First Epistle of Clement is simply an example of the overall concern which individual churches took for the well being and care of one another.

The second piece of evidence is the reference to the church at Rome which Irenaeus makes in his work *Against Heresies*. He uses this church as the supreme example of the ability of apostolic churches to trace their teaching and authority back through the succession of bishops to the apostles, thereby validating them as being truly apostolic. He does this in answer to gnostic claims that they possess a secret oral tradition which had been handed down from the apostles. He points out Rome as a church singular in honour in that, he says, it was founded by Peter and Paul, and was one with whom all churches must agree in doctrine. But while he focuses his attention solely on Rome he states that Rome is not unique, for all that can be said of Rome can also be said of any of the other churches founded by the apostles. He in no way suggests that Rome held a position of pre-eminence over the other churches. As the Roman Catholic historian Robert Eno has commented:

The context of Irenaeus' argument does not claim that the Roman Church is literally unique, the only one of its class; rather, he argues that the Roman Church is the outstanding example of its class, the class in question being apostolic sees. While he chose to speak primarily of Rome for brevity's sake, in fact, before finishing, he also referred to Ephesus and Smyrna.[1]

Another historical fact which undermines the claims of Vatican I relative to the universal practice of the Church is that the Fathers often opposed the bishops of Rome in both a teaching and ruling capacity, for they refused to submit to their decrees.

An example of this is the dispute between the North African Church and Pope Zosimus (417-418). A presbyter called Apiarius had been deposed by a bishop who was a friend of Augustine. Apiarius appealed to Rome over the authority of the North African Church to seek a reversal of their decision. Zosimus sided with Apiarius and judged that he should be reinstated. But the North African Church resolutely refused to submit to this decision of the bishop of Rome. Zosimus appealed to the canons of the Sardican Synod of 342 A.D. as the basis for his authority, mistakenly thinking they were part of the canons of Nicea. The North African Church could not find these particular decrees in their record of the Nicene canons, but declared that they were willing to submit to the ruling of the bishop of Rome if it could be proved that the canons were genuinely Nicean.

When it was finally determined that they were not from Nicea, the North Africans rejected these canons as giving the bishop of Rome any authority to interfere in the sphere of their jurisdiction. Significantly, in 424 A.D. at a synod at Carthage, the Church then passed a number of decrees forbidding all appeals in Church controversies to other sees apart from their own, especially the See of Rome. In other words, in their minds, except for the authority of a general council, there was no higher authority or court of appeal than the bishop of one's own locality. If it were the common belief, teaching and practice of the Church that the bishop of Rome had been granted the authority of supreme ruler by Christ himself, the North African Church and Augustine would certainly have yielded obedience, and would not have prohibited appeals to any other see but their own. They were willing to yield implicit obedience to the decrees of a general council, but not to the bishop of Rome.

Papal Authority and Infallibility: The Test of History

Another incident which reveals that the overall Church did not view the bishop of Rome as possessing primacy of rule is the conflict between Pope Julius and the Eastern bishops at the Sardican Council in 342. The Eastern bishops had deposed Athanasius, the bishop of Alexandria and champion of Nicene theological orthodoxy, while the West had offered him refuge. This caused a great conflict with the Eastern bishops. They held a synod at Antioch in 341, completely independent of the bishop of Rome, in which they passed twenty-five canons which were later adopted by the Council of Chalcedon and thus came into the code of the universal Church. The bishops refused to take part in the Sardican Council as long as Rome recognized Athanasius and demanded that the Roman See recognize the Eastern Church's authority in its own jurisdiction and not interfere with its decisions. They openly defied the bishop of Rome and clearly expressed the attitude that they considered all the bishops in the Church to be on an equal footing. The Sardican Council did pass certain canons giving bishops the right to appeal to Rome if they felt their case was unjustly dealt with, but these canons were applicable only in the West since the Council itself was strictly a Western one. These decrees were completely rejected by the Eastern Church as well as by the North African Church.

In the middle of the third century Cyprian wrote a letter (254 A.D.) to the bishops of the Spanish Church.[2] They had deposed two unworthy bishops who had subsequently appealed to the bishop of Rome. He then reversed the judgment and demanded that the individuals be reinstated. Cyprian openly defied the bishop of Rome's ruling by advising the Spanish bishops to disregard this order and adhere to their original decision.

Another significant illustration of the lack of recognized authority held by the bishop of Rome is provided by the Council of Carthage in 256 A.D., in which Cyprian along with eighty-six other bishops formally decreed their steadfast opposition to the teaching of Pope Stephen on baptism. What is so significant about this opposition is that it was made in the context of Stephen applying Matthew 16:18 to himself as Peter's successor, and claiming to be the bishop of bishops in the Church and therefore due implicit obedience to his judgments. This demand, and the interpretation of Scripture upon which it was based, were soundly and unanimously repudiated by the bishops:

> It remains that we severally declare our opinion on this same subject, judging no one, nor depriving any one of the right of communion, if he differ from us. For no one of us setteth himself up as a Bishop of Bishops, or by tyrannical terror forceth his Colleagues to a necessity of obeying; inasmuch as every Bishop, in the free use of his liberty and power, has the right of forming his own judgment, and can no more be judged by another than he can himself judge another. But we must all await the Judgment of our Lord Jesus Christ, Who Alone, has the power both of setting us in the government of His Church, and of judging of our acts therein.[3]

What was the attitude of the ecumenical councils[4] towards the bishops of Rome? They never viewed the position of the bishop of Rome as one of supreme authority over the Church. The councils, in fact, always operated independently of Rome and with an authority derived, in their view, directly from the Holy Spirit and not in any sense dependent on Roman approval. The canons passed by these councils over the centuries viewed the bishops of Rome as possessing a primacy of honour within the Church, but on an equal footing with the other major sees in authority and able to exercise the authority of jurisdiction only within well defined geographical limits. As Döllinger has pointed out:

> The popes took no part in convoking Councils. All the great Councils, to which bishops came from different countries, were convoked by the Emperors, nor were the Popes ever consulted about them beforehand . . . They were not always allowed to preside, personally or by deputy, at the Great Councils. At Nice, at the two Councils of Ephesus in 431 and 449, and at the Fifth Great Council in 553, others presided; only at Chalcedon in 451, and Constantinople in 680, did the Papal legates preside. And it is clear that the Popes did not claim this as their exclusive right . . . Neither the dogmatic nor the disciplinary decisions of these Councils required Papal confirmation, for their force and authority depended on the consent of the Church, as expressed in the Synod, and afterwards in the fact of their being generally received.[5]

Papal Authority and Infallibility: The Test of History

The councils from time to time opposed the authoritative decrees of the bishops of Rome and also emphasized their superior authority by passing a number of canons which dealt directly with the issue of jurisdiction within the Church and the authority of the Roman See.[6]

It is apparent from the Councils of Nicea, Constantinople and Chalcedon that Rome was given a primacy of honour in the Church because it was located in the capital city of the empire and had witnessed the martyrdom of Peter and Paul. But the canons of Constantinople and the 28th canon of Chalcedon elevated Constantinople as the new capital of the empire, to be given the place of primacy next to Rome, and further specified that the sees of the different patriarchates were to hold equal authority within well defined limits.

One of the Constantinopolitan canons also forbade the bishops at the head of the great ecclesiastical divisions to meddle in affairs outside their own provinces. We can see that this canon was still being honoured in the seventh century in a series of letters written by Gregory, bishop of Rome (590-604), to John, the patriarch of Constantinople.[7] Considered to be one of the last of the true Church Fathers and one of the greatest popes by the Roman Catholic Church, Gregory attacked John for claiming for himself the title of Universal Bishop of the entire Church because Constantinople was the capital city of the present empire. His anger was not because the prerogatives which supposedly belonged exclusively to Rome were being stolen by an impostor, but because, according to Gregory, such a title was an innovation, an expression of diabolical pride which promoted disunity and should have no place in the Church. Gregory repudiated the idea that any bishop could be the supreme ruler in the Church, and explicitly stated that all the present bishops were equal:

Peter, the first of the apostles, himself a member of the holy and universal Church, Paul, Andrew, John . . . were but heads of particular communities . . . and yet all were members under one Head . . . Now let your Holiness acknowledge to what extent you swell within yourself in desiring to be called by that name by which no one presumed to be called who was truly holy.

In a passage remarkable because of the claims of Gregory's distant successors, he declared:

> Now I confidently say that whosoever calls himself, or desires to be called, Universal Priest, is in his elation the precursor of Antichrist, because he proudly puts himself above all others. Nor is it by dissimilar pride that he is led into error; for, as that perverse one wishes to appear as God above all men, so whosoever this one is who covets being called sole priest, he extols himself above all other priests.[8]

Obviously, Roman Catholic claims that the papacy was a reality in the Church from the very beginning are historically untenable. There has never been a supreme ruler in the Church, as the split between East and West makes abundantly clear.

But given this mass of historical data, how did later popes manage to assert their authority over the Western Church? As long as the true facts of Church history were well known they served as a preservative against unlawful ambitions. Part of the answer lies in the political vacuum created by the collapse of the Roman Empire, and another part in a notorious ninth-century literary forgery which completely revolutionized the primitive government of the Church and laid a legal foundation for the ascendancy of the papacy in Western Christendom. This forgery is a collection of documents written around 845 A.D. and known as *The Pseudo-Isidorian Decretals*. These contain a fabrication of Church history which set forth precedents for the exercise of sovereign authority by the popes over the universal Church through the centuries. Pope Nicholas I (858-867) was the first to use them as the basis for advancing his claims of authority, but it was not until the eleventh century, with Pope Gregory VII, that these Decretals were used in a really significant way to alter the government of the Western church. At that time the Decretals were combined with two other major forgeries, *The Donation of Constantine* and *The Liber Pontificalis*, as well as other falsified writings, and codified into a system of canon law which elevated Gregory and all his successors to the position of absolute monarch over the Church in the West. These writings were then utilized by Gratian and incorporated into his *Decretum* in the twelfth century. By this means they became the basis of all canon law in the Church as well as the foundation for all scholastic theology relating to the Church.

PAPAL INFALLIBILITY

Having examined the facts of history relative to the claims of Vatican I for papal primacy, we now want to turn our attention to an analysis of the historical facts as they relate to Vatican I's claims for papal infallibility. We want to begin by defining our terms.

Infallibility means that the pope is guaranteed immunity from error when exercising his teaching authority on matters of faith and morals. But this immunity from error only applies when the pope is speaking as an authoritative teacher—that is, when making what the Roman Church calls *ex cathedra* statements. Infallibility, according to Rome, does not mean that the pope is sinless. It simply means that he cannot err when authoritatively teaching on faith and morals.

The facts of history are a sure test of the truthfulness of this theory. If the claims for papal infallibility based on the interpretation of a select group of scriptural references are true, then they would surely be validated by history. Vatican I itself appeals to history for a demonstration of its claims when it states that the dogma has been the perpetual belief and practice of the Church in its ecumenical councils, that it had the universal consent of the Fathers and that the See of Rome had maintained perpetual freedom from every doctrinal error. Roman Catholic writers have admitted that some popes have contradicted other popes in their private opinions or their disciplinary rulings, but they still argue that 'never has any Pope officially contradicted what an earlier Pope officially taught about faith or morals. The same can be said of ecumenical councils, which also teach infallibly'.[9] This is an impressive assertion, but it is not true. The claims of papal infallibility can be held only by ignoring or distorting historical facts. We have already seen that part of Vatican I's claims for historical validation have been proven false in that there is no unanimous consent of the Fathers relative to the interpretation of the relevant passages of Scripture which form the foundation for the dogma. And what is true in terms of Scripture interpretation is true for history as well. Popes have erred indeed and the Fathers and councils never believed the bishops of Rome to be infallible.

It was the facts of history which compelled many of the bishops of Vatican I to oppose the decisions of the Council. The bishops were far from unanimous in their decisions. Joseph Ignaz von Döllinger, one of the most renowned historians of the Church, was completely opposed to the Council's decrees on this subject. In protest, he wrote a book on Church history to demonstrate the fallaciousness of the claims of Vatican I. The following are some historical examples which undermine the Roman Catholic claims for papal infallibility:

1. *Pope Liberius (352–366)*

Liberius was the pope during the Arian controversy. Arians taught that Christ was a created being and not God. The Council of Nicea in 325 officially condemned this teaching and affirmed the truth of the deity of Christ. Pope Liberius was initially a defender of the Nicene faith and an opponent of Arius' teachings, for which he was deposed and banished by the emperor, Constantius II. In his place, the Roman clergy elected an Arian, Felix II. Eventually Liberius acquiesced to Arian demands by signing an Arianizing confession and agreeing to the excommunication of Athanasius, the champion of Nicene orthodoxy. On these conditions he was allowed to return to Rome and resume his position as bishop of Rome. He later reversed his position again, but it cannot be denied that Liberius temporarily endorsed at least a semi-Arian confession, and did so as the legitimate pope. This is verified by Athanasius, Hilary and Jerome. Liberius obviously apostatized for personal and political reasons, but if the Roman Catholic Church's interpretation of Matthew 16:18-19 were correct, and if the Holy Spirit guarantees that no heresy will infect the papacy, then this incident would never have occurred.

Papal Authority and Infallibility: The Test of History

2. Pope Zosimus (417–418)

During the Pelagian controversy, in an encyclical letter and therefore when he was speaking authoritatively on a matter related to faith and morals, Pope Zosimus rebuked Augustine and the North African Church for their condemnation of Pelagius and his teachings.[10] He declared Pelagius and his main disciple, Celestius, to be orthodox in their teaching and demanded that the North African Church change its views and submit to his judgment and authority. What is particularly significant is that this was done in opposition to the opinion and authoritative judgment of Pope Innocent, Zosimus's predecessor.

The African bishops warned Zosimus that he was being misled by Pelagius and Celestius, and appealed to him to uphold the official judgment of Pope Innocent. He wrote back to them saying that he had already given the whole affair his thorough consideration. The North Africans then assembled a general synod of their own at Carthage in 418 A.D., at which some two hundred bishops were present. They passed a number of canons specifically condemning the teachings of Pelagius. This was done in defiance of the decrees of Zosimus, giving clear evidence that the early Church did not believe the bishops of Rome were infallible. As a result of their opposition, Pope Zosimus reversed his position and condemned the Pelagian heresy.[11]

This is not a case of a pope expressing a private opinion, then becoming better informed and changing his mind. This pope not only reversed the judgment of a previous bishop of Rome, but also officially contradicted himself. He retracted what he had previously authoritatively announced in an encyclical letter on an issue of major doctrinal importance. Here is a case of a pope being rebuked for error and instructed by bishops on a major doctrinal issue, and subsequently submitting himself to their judgment—surely a devastating blow to claims for an 'infallible' pope?[12]

3. Pope Vigilius (537–555)

In 553 A.D. the Emperor Justinian convened the Fifth Ecumenical Council at Constantinople without the assent of the pope. One of the chief objectives of the Council was to examine the orthodoxy of what has become known as 'The Three Chapters'. This refers to certain writings of Theodore of Mopsuestia, Theodoret of Cyrrhus, and Ibas of Edessa. Earlier, Pope Vigilius had issued an official papal decree, known as 'The Judicatum', in which he opposed and anathematized these men and their writings. But while the council was in session Vigilius reversed his first decree and issued another entitled 'The Constitutum', in which he refused to condemn the authors of 'The Three Chapters', leaving it to the judgment of God since they were already dead. 'The Constitutum' closes with the words:

> We ordain and decree that it be permitted to no one who stands in ecclesiastical order or office to write or bring forward, or undertake, or teach anything contradictory to the contents of this Constitutum in regard to the three chapters, or, after this declaration, begin a new controversy about them. And if anything has already been done or spoken in regard of the three chapters in contradiction to this our ordinance, by any one whomsoever, this we declare void by the authority of the apostolic See.[13]

The Council, however, ignored this papal decree; condemned 'The Three Chapters'; and anathematized the authors, as well as those who refused to condemn them—an implicit attack on Pope Vigilius himself. Since both the ecumenical councils and the pope are considered to be infallible in Roman Catholic theology, the anathematizing of one by the other offers a startling contradiction. The crisis was only defused when, seven months after the Council had ended, Vigilus reversed his position again by submitting to its decrees, repudiating 'The Constitutum', and issuing a second 'Constitutum' in 554. So Pope Vigilius twice revoked his earlier 'infallible' decrees and ultimately submitted himself to the authority and judgment of the Council which had opposed him.

Interestingly, Vigilius appealed to Augustine's *Retractationes* as an example of an eminent Father who had been forced to recognize earlier errors. But it is one thing for Augustine, who was not infallible, to write retractions, and quite another for a supposedly 'infallible' pope to do so. Although later Roman Catholic theology would promote the dogma of infallibility, Vigilius's defence makes it clear that he did not believe he was infallible, and obviously neither did the Church councils.

4. Pope Honorius (625–638)

In a number of letters written to Sergius I, Patriarch of Constantinople, and several other individuals, Honorius officially embraced the heresy of monothelitism—which teaches that Christ had only one will, the divine.[14] For this, Honorius was condemned as a heretic by the Sixth Ecumenical Council (680-681), which was ratified by two succeeding ecumenical councils.[15] He was also condemned by Pope Leo II, as well as by every pope until the eleventh century who took the oath of papal office.

The significance of these facts cannot be overstated. An ecumenical council, which is considered infallible by the Roman Catholic Church, as well as Pope Leo II, have condemned and anathematized an 'infallible' pope for heresy. In the light of this historical evidence, the theory of papal infallibility is bankrupt, as Roman Catholic historian Johann von Döllinger admits:

> This one fact—that a Great Council, universally received afterwards without hesitation throughout the Church, and presided over by Papal legates, pronounced the dogmatic decision of a Pope heretical, and anathematized him by name as a heretic—is a proof, clear as the sun at noonday, that the notion of any peculiar enlightenment or inerrancy of the Popes was then utterly unknown to the whole Church.[16]

Roman Catholic apologists generally attempt to salvage the dogma of papal infallibility by claiming that Honorius was not giving an *ex cathedra* statement but merely his opinion as a private individual. He was therefore not condemned in his official capacity as the pope. However, the text of the official decrees of the Sixth Ecumenical Council proves that it thought otherwise. It condemns Honorius as a heretic in his official capacity as pope, not as a private individual, for being used by Satan for actively disseminating a heresy which would be a stumbling block for all orthodox people. In other words, it condemns the pope as a heretic on the basis of pronouncements which the Church would later define as meeting the conditions of *ex cathedra* statements.

5. Pope Boniface VIII (1294–1303)

In 1302 Boniface VIII issued his famous bull, *Unam Sanctam*.[17] As pope he authoritatively declared that the papacy has ultimate authority not only over the spiritual affairs of men but also over the temporal powers as well, so that they were therefore to be subject to the Roman pontiff. It also declared that for every human being the condition for salvation was submission and obedience to the pope. This was later re-affirmed by Leo X, Pius IX and Vatican I. Anyone who refused to submit to the pope, in either temporal or spiritual affairs, was a heretic and forever lost.

This was the *ex cathedra* declaration (according to Roman Catholic theology) of an infallible pope, and was a decree specifically related to salvation. No one could be saved who refused to submit to the Roman pontiff. Yet today, the official teaching of Vatican II is that non-Catholics can experience salvation, a direct contradiction of Pope Boniface VIII's bull.

6. Pope Eugenius IV (1431–1447)

In 1431 the Council of Basel was convened despite the opposition of Eugenius IV. The pope issued three bulls in an attempt to stop the proceedings of the Council, but it continued to meet and to assert its authority. The members of the Council justified their disobedience by appealing to the authority and legitimacy of the Council of Constance, which thirteen years earlier had healed the great schism in the Western Church when three different popes vied for recognition as its true leader. The Council of Constance had deposed two of the popes and ensured the other abdicated, allowing a new pope to be elected. It had also reaffirmed the superiority of councils over popes and that popes were to be subject to them.[18] These decrees were officially sanctioned and ratified by Pope Martin V (1417-1431).

Facing the possibility of a renewed schism and a crisis in his own authority, Eugenius IV finally accepted and fully approved the Council of Basel, which had reaffirmed the decrees of the Council of Constance revoking his previous bulls in opposition to it. The legates appointed by the pope swore to accept and defend its decrees. In this bull, Pope Eugenius IV affirmed the Council's teaching of the superiority of General Councils.

The decrees of Martin V and Eugenius IV were disregarded by subsequent popes and ultimately abrogated by the First Vatican Council of 1870—an infallible Council setting aside infallible papal decrees as well as the decrees of previous infallible councils: Constance and Basel.

Just before he died Eugenius issued four bulls. The last one declared that if his successors found the concessions granted in the previous three were in any way contrary to the doctrine of the Fathers, they were to be considered void. If papal infallibility were a reality and if the popes have always believed in such a doctrine, why would Eugenius find it necessary to issue such a bull?

7. *Paul V (1605–1621) and Urban VIII (1623–1644)*

In the seventeenth century, in the reigns of Paul V and Urban VIII, the Roman Catholic Church officially censured, and then condemned, Galileo for teaching the Copernican theory of the solar system. The Church was not claiming authority over areas of science. Rather, it condemned the theory because, in its view, it was contrary to the teachings of Scripture and the Church possessed the infallible right to determine the proper interpretation of Scripture. With the full approval and authority of the pope, the Church declared and defined an issue of faith which was subsequently shown to be wrong. It was not that the Bible itself was wrong, but that the particular interpretation the Roman Catholic Church had adopted was wrong. As Dr. George Salmon concluded: 'The history of Galileo makes short work of the question: Is it possible for the Church of Rome to err in her interpretation of Scripture, or to mistake in what she teaches to be an essential part of the Christian faith? She *can* err, for she *has* erred.'[19]

If the Lord Jesus Christ had, in fact, endowed the bishops of Rome with the gift of infallibility, this would have become self evident in the course of Church history. We would see the popes continually exercising this gift on behalf of the Church by being the primary influence in settling doctrinal disputes and in protecting the Church from heresy. But our survey of just a small part of ecclesiastical history shows the fallaciousness of the claim of papal infallibility. As we have seen, some of the popes themselves have taught error and have been condemned for it. But it is also highly significant that in the major doctrinal controversies which engaged the Church for the first seven centuries, there is only one pope who played an active and dominant part in dealing with heresy—Leo I at the Council of Chalcedon. And even then the Council did not automatically accept his teaching but subjected it to its examination. In any traditional listing of truly authoritative Church Fathers, distinguished for their obvious theological contributions, only two popes are ever mentioned—Leo I (440-461) and Gregory the Great (590-604). That is very strange indeed if the Lord Jesus vested ultimate teaching authority, as well as the gift of infallibility, in the bishops of Rome.

Vatican I claims a universal authority for ruling and teaching the Church of Jesus Christ. But our examination of the scriptural and historical evidence has proven such claims to be empty.

The Roman Church claims that it alone has been granted authority from God to interpret Scripture correctly and that it is infallible in so doing. But the patristic interpretation of Matthew 16, John 21 and Luke 22, the most important and foundational passages of Scripture for the Roman Church's authority, proves this to be false. Here we are dealing with a matter of Scripture interpretation and the early Fathers in both the East and West, who supposedly make up the infallible *magisterium* of the Church, give an interpretation of these passages which agrees, not with the Roman Catholic Church, but with the Protestant Reformers. This totally undermines the claims of the Roman Church to be an infallible interpreter of Scripture. How can the Roman Church be an infallible interpreter, when the interpretation it gives to such important passages contradicts, from a Roman Catholic perspective, the infallible *magisterium* of the patristic age—something which Trent and Vatican I both declare it is unlawful to do? And it proceeds to anathematize anyone who would reject the interpretation it imposes on Matthew 16 and John 21. In so doing Vatican I has condemned Augustine and the majority of the Fathers.

Once again, as with its teaching on tradition, the Church of Rome has demonstrated that it has departed from the faith of the early Church and has introduced teachings as dogmas of the faith which it says are necessary for salvation, but which were never taught in the early Church. The Roman Church never tires of charging the Protestant and Eastern churches with promoting division and schism. However, it is the Roman Church which has been chiefly responsible for promoting the divisions, for it is this Church which has twisted the facts of history. Through long centuries it has arrogated to itself a false authority and has subjected the Church of Jesus Christ to false teaching.

The Roman Catholic teaching of authority in its exaltation of tradition, the papacy and the Church, is a depreciation of the authority of Scripture and the supreme authority of Jesus Christ. It supplants divine authority with human authority. The charge that Christ brought against the Jews in this issue of authority applies likewise to the Church of Rome: 'You invalidated the word of God for the sake of your tradition . . . teaching as doctrines the precepts of men' (*Matt.* 15:6, 8).

6

Marian Dogmas

The Roman Catholic Church teaches some unique things about Mary, the mother of Christ. According to its official dogma, Mary is the only person apart from Christ who was born free of original sin and as a consequence was able to live a sinless life. She also, though married to Joseph, lived a life of perpetual virginity, bearing no children other than the Lord Jesus. When her sojourn on earth was completed she was assumed into heaven by God and, according to the Roman Church, has been crowned the Queen of Heaven and given the title and office of mediatrix. It is accordingly supposed that she co-operates with the Lord Jesus in mediating salvation to sinners. Mary is to receive prayer and devotion, and is able to dispense grace to those who call upon her.[1]

These dogmas are the result of a gradual process of historical development. While the Roman Catholic Church claims that it does not believe in nor teach new revelations, its distinctive teachings on Mary's immaculate conception, her assumption into heaven and her present mediatorial role are found neither in the Word of God nor in the historic tradition of the early Church. Yet in 1854 and 1950 these dogmas were declared authoritatively as truths revealed by God, and necessary to be believed for salvation. The Roman Church's basis for these beliefs, while appealing to Scripture indirectly, rests chiefly on the reception of new revelation.

From the early years of the Church, some writers such as Irenaeus began to stress Mary's humble obedience to God as the antithesis of Eve's folly, thus elaborating upon the biblical antithesis between Christ and Adam. At a time when there was the growing veneration of martyrs, Mary also began to be viewed as one who should be specially honoured because of her unique relation to the Lord, and slowly she became more and more exalted in the consciousness of the people. She was therefore accorded *hyperdulia*, the highest degree of veneration, as opposed to mere *dulia*, which belongs to all saints and angels, and *latria*, which is due to God alone.

Yet there is not the slightest evidence that there was a cult of Mary or a worship of her person in these early centuries. The real turning point in the doctrine of Mary came with the Council of Ephesus in 431 A.D., when Mary was declared to be the 'Mother of God' (*theotokos*). This was not initially intended to exalt Mary so much as to exalt the Lord Jesus Christ and preserve the truth of his divinity. However, just as the portrayal of Mary as being antithetical to Eve was distorted by the unbiblical way in which Mary was seen to contribute to our salvation, so this changed emphasis opened up the possibility of a growing exaltation of Mary herself. The veneration became so great that eventually she was believed to have been immaculately conceived. The next step was for her to be exalted to the position of co-redemptrix and co-mediatrix with Christ. Mariology had clearly led to Mariolatry.

The alleged scriptural basis for the teaching of the immaculate conception lies on extremely shaky foundations. Luke 1:28 records the salutation of the angel Gabriel to Mary as: 'Hail, full of grace, the Lord is with you.' Roman Catholic writers claim that the term 'full of grace' is unique and that it could only mean Mary must have been born free of original sin and was able to live a sinless life. As she was to be the mother of Jesus, he could not be born of one who had been defiled by sin. The Greek word that is translated 'full of grace' is *kecharitomene*, which is the perfect passive participle of the verb *charitoo*. This can be more simply translated as 'highly favoured'. This verb form is found only twice in the New Testament: in Luke 1:28 and Ephesians 1:6. Roman Catholic apologists, such as Karl Keating, assert that in its use by the angel Gabriel:

> The sense is not just 'to look upon with favour, but to transform by this favour or grace'. *Kecharitomene*, then, signifies a plenitude of

favour or grace . . . The Greek indicates a perfection of grace. A perfection must be perfect not only intensively, but extensively. The grace Mary enjoyed must not only have been 'full' or strong or complete as possible at any given time, but it must have extended over the whole of her life, from conception. That is, she must have been in a state of sanctifying grace from the first moment of her existence to have been called 'full of grace' or to have been filled with divine favour in a singular way. This is just what the doctrine of the Immaculate Conception holds: that Mary, in the first instance of her conception was, by a singular grace and privilege of Almighty God in view of the mercies of Jesus Christ, the Saviour of the human race, preserved exempt from all stain of original sin.[2]

This explanation of the uniqueness of the Greek word and what it supposedly signifies is intended to settle the matter. Unfortunately, Keating's interpretation of this verse leads him into a position which undermines his whole premise. Scripture must always be interpreted within its immediate context and within the larger context of the totality of Scripture—to isolate a passage of Scripture from its context and interpret it independently of the rest of Scripture can lead to dangerous errors. And so here, as we can see if we look at the other incidence of the Greek verb *charitoo* in Ephesians 1:6.

Here, the reference is to the entire Ephesian church: 'to the praise of the glory of His grace, which He freely bestowed on us in the Beloved'. The term 'freely bestowed' refers to the grace of God and is the word *echaritosen*, which is simply a different tense of the same verb used in Luke 1:28 for Mary. If we accept Keating's interpretation of Luke 1:28, and apply it to Ephesians 1:6, we must conclude that those who comprised the Ephesian church were born free of original sin and had always lived sinless lives.

It is obvious that the term in Ephesians does not mean what Keating suggests. For the members of the Ephesian church are also described in Ephesians 2:1-3 as those who once were dead in sin under the authority of Satan, who walked in sin and were under the wrath of God. Yet here they are described as those who have become the recipients of the grace of God in the same sense as Mary had. The correct interpretation must be that each one had been transformed and highly favoured by God, not that they were born free of original sin and lived sinless lives. In Luke 1:46-47, Mary herself gave personal testimony to the fact that she needed a Saviour when she sang: 'My soul exalts the Lord, and my spirit has rejoiced in God my Saviour.' She was no different from other Christians who have become the recipients of the grace of God.

Roman Catholic authors admit that the Marian doctrines cannot be verified from the early tradition of the Church in the writings of the Church Fathers. 'Theologically, we must face up to an evolution,' says Juniper Carol: 'From the extant philological data it does not seem that the personal sinlessness of Mary or her Immaculate Conception were explicitly taught as Catholic doctrine in the patristic West.'[3] Irenaeus, Tertullian, Origen, Hilary of Poitiers, Marius Victorinus, Ambrosiaster, Basil the Great and Chrysostom all stated that Mary was not sinless. So what we find as we examine the patristic teaching of the early centuries is conflicting opinion over the extent of the sanctity of Mary. Some viewed her to have been sinless, others to have been imperfect in her moral life.

But while there was conflicting opinion in the early Church regarding the sinlessness or non-sinlessness of the life of Mary, there was universal rejection of the doctrine that she was immaculately conceived and therefore born free of original sin. This teaching was introduced for the first time by Pelagius and his disciple Celestius, yet not one Father in the early Church agreed with his teaching. Vincent of Lérins, writing in the middle of the fifth century, states his opposition in the treatise *A Commonitory*. He argues that this teaching contradicts the tradition handed down from the Fathers and was thus contradictory to the Catholic faith. He clearly states that the universal teaching of the Church up to the time of Pelagius was that the entire human race was subject to the sin of Adam or original sin. And he does not add any exceptions with respect to Mary.[4] In the same treatise, Vincent states that the one unique prerogative of grace and special glory of Mary was that she should be called the mother of God (*theotokos*), not that she was immaculately conceived.

Roman apologists often attempt to claim Ambrose as a

proponent of the doctrine of the immaculate conception, but such an assertion is contrary to the historical facts. Pelagius also appealed to Ambrose as an authority for his doctrine and interpreted Ambrose's teaching in such a way that it supported his views on original sin. But Augustine himself rebukes Pelagius for his appeal to Ambrose saying that Pelagius had misrepresented him and that he had never denied the universality of original sin. Augustine gives the following statements from Ambrose in support of his claims:

> No man born of a man and a woman, that is, by means of their bodily union, is seen to be free from sin. Whoever indeed is free from sin, is free also from conception and birth of this kind . . . For the Lord Jesus alone of those who are born of woman is holy, inasmuch as He experienced not the contact of earthly corruption, by reason of the novelty of His immaculate birth.[5]

We find this same repudiation in the writings of numerous popes and eminent theologians in the West (Pope Leo I, Gregory the Great, Bernard of Clairvaux, Bede, Anselm, Hugo of St. Victor, Albertus Magnus, Bonaventura and Thomas Aquinas) and in the Fathers and theologians of the Eastern churches.

Even more importantly, this theory is a direct contradiction of Scripture—which constantly proclaims that every human being is a sinner, subject to original sin and in need of a Saviour: 'For all have sinned and fall short of the glory of God . . . There is none righteous, not even one . . . In Thy sight no man living is righteous . . . If we say that we have no sin, we are deceiving ourselves, and the truth is not in us' (*Rom.* 3:23, 3:10; *Psa.* 143:2; *1 John* 1:8).

The only grounds on which the Roman Catholic Church can attempt to legitimise its demand that the faithful believe in the immaculate conception of Mary is by claiming that it is a dogma formulated by an 'infallible' pope. The ultimate authority is not Scripture or even tradition, but the Church and the pope. The significance of these facts can scarcely be overstated. The Roman Church has committed itself to adhering to and promoting only those teachings which can be validated by the test of the unanimous consent of the Fathers as proof of its catholicity and apostolic authority. But this is a doctrine which was first introduced by a heretic and unanimously rejected by popes, Fathers and theologians of the Catholic Church for centuries. Yet the Church of Rome now teaches that this doctrine must be believed for salvation and anyone rejecting it is anathematized by the Church.

A PERPETUAL VIRGIN?

The Roman teaching of Mary's perpetual virginity must also be rejected. Mary was certainly a virgin until the time of Christ's birth, but the Roman Church has continued to maintain that she did not enter into a normal sexual relationship with Joseph after that. There are a number of reasons for disputing this theory.

First, it cannot be supported by the only contemporary documents on the life of Mary—the Scriptures. In the early centuries of the Christian Church, monasticism and asceticism, and in particular virginity, were seen as a means of sanctification. Celibacy became viewed as a higher state of holiness than marriage and sexual intercourse within marriage was regarded as sinful and defiling. For example, Origen, who taught that Mary was a perpetual virgin, actually castrated himself. It was unthinkable, therefore, for those who held such presuppositions to believe that Mary could have had normal marital relations and given birth to other children. This prevailing view towards sex and marriage greatly influenced interpretations of Scripture, and Marian myths became a powerful reinforcing factor. As one commentator has noted:

> Many of the most enthusiastic promoters of the cult of the Virgin have been celibate male clerics. Moreover, the Church has from the earliest times consistently and explicitly taught the superiority of the virginal state over that of marriage, and it has ever been held that no sexual acts, even those of married people, are entirely without sin. In endorsing all this the cult of the Virgin Mother has undoubtedly played a part.[6]

The idea that celibacy is a higher spiritual state than that of marriage, and that sexual intercourse within marriage is inherently sinful is totally contrary to Scripture. Paul dealt with the whole issue of asceticism in a number of epistles and clearly stated that the promotion of celibacy and asceticism was false teaching and contrary to the will of God:

> If you have died with Christ to the elementary principles of the world, why, as if you were living in the world, do you submit yourself to decrees, such as, 'Do not handle, do not taste, do not touch!' (which all refer to things destined to perish with the using)—in accordance with the commandments and teachings of men? These are matters which have, to be sure, the appearance of wisdom in self made religion and self-abasement and severe treatment of the body, but are of no value against fleshly indulgence (*Col.* 2:20-23).
>
> But the Spirit expressly says that in later times some will fall away from the faith, paying attention to deceitful spirits and doctrines of demons, by means of the hypocrisy of liars seared in their own conscience as with a branding iron, men who forbid marriage and advocate abstaining from foods, which God has created to be gratefully shared in by those who believe and know the truth. For everything created by God is good, and nothing is to be rejected, if it is received with gratitude (*1 Tim.* 4:1-4).

Paul says that this kind of asceticism is false teaching which leads to a false spirituality. Celibacy is not a higher state of spirituality. Within the will of God the married state is good and sexual intercourse is not sinful. On the contrary, Scripture says that marriage is to be held in high esteem and that the marriage bed is undefiled (*Heb.* 13:4). Scripture also strictly forbids continued sexual abstinence within marriage (*1 Cor.* 7:3-5). Had Mary been a perpetual virgin she would clearly have been sinning against God's design for marriage in the New Testament as well as in the Old.

Even where Scripture explicitly talks about Mary, it is clear that she was not a perpetual virgin. Matthew 1:24-25 says, 'And Joseph arose from his sleep, and did as the angel of the Lord commanded him, and took her as his wife, and he kept her a virgin until she gave birth to a Son; and he called His name Jesus.' Joseph kept Mary a virgin until she had given birth to Jesus. The natural implication of the word is that after Jesus' birth he and Mary began a normal marriage relationship. The Greek word translated 'until' is *heos*. Thayer's *Greek-English Lexicon of the New Testament* says the word as it is used in Matthew 1:25 has the force of a conjunction specifying a certain period of time in which a course of action is carried on and then ends, and another action begins. Therefore, the proper interpretation of this passage is that Mary was a virgin up to the time of the birth of Jesus, but after that time she and Joseph entered into the normal sexual relationship.

In addition to this, Scripture actually teaches that Mary and Joseph had several other children. Luke 2:7 says, 'And she gave birth to her first-born son; and she wrapped Him in cloths, and laid Him in a manger, because there was no room for them in the inn.' The Greek word for 'first-born' is *prototokos*. When referring to children it means the first to be born. And this view is further strengthened by the statements that Jesus had brothers and sisters. There are a number of passages which speak of certain relatives of Jesus and some translations, such as the King James Version, refer to those relatives as his 'brethren', which can mean specifically his brothers and sisters as well as more distant relations. The Roman Catholic Church, however, teaches that the word means exclusively the 'cousins' of Jesus. But where the English term 'brethren' may be ambiguous, the Greek text is not. It does not say that the relatives of Jesus were his cousins, it says they were his brothers and sisters. This is why those translations of the Scriptures which are more literal in their translation of the Greek text translate those passages, not as cousins, but as brothers and sisters.

In the Hebrew language, the word translated 'brother' in the older English translations is used in the broadest sense of a family relationship. The term could mean a literal brother or simply a relative. For instance, in Genesis 14:14 Lot is described, in some translations, as Abraham's 'brother', although the word would be better rendered 'relative'. So one Hebrew word is used to describe a multiplicity of family relationships and can be translated by several different English words. The Hebrew language does not have a word for 'cousin', for example.

However, when we come to the New Testament and the Greek language we find a completely different situation. Whereas the Hebrew language can be somewhat ambiguous, the Greek language is extremely precise. It makes a clear distinction between the words used to describe family relationships and has specific words for 'brother', 'sister', 'mother', 'father' and 'cousin'. When referring to someone who is a cousin or other relative not of the immediate family, the New Testament uses the Greek word *sungenes*. Sometimes the word is translated 'kindred' and covers the concept of near relations such as aunts, uncles, nephews, nieces and cousins (Cf. *Luke* 1:36, 58, 61, 2:44, 21:16; *John* 18:26). But when referring to a person's brother or sister within a family, it consistently uses the masculine or feminine form of the Greek word *adelphos* (Cf. *Luke* 3:1, 6:14; *Mark* 3:17; *John* 11:1-2). Thus Luke 21:16 uses the two words *adelphos* and *sungenes* in the same sentence when it says: 'But you will be delivered up by parents and *brothers* and *relatives* and friends...'.

The overwhelming declaration of the New Testament documents is that after the birth of Jesus, Mary and Joseph entered into a normal marriage relationship and that Jesus had brothers and sisters. One cannot teach the perpetual virginity of Mary without doing violence to these scriptural texts. If cousins or other relatives of Jesus were meant, the writers of the Gospel narratives would surely have used the specific word that refers to cousins.

Cultural considerations also work against the doctrine of Mary's perpetual virginity. In Jewish society in Palestine, there was no religious or cultural reason for her to have taken a vow of chastity. She was engaged to be married and was committed to a normal life of marriage—to be a wife and mother. Celibacy was not esteemed within Jewish culture. It was not viewed as a higher state of spirituality. What was highly esteemed in the Jewish culture was the family, and a sign of God's blessing to a Jewish wife was conceiving and bearing children. To infer that Mary had taken a vow of celibacy is absurd. It would contradict everything she esteemed and valued most highly as her role within family life. To extol the values of celibacy and then refer this to Mary is reading later history back into Jewish and biblical culture. The only reasonable conclusion that one can come to in the face of Roman claims for the life-long virginity of Mary is that they have no foundation. These teachings are clearly contradictory to Scripture and cannot be held with integrity in light of the facts.

THE ASSUMPTION OF MARY

The Roman Catholic doctrine of the assumption of Mary is similarly bereft of any kind of convincing evidence.[7] This teaches that she was assumed body and soul into heaven, either without dying or shortly after death. This extraordinary claim was only officially declared to be a dogma of Roman Catholic faith in 1950, though it had been believed by many for hundreds of years. To dispute this doctrine, according to Rome's teaching, would result in the loss of salvation. Yet there is no scriptural proof for it, and even the Roman Catholic writer Eamon Duffy concedes that, 'there is, clearly, no historical evidence whatever for it . . .'[8]

For centuries in the early Church there is complete silence regarding Mary's end. The first mention of it is by Epiphanius in 377 A.D. and he specifically states that no one knows what actually happened to Mary. He lived near Palestine and if there were, in fact, a tradition in the Church generally believed and taught he would have affirmed it. But he clearly states that 'her end no one knows'.[9] In addition to Epiphanius, there is Jerome who also lived in Palestine and does not report any tradition of an assumption.

Isidore of Seville, in the seventh century, echoes Epiphanius by saying that no one has any information at all about Mary's death. The patristic testimony is therefore non-existent on this subject. Even Roman Catholic historians readily admit this fact:

In these conditions we shall not ask patristic thought—as some theologians still do today under one form or another—to transmit to us, with respect to the Assumption, a truth received as such in the beginning and faithfully communicated to subsequent ages. Such an attitude would not fit the facts.[10]

How then did this teaching come to have such prominence in the Church that eventually led it to be declared an issue of dogma in 1950? The first Church father to affirm explicitly the assumption of Mary was Gregory of Tours in 590 A.D. But the basis for his teaching was not the tradition of the Church but his acceptance of an apocryphal Gospel known as the *Transitus Beatae Mariae* which we first hear of at the end of the fifth century and which was spuriously attributed to Melito of Sardis.

There were many versions of this literature which developed over time and which were found throughout the East and West but they all originated from one source. Thus, the *Transitus* literature is the real source of the teaching of the assumption of Mary and Roman Catholic authorities admit this fact. Mariologist, Juniper Carol, for example, writes: 'The first express witness in the West to a genuine assumption comes to us in an apocryphal Gospel, the *Transitus Beatae Mariae* of Pseudo-Melito.'[11] It was through these writings that teachers in the East and West began to embrace and promote the teaching. But it still took several centuries for it to become generally accepted. The earliest extant discourse on the feast of the Dormition affirms that the assumption of Mary comes from the East at the end of the seventh and beginning of the eighth century.[12] The *Transitus* literature is therefore highly significant and it is important that we understand the nature of these writings. The Roman Catholic Church would have us believe that this apocryphal Gospel expressed an existing, common belief among the faithful with respect to Mary and that the Holy Spirit used it to bring more generally to the Church's awareness the truth of Mary's assumption.

The historical evidence would suggest otherwise. The truth is that, as with the teaching of the immaculate conception, the Roman Church has embraced and is responsible for promoting teachings which originated, not with the faithful, but with heretical writings which were officially condemned by the early Church. History proves that when the *Transitus* teaching originated the Church regarded it as heresy. In 495 A.D. Pope Gelasius issued a decree entitled *Decretum de Libris Canonicis Ecclesiasticis et Apocryphis*. This decree officially set forth the writings which were considered to be canonical and those which were apocryphal and were to be rejected. He gives a list of apocryphal writings and makes the following statement regarding them:

> The remaining writings which have been compiled or been recognised by heretics or schismatics the Catholic and Apostolic Roman Church does not in any way receive; of these we have thought it right to cite below some which have been handed down and which are to be avoided by catholics.[13]

In the list of apocryphal writings which are to be rejected Gelasius signifies the following work: *Liber qui apellatur Transitus, id est Assumptio Sanctae Mariae, Apocryphus.*[14] This specifically means the *Transitus* writing of the assumption of Mary. At the end of the decree he states that this and all other listed literature is heretical and that their authors and teachings and all who adhere to them are condemned and placed under eternal anathema which is indissoluble. And he places the *Transitus* literature in the same category as the heretics and writings of Arius, Simon Magus, Marcion, Apollinaris, Valentinus and Pelagius. These are his comments:

> These and [writings] similar to these, which ... all the heresiarchs and their disciples, or the schismatics have taught or written ... we confess have not only been rejected but also banished from the whole Roman and Apostolic Church and with their authors and followers of their authors have been condemned forever under the indissoluble bond of anathema.[15]

Pope Gelasius explicitly condemns the authors as well as their writings and the teachings which they promote and all who follow them. And significantly, this entire decree and its condemnation was reaffirmed by Pope Hormisdas in the sixth century. These facts prove that the early Church viewed the assumption teaching, not as a legitimate expression of the pious belief of the faithful but as a heresy worthy of condemnation.

There are those who question the authority of the so-called Gelasian decree on historical grounds saying that it is spuriously attributed to Gelasius. However, the Roman Catholic authorities Denzinger, Charles Joseph Hefele, W. A. Jurgens and the *New Catholic Encyclopedia* all affirm that the decree derives from Pope Gelasius,[16] and Pope Nicholas I in a letter to the bishops of Gaul (*c.* 865 A.D.) officially quotes from this decree and attributes its authorship to Gelasius.

Pius XII, in his decree in 1950, declared the assumption teaching to be a dogma revealed by God. But the basis upon which he justifies this assertion is not that of Scripture or patristic testimony but of speculative theology. He concludes that because it *seems* reasonable and just that God should follow a certain course of action with respect to the person of Mary, and because he has the power, that he has in fact done so, and that therefore, we must believe that he really acted in this way. Tertullian dealt with similar reasoning from certain men in his own day who sought to bolster heretical teachings with the logic that nothing was impossible with God. His words stand as a much needed rebuke to the Roman Church of our day in its misguided teachings about Mary:

> But if we choose to apply this principle so extravagantly and harshly in our capricious imaginations, we may then make out God to have done anything we please, on the ground that it was not impossible for Him to do it. We must not, however, because He is able to do all things, suppose that He has actually done what He has not done. But we must inquire *whether He has really done it* . . . It will be your duty, however, to adduce your proofs out of the Scriptures as plainly as we do . . .[17]

Tertullian says that we can know if God has done something by validating it from Scripture. Not to be able to do so invalidates any claim that a teaching has been revealed by God. This comes back again to the patristic principle of *sola scriptura,* a principle which has been repudiated by the Roman Church and which has resulted in its embracing and promoting teachings, such as the assumption of Mary, which were never taught in the early Church.

The only grounds the Roman Catholic faithful have for believing in the teaching of the assumption is that the 'infallible' Church declares it. But given the above facts the claim of infallibility is shown to be completely groundless. How can a Church which is supposedly infallible promote teachings which the early Church condemned as heretical? Whereas an early papal decree anathematized those who believed the teaching of an apocryphal Gospel, now papal decrees condemn those who disbelieve it. The conclusion has to be that teachings such as Mary's assumption are the teachings and traditions of men, not the revelation of God.

MARY A MEDIATRIX?

Scripture asserts quite plainly that 'there is one God, and one mediator also between God and men, the man Christ Jesus' (*1 Tim.* 2:5). Yet the Roman Church changes this. While it agrees that Christ is the ultimate mediator, Rome teaches that Mary has been assigned the role by God of co-operating with the Lord Jesus Christ in the mediation of grace. It is argued that just as Christians pray to God on behalf of one another and in this sense can be called mediators, so Mary acts as a mediatrix or mediatress for Christians still on earth. She intercedes on their behalf before God.

The argument sounds innocent enough. After all, Christians do pray to God for one another. But there is a fallacy in this proposed defence. In praying to God on behalf of other individuals, the Christian is not a mediator. Of course, we intercede for others with God—but when Scripture speaks of Jesus as mediator, it stresses that he alone is the mediator who can reconcile God and man. It is through Christ and him alone that God mediates his saving grace to mankind. It is through Christ alone that men and women are granted access into the presence of God. When Christians pray for other men and women, they go directly to God through Jesus Christ and offer their intercession. In no way are they acting as mediators who can mediate grace to other men. If someone asks me to pray for them they do not look to me as a channel of grace which they can depend upon to meet their spiritual need.

To pray for someone is one thing, to be a mediator in the biblical sense is quite another. The one is sanctioned in Scripture, the other is strictly forbidden—for there is only one mediator, the Lord Jesus Christ. The position that the Roman Church assigns to Mary far exceeds the simple and innocent illustration of someone who prays for someone else. In its theology, she is a mediatrix with all the powers and prerogatives which are given to Jesus Christ in Scripture. She is placed on a par, equal in dignity, honour and function with the Lord of glory.[18] Mary is a channel of grace to men; God has ordained that all the grace that Christ has won should be mediated through Mary. Roman Catholic apologist Karl Keating is explicit on this point: 'No grace accrues to us without her intercession . . . Through God's will, grace is not conferred on anyone without Mary's co-operation.'[19]

And not only is it taught that she is a mediatrix in the sense that she is God's ordained channel of grace to men, but she is also a co-redemptrix in the sense that she also co-operated with the Lord Jesus Christ in making atonement for sin. This is validated from the teaching of a number of popes. For example:

LEO XIII: When Mary offered herself completely to God together with her Son in the temple, she was already sharing with him the painful atonement on behalf of the human race . . . (at the foot of the cross) she was a co-worker with Christ in His expiation for mankind and she offered up her Son to the divine justice dying with him in her heart.'[20]

PIUS XI: Mary, by giving us Christ the Redeemer, and by rearing him, and by offering him at the foot of the cross as Victim for our sins, by such intimate association with Christ, and by her own most singular grace, became and is affectionately known as Reparatrix.'[21]

BENEDICT XV: 'Thus she [Mary] suffered and all but died along with her Son suffering and dying—thus for the salvation of men she abdicated the rights of a mother toward her son, and insofar as it was hers to do, she immolated the Son to placate God's justice, so that she herself may justly be said to have redeemed together with Christ the human race.'[22]

PIUS IX: 'With her Son, the Only-begotten, she is the most powerful Mediatrix and Conciliatrix of the whole world.'[23]

According to papal authority Mary co-operates with Christ in redemption by personal merit, satisfaction, sacrifice and in offering a personal ransom price and she is now the one authorized to dispense the grace of salvation to men.

In the famous and widely read book, *The Glories of Mary*, a paean of praise to Mary written by Alphonsus de Liguori (1696-1787), it is taught that she has been given one half of the kingdom of God over which to rule. Jesus rules over the kingdom of justice and Mary rules over the kingdom of mercy. Mary is considered a source of salvation and a true mediator between God and man. She is represented as one to whom men pray as a mediator and one to whom men are to look as an object of trust for answered prayer. The book even claims that outside of Mary there is no salvation. She has now become a Sovereign who reigns and rules with her Son over the kingdom of God, to whom men are to render submission, devotion, service, worship and obedience.

There are some who suggest that Liguori's views are extreme and not representative of the Church. However, he was declared to be a doctor of the Church, canonized as a saint and his book is openly and officially promoted by the Roman Church. In addition to this, the three volume work, *Mariology*, edited by Juniper Carol, affirms the teaching of Liguori in every aspect, demonstrating that these teachings are not relegated to a minority position within the Church. All the fine theological distinctions advanced by Roman Catholic theologians between *latria, dulia* and *hyperdulia* are really meaningless on a practical level. There are millions of people throughout the world today who, in their practical lives, live out the teachings espoused by Liguori and Carol. Until the Roman Church officially repudiates these authors and their writings, it is rightly charged with actively embracing and promoting these teachings.

What is stunning is that in making these claims for Mary, the Roman Catholic Church is effectively stealing the titles and role which Scripture unequivocally states belong to Jesus alone as the Lord and Sovereign of heaven. By being granted all the attributes, honours and functions of Jesus Christ, Mary is *de facto* elevated to a position of equality with the Son of God. To teach that Mary is omnipotent, as Liguori's book states, even in a derived sense, is to grant her divine attributes—for there is none who can be omnipotent but

God. Not even God's grace can make a creature omnipotent, for that would be to elevate the creature to the status of deity.

Throughout the history of the development of Marian theology a definite process is evident: the gradual exalting of the person of Mary to equality with Jesus Christ. This is clear from the following parallels between the Lord Jesus and the Roman Catholic teaching on Mary: Christ was immaculately conceived—as was Mary; Christ was sinless—so was Mary; Christ accomplished a work as redeemer and mediator—as did Mary; Christ was assumed body and soul into heaven—likewise Mary; Christ is the source of life—so is Mary; Christ is Lord and King—Mary is Queen and Sovereign; Christ is the mediator in dispensing grace—so is Mary; Christ is an object of prayer and trust and supreme devotion—so is Mary.

The Roman Catholic Church has allowed the cult of Mary to develop into Mariolatry which it openly promotes in its art, its festivals, its liturgy, its teaching and its worship. The veneration of Mary promoted by Roman Catholicism is pure idolatry, for God alone is worthy of such devotion, adoration, praise, thanksgiving, submission and entreaty. All that is taught about Mary is a fabrication which steals glory from God and gives it to a creature, for Mary has often displaced Jesus as the true object of worship and devotion. Yet the testimony of Scripture, the early Church and the early Fathers is unanimous and clear:

> Christ alone is the sinner's Saviour, advocate, and source of mercy.
>
> Christ alone is to be our joy and peace, and the supreme love of our lives.
>
> Christ alone is to be served, and to him alone are we to be consecrated.
>
> Christ alone is our protector and deliverer from Satan, and he alone is the sovereign Ruler over the Church and the universe.

Marian Dogmas

The self-appointed successors of Peter have deliberately disobeyed his ringing declaration at Pentecost, that 'there is salvation in no one else; for there is no other name under heaven that has been given among men, by which we must be saved' (*Acts* 4:12). Even more tragically, they have cast aside the Son of God himself, who testified: 'I am the way, and the truth, and the life; no one comes to the Father, but through Me' (*John* 14:6).

7

Salvation and the Sacramental System

The ultimate question facing us is how we can obtain forgiveness of sins. The Bible teaches that God has achieved a work of salvation for men and women and now offers forgiveness of sin through the Lord Jesus Christ. This is the main message of the gospel and the major reason why it means 'good news.' Throughout history, the fact that Christ has successfully completed a work of salvation has never been disputed in the Christian Church. Since the time of the writings of the Apostolic Fathers, Christ has been set forth as Redeemer, Teacher, Example, Mediator, Lord and Saviour of mankind. But while the Roman Catholic Church has held to orthodox teaching about the person of Christ, it has wandered far from that teaching on how the benefits of the work of Christ are appropriated.

Over time, the Roman Catholic Church has abandoned biblical teaching on faith and on God's means of communicating saving grace and established instead a full blown sacramental system as the means by which salvation comes to man. The Council of Trent's decree in 1547 is explicit about the importance of the sacraments:

Canon IV. If anyone saith, that the sacraments of the New Law are not necessary unto salvation, but superfluous; and that, without them, or without the desire thereof, men obtain of God, through faith alone, the grace of justification;—though all [the sacraments] are not indeed necessary for every individual: let him be anathema.[1]

According to the Roman Catholic Church, there are seven

Salvation and the Sacramental System

sacraments given by God for the salvation and nurture of the Church. These sacraments consist of baptism, confirmation, the eucharist, penance, ordination, marriage and extreme unction. The precise number of sacraments was a source of great controversy in the Church for many hundreds of years, until the seven were finally established in the twelfth century.

In the following two chapters we will examine in detail these sacraments which the Roman Catholic Church claims are the means by which salvation is brought to the individual, then in chapter nine we will go on to explore the alternative, biblical view that a person is justified (made right) with God through faith alone.

What was the historical position of the early Church and the Fathers on this fundamental issue?

*   *   *

ORDINATION AND THE PRIESTHOOD

In the New Testament and the writings of the Apostolic Fathers there is no mention made of a special group of men set apart to minister as priests. The New Testament specifically teaches that Christ has become the fulfilment of the Old Testament priesthood and he is now the only mediator between God and man (*1 Tim.* 2:5). The New Testament unambiguously states that the human priesthood which God established under the Mosaic law was set aside once Christ came. This is the truth drawn in the parallel between Christ and Melchizedek in the seventh chapter of Hebrews:

> For when the priesthood is changed, of necessity there takes place a change of law also . . . For, on the one hand, there is a setting aside of a former commandment because of its weakness and uselessness (for the Law made nothing perfect), and on the other hand there is a bringing in of a better hope, through which we draw near to God (*Heb.* 7:12, 18-19).

Scripture teaches that the old system has been set aside because it was imperfect and could not accomplish what God required, but now that Christ has come he has perfectly fulfilled the requirements for salvation. He, himself, has become the ultimate and perfect sacrifice and priest. So there is no need for continuing sacrifices because he has done the work of sacrifice by his one death, and there is no need for a continuing priesthood because he is a priest forever according to the order of Melchizedek:

> What we have said is even more clear if another priest like Melchizedek appears, one who has become a priest not on the basis of a regulation as to his ancestry but on the basis of an indestructible life. For it is declared: 'You are a priest for ever, in the order of Melchizedek' (*Heb.* 7:14-17).

Christ is an eternal priest because he lives in the power of an indestructible life, and the writer to the Hebrews goes on to point out that it is also an exclusive priesthood—its functions cannot be transferred to anyone else: 'But He, on the other hand, because He abides forever, holds His priesthood permanently' (7:24). The word 'permanently' is the Greek word which means 'unchangeable, not liable to pass to a successor' (*Thayer's Greek-English Lexicon,* p. 54). As Philip Hughes has commented:

> As a priest who, in accordance with the affirmation of Psalm 110, continues for ever and who therefore holds his priesthood permanently, there is neither need nor place for any kind of priestly succession in his case. Because he does not pass away his own priesthood does not pass away, nor is it passed on to others; there can be no question of his passing on to others an office which is uniquely and uninterruptedly his.[2]

The clear and explicit teaching of these passages is that Jesus Christ could not have instituted a new order of human priesthood through the disciples because Scripture teaches that his priesthood has displaced the old order and he now exercises an exclusive and eternal priesthood, the prerogatives of which can be transferred to no one else. Accordingly the Scriptures teach that men now have direct access to God through Jesus Christ. They no longer need a human priesthood nor further sacrifices, for he has become our sacrifice and our priest.

Salvation and the Sacramental System

In the New Testament the two major human offices which are mentioned for the ongoing oversight of the Church are distinctly different from the priesthood which had gone before. These offices are those of 'elder' and 'deacon'. The 'elder' or 'overseer' is designated as the one who is called by God to teach and rule, and the 'deacon' is called to minister in a practical serving capacity. There are two terms used for 'overseer' in the New Testament—*presbuteros* and *episkopos*: although these are translated 'elder' and 'bishop' respectively, they are used interchangeably in the New Testament.[3] Paul and Peter, for example, both use the terms elder and bishop to describe the same office. The word *presbuteros* or 'elder' describes the position, while *episkopos* describes the function of the elder as one who rules or oversees. And the New Testament exhorts believers to be submissive and obedient to the elders God has placed in authority over them (cf. *1 Pet.* 5:5; *Heb.* 13:17). The New Testament does not use the term priest—*hiereus*—to refer to a separate office of Christian ministry.

Similarly, in the early writings of the Church no mention is made of priests in Christian ministry. There is a parallel sometimes drawn between the offices of the New Testament and the ministerial functions of the priesthood in the old dispensation—as found in the writings of Clement and Ignatius, for example—but they do not teach that New Testament ministry and ministers are the same as in the Old Testament. Clement in 1 Clement 40-41 uses the Old Testament priesthood as an illustration of a principle of divine calling and orderliness. At that time, God specifically called and appointed certain men to perform a specified ministry which was to be done in a particular way. He then applies that principle to his readers under the New Testament dispensation, to warn them that God still calls and appoints men to fulfil the role of pastor, elder and deacon, and that believers must be careful to submit to the authorities that God has established in the Church.

Clement never uses the term 'priest' to describe a Christian minister. This is true of all the writings of the Apostolic Fathers. Polycarp, Ignatius, Clement and *The Didache* all use the terms 'bishop' or 'presbyter' and 'deacon' when referring to those responsible for Christian ministry. These are the terms employed by the New Testament itself. When these and other writers do use the Greek term for 'priest' (*hiereus*), it is always in reference to the Old Testament or to the person of Christ. The first use of the word to refer to Christian ministers is from the writings of Origen the third century Greek Father. Clement of Alexandria, writing in the latter part of the second century, uses the word to describe all Christians in general.

It is with the fourth century Greek Fathers that we find the word *hiereus* universally applied to describe a Christian minister.[4] And it is with Tertullian in the West that the beginnings of a sacerdotal function in the Christian ministry began to become evident, for he uses the Latin term *sacerdotium* (priesthood) to describe a Christian minister. It is clear that by the beginning of the third century Christian ministers were beginning to be viewed as priests similar to those of the Old Testament. The Greek term *presbuteros* had apparently shifted in meaning from its original usage and become identified with a priestly ministry—though not entirely one characterized by what later developed into the Roman Catholic system. After sifting the evidence of the early development of the priesthood, Richard McBrien concluded that:

So long as Christians understood themselves as the renewed, not the new, Israel, they had no idea of replacing the Jewish priesthood with one of their own . . . Not until the early Christians concluded that they were indeed part of a radically new movement distinct from Judaism was there a basis for the development of a separate Christian priesthood. Other events accentuated this process: the increasing numbers of Gentile converts, the shift of leadership away from the Jerusalem church and to the churches of Rome, Antioch, Ephesus, and Alexandria, the destruction of the Temple, and, finally, Judaism's own sectarian tendencies in the post-destruction period. Concomitantly, there was a growing recognition of the sacrificial character of the Eucharist, which called for a priesthood of sacrifice distinct from the Jewish priesthood.[5]

By the time of Tertullian there was a clear differentiation between laymen and what McBrien calls 'the priesthood'. Having a separate order of men set apart for ministry is not contradictory to the biblical pattern, as we have seen, but what is contradictory is the application to this order of a sacerdotal function. It was Cyprian who crystalized this application by drawing a direct parallel between Judaism and the New Testament ministry. He directly applied the position and functions of the Old Testament priesthood to the officers of the Christian Church, and in doing so, forged the 'sacerdotal conception of the Christian ministry as one of a mediating agency between God and the people.'[6]

In the Roman Catholic view, ordination to the priesthood confers upon the individual the ability and the authority to administer the sacraments and to teach and govern the Church. It is a solemn sacrament apart from which the individual would not be able to fulfil his role as priest, for this sacrament supposedly places an indelible mark upon the individual which he can never lose. This teaching was first enunciated by Augustine, but for many years ordination was not even considered to be a sacrament. This view of ordination and the sacerdotal ministry evolved as the whole concept of salvation and sacramental grace was developed in the Church, so that eventually only an authorized priest, set apart by God as in the Old Testament, could administer the sacraments of baptism, the eucharist, confession and penance, and thereby deliver salvation to people.

It is clear from the New Testament that there is a concept of ordination for Christian ministers—the public recognition and setting aside of an individual specifically called by God to assume the role of a pastor or elder. Ordination is the public recognition by the Church of a gift sovereignly given by God and independent of any work of man. But such a role has nothing to do with an exclusive priesthood, for, as mentioned above, the New Testament teaches that *all* Christians have been set apart as spiritual priests in the kingdom of God.

Christ could not have instituted a new priesthood along Old Testament lines, for that function of mediation has been abrogated now that he has made a perfect sacrifice for sin.

BAPTISM

The doctrine of baptism is one of the few teachings within Roman Catholicism for which it can be said that there is a universal consent of the Fathers. The Council of Trent declared that baptism is the sacrament which effects remission of sins and regeneration. According to Roman theology, it is the means whereby a sinner is brought into the kingdom of God, cleansed from the guilt of original sin, given a new nature, and forgiven for all sins committed up to the point of baptism. From the early days of the Church, baptism was universally perceived as the means of receiving four basic gifts: the remission of sins, deliverance from death, regeneration, and the bestowal of the Holy Spirit.

If we compare this doctrine with the teaching found in the New Testament, however, we can see some significant differences. In the New Testament, baptism was instituted by Christ as a sacrament and commanded by him for all who would become his followers. Baptism signifies the believer's identification with Christ in his death, burial and resurrection to new life. It is a public declaration that he has repented of his sins, turned from the world and embraced Jesus Christ in self-surrender and trust as his Lord and Saviour. In other words, it signified that an individual had responded to the message of the gospel and had come to Christ. Baptism in the New Testament is always aligned with repentance and faith—it is never divorced from them. The Scriptures teach that through the regenerating work of the Holy Spirit and the gifts of repentance and faith, a person is united to Christ, forgiven for all sin, accepted by God, adopted into the family of God and given the gift of eternal life. Baptism is the outward sign of the inward reality of these spiritual truths and a seal to the believer of their reality.

Scripture does not teach that water baptism is the means of regeneration and forgiveness of sins, and the early Church's rapid slide into believing that it does reflects the same error of the Jews under the Old Testament dispensation when, as the people of God they had taught that an individual entered into God's covenant through the rite of circumcision. What may be called sacramental regeneration is the very mistake Paul clearly addressed in the epistle to the Romans. In chapters two to four he exposed the distinction between an outward, physical circumcision and a spiritual circumcision which takes place in the heart by the Spirit of God. He

Salvation and the Sacramental System

pointed out that though one may be physically circumcised as a Jew, this did not mean that one was spiritually circumcised. True circumcision of the heart, he wrote, would result in moral changes and in righteous living. Physical circumcision apart from the inner circumcision of the heart which results in a transformation of life was meaningless and empty—and could lead to the blaspheming of God because the life that was lived denied the profession that was made.

New life, Paul claimed, was not the result of a physical rite. In Romans 4 he used the Jewish patriarch Abraham as evidence to support his argument. Forgiveness of sins is appropriated not by good works or religious rites, but by faith: for Abraham was justified before circumcision was ever established by God. Circumcision was merely the seal or outward testimony to the reality of that God-given righteousness. Consequently, circumcision was not the cause of forgiveness or the means of appropriating it, but an outward sign of a spiritual reality of the heart. This was exactly what baptism in the New Testament dispensation is intended to signify. Physical circumcision identified one outwardly as being part of the visible Jewish nation. But it was the circumcision of the heart which made one a Jew spiritually, a child of God and recipient of the covenant promises. This is why Paul could say that not all Israel (recipients spiritually of the covenant promises) were descended from Israel (physical birth and circumcision). Just so, water baptism identifies one with the visible Church but it is regeneration which constitutes one a child of God and a true Christian in reality and not merely in profession. It is the Spirit-baptism in the heart and consequent union with Christ that is all important. The rite of water baptism, independent of repentance and faith, accomplishes nothing. It does not regenerate and has no special power of itself.

Although the post-apostolic Church lost the New Testament pattern for baptism, it never separated the sacrament from the exercise of repentance and faith. So while the Church came to teach baptismal regeneration, true conversion was still safeguarded by a biblical emphasis on repentance as turning from sin and the world, and faith as the giving of oneself to Christ in self-surrender and trust.

Before individuals were allowed to be baptized they went through an extensive time of preparation (between two and three years) in which they were thoroughly indoctrinated in the essential elements of Christianity and the kind of life that they would be required to live.

Toward the middle of the fourth century, Cyril of Jerusalem wrote his *Catechetical Lectures* for those who were preparing for baptism. Here we find that after the time of major instruction had been completed they had forty days in which to prepare for baptism. In this preparation the individual would confess and repent of sin. This process was known as *exomologesis* (a term for confession derived from the verbs used in Matthew 3:6 and Acts 19:18). Cyril warned his readers that apart from a sincere and thorough repentance, baptism would be of no avail and forgiveness of sins would not be granted. At the time of baptism, the individual would profess faith in Christ and verbally and publicly renounce the devil and all his works, the world, and sin; then give himself to Christ, vowing to follow him in a life of commitment. The major emphasis of the early Church, therefore, was still on the heart, but the theological protection against the baptismal ceremony degenerating into a perceived means of salvation was already very weak.

At the beginning of the fifth century, Augustine wrote a treatise entitled *Faith and Works*, in defence of the extensive catechetical instruction that was still the practice of the Church in his day. His writing reveals that there were those in the Church who were critical of the heavy emphasis on repentance and the call for a holy life as a Christian. These people wanted to emphasize the sufficiency of faith and baptism to the exclusion of repentance. They felt that such instruction should come after one had become a Christian. They taught that heart repentance, which manifested itself in the forsaking of sin, was not necessary for salvation. Augustine vigorously opposed such ideas and set forth the biblical teaching on the necessity for true repentance to accompany faith if one is to come to a saving knowledge of Christ. It is clear that he was calling men to repentance not penance, but in time, because of the flimsy theological foundations of the Church's baptismal doctrine, the differences between the two were blurred. Faith quickly degenerated into intellectual assent and repentance was displaced by penance, with the tragic result that millions of 'believers' through the centuries were given false hopes and a groundless assurance.

CONFESSION AND PENANCE

The Council of Trent taught that Christ instituted the priesthood for two primary functions: to forgive sins and to administer the sacrament of the eucharist. It declares that through confession of sin to a priest, and by his absolution and the performance of the prescribed penance, an individual can receive forgiveness of sins. The Roman Church teaches that sin requires that satisfaction be made to God and this is achieved through penance and good works; through the enduring of sufferings in purgatory; and through indulgences which are authorized by the pope. Penitential works are meritorious before God who accepts such works as a payment for the temporal punishment due to sin.[7]

Private confession to a priest (known as auricular confession); the repetitive nature of confession and penance for all known sin; the practice of private penance as a satisfaction for sin; and the necessity for the absolution of a priest are all defended by the Roman Catholic Church as the constant historical practice of the Church which can be authenticated by the unanimous consent of the Fathers. These teachings of the Roman Church can be traced back many centuries. However, a survey of the historical evidence reveals the following:

1. The early Church knew nothing of the doctrine of auricular confession, penance, purgatory or indulgences.

2. Confession in the early Church was a public matter that related to grave sin and could be done only once. There was no judicial absolution by a priest.

3. At the end of the second and beginning of the third century, penances were introduced as a means of gaining forgiveness of sins and the distinction between mortal and venial sins became prominent.

4. The seeds of purgatory came into Christianity through paganizing and philosophical influences introduced by Origen and it was later given dogmatic authority by Gregory the Great.

5. Private confession to a priest did not come into prominence until the seventh or eighth centuries and it completely displaced public confession.

6. The first recorded use of indulgences dated from the ninth century.

7. There were conflicting opinions among theologians as late as the thirteenth century on the exact nature of confession and penance, and whether or not confession to a priest was necessary to receive forgiveness of sins.

Let us document each of these points in detail.

As we have seen, the apostles taught that if men were to experience salvation they must repent and believe. The word 'repent' or 'repentance' is the Greek word *metanoia* and it means 'a change of mind'—in biblical usage meaning a fundamental change of mind and heart towards God, Christ, sin and the world. True repentance is always evidenced by a life that is lived under the will of God and marked by holiness. Such a life, however, is not one of perfection, and although the Scriptures exhort believers to holiness they also recognize that there will be a continuing need to deal with sin. Scripture, therefore, gives very clear instructions on receiving forgiveness of sins after one has become a Christian and is part of the Church.

The Roman Catholic Church claims that Christ established the priesthood for the specific purpose of dealing with men's sins through private confession, absolution, and the assigning of penances to satisfy God's justice. For biblical evidence for these claims appeal is made to Matthew 9:6, where Jesus clearly declares his right to forgive sins; Matthew 16:19, 18:18 and John 20:23, where, it is claimed, Jesus invests his followers with this same authority; and John 17:18 and 20:21, where Jesus says that as the Father had sent him into the world so he was sending the apostles into the world. Since Jesus was sent by the Father to forgive sins, it is argued, he has granted his followers this same authority through the powers of binding and loosing, and of exercising a ministry of reconciliation through the sacrament of confession and penance (*2 Cor.* 5:18-20). The Roman Church also appeals to James 5:16 and 1 John 1:9 which commands Christians to confess their sins.

The argument looks convincing, yet its logic is flawed for it rests on a false foundation and a false interpretation of Scripture.

First, we have seen that Scripture teaches that the whole order of priesthood has been completely eliminated since Christ himself has assumed that position. The authoritative office in the New Testament is now that of an elder or pastor (*presbuteros*) who functions as an overseer (*episkopos*), and not as a priest.

Second, we have seen that the major passages relating to binding and loosing teach that Jesus was granting a declarative authority to the apostles to proclaim the gospel of Christ and offer the free forgiveness of sins to men if they would come to him in repentance and faith—not the authority to hear confession and grant absolution. This is the ministry of reconciliation (*2 Cor.* 5:18-20) which has been given to the apostles and the followers of Christ.

Jesus has authority, as God, to forgive sins and he exercised that prerogative as a personal right. But when he sends the apostles out into the world as the Father sent him, we must make a clear distinction between what Christ can do as God and what he has authorized his followers to do in his name. For example: Christ also came to make atonement for sin and was sent by the Father for that purpose. But it would be a blasphemy to claim that the apostles were likewise given authority to make an atonement for sin. Christ was also sent by the Father to proclaim the gospel and the free forgiveness of sins on condition of repentance and faith (*Luke* 4:18; *Mark* 1:15)—it is in this sense that the apostles are sent into the world as Christ was sent into the world. The authority granted to the apostles is strictly related to the proclamation of the gospel.

Third, the passages which call for personal confession have nothing to do with priestly confession and absolution. Men are called upon to confess their sins directly to God, through Christ alone as their priest, and to rest in the finished work of Christ as a payment for those sins. Hebrews 10:19-22 clearly states that men can go directly to God in confession of sin and receive forgiveness directly from him without going through a priest and without doing penances to make satisfaction for their sins:

Since therefore, brethren, we have confidence to enter the holy place by the blood of Jesus, by a new and living way which He inaugurated for us through the veil, that is, His flesh, and since we have a great priest over the house of God, let us draw near with a sincere heart in full assurance of faith, having our hearts sprinkled clean from an evil conscience and our bodies washed with pure water.

This should be clear as well from an analysis of the priesthood in the Old Testament. There is not the slightest hint that these priests heard the people's sins and judicially absolved them from their sins. Men confessed their sins directly to God on the basis of an atoning sacrifice which was slain in their place. God has *never* ordained that confession of sin be made to a priest or the performance of penance to receive forgiveness.

The heart of any true confession of sin is the element of repentance. This is completely different from the idea of penance as personal works by which a man earns forgiveness for sins. This is not taught in Scripture. Forgiveness is based solely on the work of the Lord Jesus Christ and his finished work in making a complete atonement for all sin. To teach that a man can gain forgiveness through works of penance is to pervert the gospel of grace by teaching that man's work must somehow supplement the work of Christ. Scripture does teach that men are to bring forth fruits in keeping with repentance (*Acts* 26:20; *Matt.* 3:8) but what the Word of God means is that the life must demonstrate true repentance by the fruits of holiness.

We are also enjoined to confess our sins to one another (*James* 5:16; *Matt.* 5:23-24). This means that we are to confess to a brother or sister where we have sinned against them and

Salvation and the Sacramental System

be reconciled with them, and also to open our hearts to fellow believers that they might pray for us and we for them. Christians are to deal very seriously with sin, for the Church is a holy body and the bride of Christ. Jesus and Paul both teach that the Church leadership is to confront sin and deal with it in the lives of those who are guilty. For example, Jesus gives the following specific instructions for dealing with sin in the Church:

If your brother sins, go and reprove him in private; if he listens to you, you have won your brother. But if he does not listen to you, take one or two more with you, so that by the mouth of two or three witnesses every fact may be confirmed. And if he refuses to listen to them, tell it to the church; and if he refuses to listen even to the church, let him be to you as a Gentile and a tax-gatherer. Truly I say to you, whatever you shall bind on earth shall be bound in heaven; and whatever you loose on earth shall be loosed in heaven (*Matt.* 18:15-18).

The objective in confronting such an individual is to bring repentance and restoration in the person's relationship with God. The seriousness of the danger of condoning sin within the body of the Church is clearly shown by Jesus' injunction on the power to bind and loose. If the individual in question refuses to repent, then Jesus says that person is to be excommunicated from the fellowship of the Church and be treated as an unbeliever. The judgment rendered by the Church will be likewise rendered in heaven, for the Church here is simply passing a judgment upon an individual which has already been passed in heaven. Binding and loosing here is a public matter which is strictly disciplinary in nature—it has nothing to do with private confession to a priest with judicial power to absolve men from sin.

Paul in 1 Corinthians 5 also states that Church members whose lives are characterized by certain sins are to be excommunicated from the fellowship of the Church. Only when they have demonstrated true repentance by forsaking their sin are they to be restored. He says absolutely nothing about restoration being conditional on the performance of penance because the idea of repentance as penance was anathema to him (see *Eph.* 2:8-10).

Similarly, the writings of the Apostolic Fathers are full of exhortations to holy living and appeals to the readers to prove the validity of their faith by good works. These writings clearly teach that true saving faith is evidenced in good works and a holy life, but that good works are in no way meritorious in salvation. Clement of Rome, for example, clearly states that forgiveness and salvation are gifts of God given completely independently of human works:

> We who by his will have been called in Christ Jesus, are not made righteous by ourselves, or by our wisdom or understanding or piety or the deeds which we have wrought in holiness of heart, but through faith, by which Almighty God has justified all men from the beginning of the world; to him be glory for ever and ever. Amen.[8]

Clement's teaching is a fair summary of the writings of the Apostolic Fathers as a whole. There is no mention in the writings of Ignatius, *The Didache*, Clement, Polycarp, Justin Martyr or Irenaeus of confession of sins to a priest or anyone other than God himself, of penance, purgatory or indulgences. The whole system of sacramental forgiveness devised by the Roman Church can find no confirmation in these early writings.

However, by the end of the second century there had developed a penitential discipline in the Church known as confession or *exomologesis*. But it had a very distinct meaning and character: it was done for only a certain type of sin; it was generally public; the works of penance were strictly a public affair which could only be done once; and there was no judicial absolution. Let us examine each of these points more closely.

The early Church dealt severely with those sins among its members that it considered to be very grave such as adultery, fornication, murder, heresy and denying Christ in persecution. Such sins would be dealt with by excommunication. Sins were therefore classified according to their gravity quite early in the life of the Church, but it was Tertullian in the latter half of the second century who introduced the distinction of mortal and venial sins. The Church adopted this teaching and it was then applied universally. For those individuals who had committed mortal sin, in order to be forgiven and restored to the Church it was necessary for them publicly to confess their sins and submit themselves to an extensive penitential discipline of personal humiliation. This could only be done once in any individual's lifetime. They would be excluded from communion and undergo weeping, fasting and other disciplines requiring protracted ascetic and religious exercises.

Some kind of private consultation with the bishop or presbyter was not uncommon in which the individual would admit his sin and the nature of the public penance would also be assigned, but the primary idea behind the actual confession of sin was that it was a personal acknowledgement of sin in prayer to God himself. This is the teaching of Cyprian and he states specifically that priests did not grant remission of sins but were responsible for consulting with offenders of grave sin and assigning the proper penance:

> That for brethren who have lapsed, and after saving Baptism have been wounded by the devil, a remedy may by penance be sought: not as if they obtained remission of sins from us, but that through us they may be brought to a knowledge of their offences, and be compelled to give fuller satisfaction to the Lord.[9]

By the time of the Council of Nicea, this penitential discipline had been systematized into categories of penitents (Canon 11) in which the degree of exclusion from the worship services and the exact nature of the penance was regulated by the class of penitent one was designated.[10] If an individual, after penance, committed the same grave sins again, there was no forgiveness available through the Church and he was excommunicated. The lighter sins which Christians committed were not subject to this confession but were dealt with on a personal basis through personal prayer, good works and private penance. These sins were never confessed privately to a priest and absolved by him, but were confessed directly to God.

That there was only one occasion for repentance made available through the Church for grave sins is also affirmed by the writings of The Shepherd of Hermas, Origen, Tertullian, Clement of Alexandria, Ambrose, Pacian and by numerous canons of different councils of the Church. These writings range from the immediate post-apostolic age until the sixth century, demonstrating that the practice of the Church for many centuries was very different from that which was decreed by the Council of Trent. The severity of this process of confession, repentance and penance perhaps inevitably generated pressures for it to be ameliorated or reduced. Over time there was a gradual change in this practice, so that eventually no matter how often an individual might sin he could seek reconciliation through the presbyter.

This trend toward a lenient view of sin and its forgiveness relative to the practice of confession and penance in the Church became so pronounced that the third Council of Toledo (589 A.D.) felt duty-bound to condemn outright the practice of frequent confession and penance. In Canon 11 it stated that:

> In some churches of Spain, disorder in the ministry of penance has gained ground, so that people sin as they like, and again and again ask for reconciliation from the priest. This must no longer happen; but according to the old canons everyone who regrets his offence must be first excluded from communion, and must frequently present himself as a penitent for the laying on of hands. When his time of penance is over, then, if it seems good to the bishop, he may again be received to communion; if, however, during his time of penance or afterwards, he falls back into his old sin, he shall be punished according to the stringency of the old canons.[11]

Regardless of the protests and attempts of certain parts of the Church to retain the ancient practice, the penitential discipline did change. By the later Middle Ages penance had developed into a very regulated affair in which certain punishments were prescribed for specific sins. These were written down in penitential books which document for us the penitential practice of the Church from the seventh century onwards. As McNeil and Gamer have noted, these clearly chart an important shift:

> This public procedure, in which the penitent, in his humiliation, implored the intercession of 'all the brethren', was later to be replaced by a private and secret rite involving confession to and absolution by a priestly confessor and entailing acts of penance that were often mainly or wholly private ... In the vast majority of cases,

penance became wholly private in the sense of being dissociated from the assembled church, there was no public *exomologesis* and no corporate knowledge of the matter on the part of the congregation.[12]

The introduction of penance as a vital element of true repentance gradually corrupted the biblical concept of repentance so that it degenerated into an external, legalistic system of works by which an individual made reparation to God for his own sins. Thus what was initially seen as the evidences or fruits of true repentance was eventually viewed as efficacious in their own right. It was a small step from this position to one where any kind of good works were believed to accrue merit before God. Tertullian was one of the first to teach that human works such as fasting, alms-giving etc. rendered satisfaction to God and merited forgiveness for sins which were not mortal.[13] His disciple, Cyprian, further amplified this doctrine by stating that sins after baptism were not forgiven through the atoning work of Christ alone but through the works of penance. He maintained that such works appeased the wrath of God and merited forgiveness and the restoration of lost grace and eternal life.

The result of this teaching was that the concept of penance soon displaced the biblical meaning of repentance and the two became synonymous terms. The work of Tertullian and Cyprian laid the foundations of the whole system of penance and works which was later built on by the Roman Catholic Church. Today, the Catholic Church still claims that men and women can earn God's favour. John Hardon, whose catechism was written in 1981 and has the official authorization of the Vatican, affirms this in these statements:

Penance means repentance or satisfaction for sin . . . Penance is also necessary because we must expiate and make reparation for the punishment which is due for our sins . . . Satisfaction is remedial by meriting grace from God.[14]

This dogma of penance is the antithesis of the biblical teaching of repentance, for it denies the very essence of the meaning of grace itself. Hardon states that penance *merits* grace while the biblical meaning of grace is that of *unmerited* favour. Repentance means a heart forsaking of sin and a turning to Christ for forgiveness by trusting in his finished work. Christ has made a full atonement for sin. He has borne the full wrath of God against it. We are, therefore, called upon to confess our sins directly to God and to recognize and appropriate the forgiveness already secured in the death of Christ. To add one's own satisfaction for sin through one's own works is to pervert the atonement of Jesus Christ.

We have seen that the early practice of confession in the Church gradually changed over time so that it became a common and private practice rather than a one time and public affair, but even as late as the twelfth century we find evidence of a continuing dispute about the sacrament of penance. For at that time Peter (the) Lombard revealed that there was considerable disagreement on a number of aspects relating to it, not least whether confession to a priest was essential for forgiveness (the bed-rock doctrine of the Tridentine decrees). Peter accepted the prevailing view of the Church until then, which defined the absolution as merely a declarative announcement. Yet in the next generation Alexander of Hales would be one of the first theologians who pronounced the absolution a judicial sentence.[15] In this instance, Alexander's view would prevail.

The Council of Trent's claims that from the beginning the Church has practised secret confession to a priest who administered judicial absolution for forgiveness of sins is unsupported by the historical evidence. It was not until the beginning of the eighth century that private confession began to displace the public form, and it did not become a universal practice until the Middle Ages. Similarly, the necessity of priestly absolution was not fully recognized until the thirteenth century.

This was all part of the drift of Christianity during the centuries after Christ's death to an externalization of religious practice. Repentance became identified with outward acts which supposedly made expiation for sin—a trend which went hand in hand with the rise of asceticism in which men sought to achieve merit before God by living a life consisting of monastic withdrawal from the world, voluntary poverty, celibacy, and harsh treatment of the body. These works supposedly brought an individual into a higher state of spirituality and enabled him to earn or merit the grace of God and enter heaven on the basis of his good works.

INDULGENCES

With the rise in the belief that certain works could gain merit with God came the teaching, relatively late in Church history, of the ability of the saints and martyrs to gain extra merit above what was necessary for them personally to earn eternal life. These were called the works of supererogation. According to Roman Catholic theology, these merits are stored in a treasury from which the Church, by authorization of the pope, can draw and apply to individual Christians. Thus according to the Roman Church, the pope has the power to grant indulgences and remit the temporal punishment due to sin based on the accumulated merit of Christ and the saints. Generally, these indulgences are granted to individuals who perform a prescribed work or pay a certain sum of money as a substitute for works of penance. There are two kinds of indulgences: plenary and partial. A plenary indulgence removes all the temporal punishment due to sin; a partial indulgence removes only a portion of the temporal penalties still owed to God after he forgives our sins.

This teaching embraces a concept of vicarious atonement in which individual saints, in addition to the atonement of Christ, are able to make atonement for the sins of other believers. We should understand clearly that the official dogma of the Church is that indulgences do not forgive sins, they merely remit the temporal punishment due to them. Indulgences are not meant to be a substitute for confession, repentance and absolution.

But this theory of indulgences and of a treasury of merit developed very late in the history of the Church. It was not until the thirteenth century that the whole idea of a treasury first emerged. Ludwig Ott affirms this fact in this statement:

The teaching of the existence of the *thesaurus Ecclesiae* and of the Church's power over it was developed by the Scholastic

Theologians at the beginning of the 13th century (Hugo of St. Cher), and was officially proposed by Pope Clement VI in the Jubilee Bull *'Unigenitus Dei Filius'* (1343), and later by Pope Leo X in the Indulgence Decretal *'Cum postquam'* (1518), but was not defined.

Indulgences were first introduced in the eleventh century and initially were granted on the basis of the Roman interpretation of the power of the keys and later there developed the theory of the treasury of merit. Popes began to offer them in order to raise money for personal projects such as building projects, or for the promotion of personal causes such as the Crusades or the extermination of heresy. They eventually became corrupted to the point where the Church taught that by the payment of money one could buy an indulgence and secure the release of souls in purgatory.

The theory and practice of indulgences and the treasury of merit certainly finds no sanction in the Scriptures or writings of the Church Fathers. It is non-existent in these sources and therefore can claim no biblical or historical validation. And the harm that indulgences have produced can scarcely be calculated. They became a ready source of income and a horribly corrupting influence on the papacy and the Church as a whole. Just as importantly, their influence on the individual Church member was equally corrosive spiritually, as men came to believe that they could, in effect, buy forgiveness of sins. Philip Schaff mentions that by the close of the thirteenth century indulgences were not only associated with remitting the temporal punishment for sin but also the guilt as well.[16] The indulgence teaching is the logical outcome of a corrupt theology. It is a serious depreciation of the sufficiency and exclusive nature of the atonement of the Lord Jesus Christ.

PURGATORY

Where the works of merit, penance, indulgences and the eucharist have been insufficient to deal with the temporal punishment due to sin, the Roman Catholic Church teaches that the sufferings of purgatory are required to 'purge' the soul from the last remnants of sin and thereby enable the individual to enter heaven.

There are three main passages of Scripture to which the Church of Rome appeals as a basis for its teaching on purgatory, but it is a passage from the Apocrypha which is the real foundation for this doctrine. We have already discussed the false claims of the Apocrypha to be considered as the Word of God in chapter one. But in actual fact, the existence of purgatory as defined by Roman Catholic doctrine cannot even be inferred from the relevant passage, 2 Maccabees 12:38-45. It tells the story of a group of Jewish soldiers, under the command of Judas Maccabaeus, who were slain in battle:

> Judas then rallied his army and moved on to the town of Adullam, and since the seventh day of the week had arrived they purified themselves according to the custom and kept the sabbath in that place. The next day they came to Judas (since the necessity was now urgent) to have the bodies of the fallen taken up and laid to rest among their relatives in their ancestral tombs. But when they found on each of the dead men, under their tunics, amulets of the idols taken from Jamnia, which the Law prohibits to Jews, it became clear to everyone that this was why these men had lost their lives. All then blessed the ways of the Lord, the just judge who brings hidden things to light, and gave themselves to prayer, begging that the sin committed might be fully blotted out. Next, the valiant Judas urged the people to keep themselves free from all sin, having seen with their own eyes the effects of the sin of those who had fallen; after this he took a collection from them individually, amounting to nearly two thousand drachmae, and sent it to Jerusalem to have a sacrifice for sin offered, an altogether fine and noble action, in which he took full account of the resurrection. For if he had not expected the fallen to rise again it would have been superfluous and foolish to pray for the dead, whereas if he had in view the splendid recompense reserved for those who make a pious end, the thought was holy and devout. This was why he had this atonement sacrifice offered for the dead, so that they might be released from their sin (*2 Macc.* 12:38-45).[17]

There are a number of important facts in this passage which are inconsistent with the Roman Catholic assertion that it teaches the existence of purgatory:

First, these soldiers were idolaters and it is explicitly stated that their deaths were a direct result of the judgment of God for idolatry. In Roman Catholic theology, this is a mortal sin which condemns an individual to hell. Consequently, these men could not be in purgatory, for purgatory is supposedly the abode of those who die in venial sin only.

Second, the Roman Church teaches that since Judas Maccabaeus offered sacrifice and prayed for the dead to be released from their sin, this must have been the accepted practice of the Jews.

But this cannot be supported from any other passage of Scripture. The Old Testament contains extensive and meticulous instructions to the Jewish people on the form and nature of the sacrifices God demanded, but nowhere did God ordain that sacrifice and prayers be made for the dead. Nor are they sanctioned by Jewish custom or law. What is evident from this account is that Judas was not doing the prescribed will of God in offering sacrifices and prayers for the dead soldiers. As the 'main' proof the Roman Catholic Church sets forth in support of its teaching on purgatory, this passage is extremely tenuous. Any rational believer would expect such a fundamental doctrine to be revealed and explained throughout God's Word, and yet the Roman Catholic Church admits that there are only a handful of New Testament references which, it claims, 'imply' the doctrine of purgatory, and none which teaches the doctrine directly.

In 1 Corinthians 3:15, Paul writes that, 'If any man's work is burned up, he shall suffer loss; but he himself shall be saved, yet so as through fire'. That the apostle should be called as a witness for a doctrine which denies the completeness of Christ's atonement is astounding, given what he has written elsewhere about the forgiveness of sins. The context of Paul's statement makes his meaning clear. He has been discussing works and teaching carried out in the name of Christ. 'Now he who plants and he who waters are one; but each will receive his own reward according to his own labour.' He specifically mentions reward for labour. And the labour has to do with ministry related to the Church. Paul says men can build on the foundation of Jesus Christ that which is acceptable to God or that which is unacceptable. He is warning those who labour in the teaching ministry to be very careful about how they build. They can build with wood, hay and stubble, or with gold, silver and precious stones. In a logical continuation of the argument, he then maintains that these works will be judged and rewards either withheld or dispensed on the basis of their passing the test of fire, which will consume all that is not glorifying to God. Paul says nothing here which implicitly or explicitly links fire with the issue of personal justification.

This concept of an individual Christian's works being weighed, tested or judged is found elsewhere in Paul's epistles. In 2 Corinthians 5:10 he writes: 'For we must all appear before the judgment seat of Christ, that each one may be recompensed for his deeds in the body, according to what he has done, whether good or bad.' All believers will stand before Christ after death and their works will be judged. If their work is burned up they will suffer loss (of what kind we are not told), but Paul is clear that they themselves will be saved. It is not the man who suffers the fire of God's judgment but his works and errors, and the fire is not purifying but destructive. This is completely different from the concept of Christians passing through purgatory.

Another classic example of the Roman Catholic Church reading a preconceived theology into a passage is its interpretation of Matthew 12:32: 'And whoever shall speak a word against the Son of Man, it shall be forgiven him; but whoever shall speak against the Holy Spirit it shall not be forgiven him, either in this age, or in the age to come.' Rome claims that Scripture implies here that some sins can be forgiven in the age to come—thereby indirectly supporting the doctrine of purgatory. Yet no mention is made of purgatory, and when this passage is compared with parallel ones from the other Gospels it is clear Jesus was talking about the extreme gravity of speaking against the Holy Spirit.[18] All of the Gospel accounts show consistency and none of them give the slightest indication or implication that there are other sins which can be forgiven after death. The rest of the New Testament is similarly unequivocal: 'It is appointed that men die once, and after death be judged' (*Heb.* 9:27). Even Roman Catholic theologian Richard McBrien concedes that:

> There is, for all practical purposes, no biblical basis for the doctrine of purgatory. This is not to say that there is no basis at all for the doctrine, but only that there is no clear biblical basis for it.[19]

So is there any historical basis for this 'traditional' doctrine? For at least the first two centuries there was no mention of purgatory in the Church. In all the writings of the Apostolic Fathers, Irenaeus and Justin Martyr there is not the slightest allusion to the idea of purgatory. Rome claims that the early Church nevertheless believed in purgatory because it prayed for the dead. This was becoming a common practice by the beginning of the third century but it does not, in itself, prove that the early Church believed in the existence of a purgatory. The written prayers which have survived, and the evidence from the catacombs and burial inscriptions indicate that the early Church viewed deceased Christians as residing in peace and happiness and the prayers offered were for them to have a greater experience of these. As early as Tertullian, in the late second and beginning of the third century, these prayers often use the Latin term *refrigerium* as a request of God on behalf of departed Christians, a term which means 'refreshment' or 'to refresh' and came to embody the concept of heavenly happiness.[20] So the fact that the early Church prayed for the dead does not support the teaching of purgatory for the nature of the prayers themselves indicate the Church did not view the dead as residing in a place of suffering.

The roots of the teaching of purgatory can be traced to pagan Greek religion and philosophy in such writings as the Roman poet Virgil's *Aeneid* and especially through the influence of Plato, whose views were introduced into the Church through Clement of Alexandria and Origen. These two leading Greek Fathers of the second and third centuries were based in Alexandria, which at the time was the centre of Christian culture, and in particular a melting pot in which Christianity and Hellenism mingled and fused. Origen, who is considered a heretic by the Roman Catholic Church, is the true founder of the doctrine of purgatory, in that he was an influential promoter of the concept of purgation through suffering after death. These views had a major influence on such Fathers as Ambrose, Jerome and most importantly Augustine—who more fully developed the Roman Catholic teaching on purgatory. He, in turn, greatly influenced Gregory the Great and is the major authority appealed to by all subsequent Roman Catholic theologians. In fact, after Augustine, there is very little that is added by others to his basic teaching on the concept and nature of purgatory.

Apart from Greek philosophical influences, the idea of purgatory was promoted and embellished by two other major influences: apocryphal literature and the accounts of visions. For example, Le Goff refers to *The Passion of Perpetua and Felicitas*, written in the third century, which tells of a vision of a Christian martyr, Dinocratus, who had died and who was in a state of suffering in some intermediary place between heaven and hell. He is finally relieved due to the prayers of his sister, Perpetua.[21] This tale greatly influenced Augustine and all who subsequently promoted the teaching of purgatory.

There were also a number of Jewish and Christian apocryphal writings from the end of the first to the middle of the third centuries, such as the *Book of Enoch*, the *Fourth Book of Ezra*, the *Apocalypse of Peter*, the *Apocalypse of Ezra* and the *Apocalypse of Paul*, which greatly influenced some of the early Church Fathers. The *Fourth Book of Ezra* is quoted by Clement of Alexandria and Ambrose, and the *Apocalypse of Ezra* and *Paul* were extensively quoted during the Middle Ages.[22] Once the authority of Augustine established the theology of purgatory and it was given dogmatic expression by Gregory the Great, the teaching was promoted and embellished through the accounts of numerous visions which were accepted at face value. Much of the authority which Gregory the Great appeals to for the existence of purgatory are visions which he says were from personal experience or claims recounted to him. He gives a number of these examples in his *Dialogues*. As the centuries passed, the accounts of visions became commonplace and continued to lend supernatural credence to the reality of purgatory.

Interestingly, even though the idea of purgatory was first introduced by Greek theologians, the Greek Church never accepted the teaching and along with the papacy, the immaculate conception of Mary and the *Filioque* it has been a major point of contention between the Eastern Orthodox and Western Roman Catholic Churches throughout the centuries. So the Roman Catholic Church cannot even claim a unanimous consent of the Fathers to the concept of purgatory (even though there is greater consensus among the Fathers than for other distinctively Roman Catholic doctrines).

Paul warns believers in Colossians 2:8 to beware of being taken captive by hollow and deceptive philosophy, which depends upon human tradition and the basic principles of this world, rather than on Christ. Purgatory is a philosophical concept which finds its source in the teachings of men, rather than the Word of God. It stems from a perversion of the biblical teaching of the sacrifice of Christ and on the way forgiveness of sins is appropriated. Scripture teaches that a believer is complete in Christ and that the work of Christ is sufficient to deal with the entire penalty for sin. It is a contradiction of this to add the works of man and the idea of expiating sin through suffering as a basis of salvation.

∞ 8 ∞

The Eucharist

The Roman Catholic doctrine of the eucharist was first given dogmatic expression at the Fourth Lateran Council in 1215, when the Church formally adopted the doctrine of transubstantiation as its official teaching. This was confirmed by the Council of Trent, which also asserted that the Lord's Supper was a propitiatory sacrifice for sin. These are the two primary and supremely important elements of the Church's teaching on the eucharist—transubstantiation and sacrifice.

The Roman Catholic Church teaches that when the priest utters the words of consecration, the bread and wine are changed into the literal body and blood of Christ. He is then offered to God on the altar as a propitiatory sacrifice for sin. The Council of Trent explicitly states that 'in this divine sacrifice which is celebrated in the mass, that same Christ is contained and immolated in an unbloody manner who once offered himself in a bloody manner on the altar of the cross'. There are thus two aspects of the Roman doctrine: *transubstantiation*, which guarantees the 'real presence' of Christ; and *the mass*, in which Christ, thus present bodily, is re-offered to God as a sacrifice. This, however, is not the only view which has been expressed in a consistent way throughout the history of the Church. From the beginning of the Church the Fathers generally expressed their belief in the Real Presence in the eucharist, in that they identified the elements with the body and blood of Christ, and also referred to the eucharist as a sacrifice, but there was considerable difference of opinion among the Fathers on the precise nature of these things, reflected in the fact that the ancient Church produced no official dogma of the Lord's Supper. Interpretation of the meaning of the eucharist in the writings of the Fathers must be done with great caution for it is very easy to take a preconceived theology of the eucharist and read it back into their comments and teachings.

What I believe an objective analysis will reveal is that the views of the Fathers are very consistent with the differing views represented by the Roman Catholic Church *and* those of the Protestant Reformers. Some of the Fathers taught that the elements are symbols of the body and blood of Christ and that his presence is spiritual, while others maintained that the elements are changed into Christ's body and blood and that his presence is physical.[1] The following examples from the writings of the Fathers of the first four centuries reveal this diversity of opinion.

The *Didache* or *Teaching of the Twelve Apostles*, as it is sometimes called, is included in the collection of works known as the Apostolic Fathers, and is one of the oldest documents from the immediate post-apostolic age that we possess. It is an early manual of Church discipline dated from between the late first century and 140 A.D., and it simply refers to the Lord's Supper as spiritual food and drink. There is no indication that the elements are transformed in any way. Ignatius of Antioch (martyred *c.* 110 A.D.), on the other hand, speaks of the eucharist as the body and blood of Christ which communicates eternal life. Justin Martyr (100/110-165 A.D.) refers to the eucharistic elements as being more than common bread and wine,[2] in that when they are consecrated they become the body and blood of Jesus; yet in his *Dialogue with Trypho* he wrote that the elements were bread and wine which were inaugurated by Christ as a memorial and remembrance of his body and blood.[3] So while he spoke of a change in the elements, it seems that in his conception, the elements still remain, in essence, bread and wine. Like Justin, Irenaeus of Lyons (140-202 A.D.) clearly believed the bread and wine became the body and blood of Jesus at consecration,[4] but he also stated that the elements were composed of two realities—one earthly and one heavenly, or spiritual.[5] He implied that at consecration, though the elements are no longer common bread and wine, they do not lose the nature of being bread and wine.

The Eucharist

Tertullian (155/160-240/250 A.D.) spoke of the bread and wine in the eucharist as symbols or figures which represent the body and blood of Christ. He specifically stated that these were not the literal body and blood of the Lord. When Christ said, 'This is my body,' Tertullian maintained that Jesus was speaking figuratively and that he consecrated the wine 'in memory of his blood' (*Against Marcion* 3.19). Some theologians have claimed that the ancient usage of the words 'figure' and 'represent' suggested that the symbols in some mysterious way became what they symbolized. But Tertullian uses the word 'represent' in a number of other places where the word carries a figurative meaning. For example, in *Against Marcion* 4.40 he says, 'He represents the bleeding condition of his flesh under the metaphor of garments dyed in red.' His interpretation of John 6 similarly indicates that when he spoke of the bread and wine as figures and symbols of Christ's body and blood, that is exactly what he meant.[6] He says that Christ spoke in spiritual terms when referring to the eating of his flesh and drinking of his blood and did not mean this literally. He holds that the eating of the flesh of Christ and the drinking of his blood means appropriating him by faith: 'He likewise called His flesh by the same appellation; because, too, the Word had become flesh, we ought therefore to desire Him in order that we may have life, and to devour Him with the ear, and to ruminate on Him with the understanding, and to digest Him by faith.'[7] Clearly he did not teach the concept of transubstantiation.

Clement of Alexandria (150-211/216 A.D.) also called the bread and wine symbols of the body and blood of Christ, and taught that the communicant received not the physical but the spiritual life of Christ.[8] Origen (185-253/254 A.D.), likewise, speaks in distinctively spiritual and allegorical terms when referring to the eucharist.

Eusebius of Caesarea (263-340 A.D.) identified the elements with the body and blood of Christ but, like Tertullian, saw the elements as being symbolical or representative of spiritual realities.[9] He specifically states that the bread and wine are symbols of the Lord's body and blood and that Christ's words in John 6 are to be understood spiritually and figuratively as opposed to a physical and literal sense.

As time passed clearer descriptions of the eucharist as the transformation of the elements into the literal body and blood of Christ emerged in the writings of Fathers such as Cyril of Jerusalem, Gregory of Nyssa, Gregory Nazianzen, Chrysostom and Ambrose. Gregory of Nyssa, for example, taught that the eucharist was the perpetuation of the incarnation and similarly Cyril of Jerusalem adopted a highly literal approach:

Since then He Himself has declared and said of the Bread, This is My body, who shall dare doubt any longer? And since He has affirmed and said, This is My blood, who shall ever hesitate, saying, that this is not His blood? He once turned water into wine, in Cana of Galilee, at His own will, and is it incredible that He should have turned wine into blood? . . . Then having sanctified ourselves by these spiritual Hymns, we call upon the merciful God to send forth His Holy Spirit upon the gifts lying before Him; that He may make the bread the Body of Christ, and the Wine the Blood of Christ; for whatsoever the Holy Ghost has touched, is sanctified and changed.[10]

At the same time, there was a continuing representation by many Fathers of the eucharistic elements as figures or symbols of the Lord's body and blood, although they also believed the Lord was spiritually present in the sacrament. Pope Gelasius I (492-496 A.D.), for example, believed that the bread and wine in substance at consecration did not cease to be bread and wine,[11] a view shared by Eusebius, Theodoret, Serapion, Jerome, Athanasius, Ambrosiaster, Macarius of Egypt, and Eustathius of Antioch.[12]

However, the theological giant who provided the most comprehensive and influential defence of the symbolic interpretation of the Lord's Supper was Augustine.[13] He gave very clear instructions and principles for determining when a passage of Scripture should be interpreted literally and when figuratively. Passages of Scripture must always be interpreted in the light of the entire revelation of Scripture, he concluded, and he used John 6 as a specific example of a passage that should be interpreted figuratively.[14]

Augustine argued that the sacraments, including the eucharist, are signs and figures which represent or symbolize spiritual realities. He made a distinction between the physical, historical body of Christ and the sacramental presence, maintaining that Christ's physical body could not literally be present in the sacrament of the eucharist because he is physically at the right hand of God in heaven, and will be there until he comes again. But Christ is spiritually with his people.[15] Augustine viewed the eucharist in spiritual terms and he interpreted the true meaning of eating and drinking as being faith: 'To believe on Him is to eat the living bread. He that believes eats; he is sated invisibly, because invisibly is he born again.'[16]

These views of Augustine are obviously in direct opposition to those of the Council of Trent. In fact, teachings such as his on the eucharist were anathematized by that Council. This highlights once again the lack of patristic consensus on the teaching of this major doctrine of the Roman Catholic Church. The view of the transformation of the elements into the literal body and blood of Christ eventually triumphed within the Church but not without consistent opposition. There were two major controversies in the ninth and eleventh centuries between the literal and more spiritualistic views and even in the Scholastic age there were many prominent theologians who rejected the doctrine of transubstantiation.[17]

In an attempt to give the impression that there has been a unanimous consent throughout the history of the Church to the Roman Catholic interpretation of the eucharist Karl Keating makes the following statement:

Whatever else might be said, it is certain that the early Church took John 6 and the accounts of the Last Supper literally. There is no record in the early centuries of any Christian doubting the Catholic interpretation. There exists no document in which the literal interpretation is opposed and the metaphorical accepted.[18]

In light of the facts given above we can see that such a claim is erroneous. The truth of the matter is that the views of the early Church on the meaning of the eucharist and its relationship to the person of Christ are very similar to those one finds today and in the days of the Reformation when one compares the different Protestant and Roman Catholic views.

There is the literal view of transubstantiation which could be that expressed by Chrysostom; the Lutheran view of consubstantiation, which could be that taught by Irenaeus or Justin Martyr; the spiritual view of Calvin, which is closely aligned with Augustine; and the strictly symbolic view of Zwingli, which is similar to that expressed by Eusebius.

A similar lack of consensus existed on the other major characteristic of the Roman Catholic position on the eucharist—that this sacrament is itself a propitiatory sacrifice. According to this teaching, in the mass Christ is physically present through the priestly consecration and he then becomes the divine victim who is immolated on the altar. The word 'immolate' specifically means 'to slay' or 'to kill' and this sacrifice is efficacious as a sin payment to satisfy God's justice.

There are some present day Roman Catholic writers who deny that the Roman Catholic Church teaches that the mass is the re-sacrifice of Christ, but the words of the Council of Trent are quite clear in their meaning:

And forasmuch as, in this divine sacrifice which is celebrated in the mass, that same Christ is contained and immolated in an unbloody manner who once offered himself in a bloody manner on the altar of the cross . . . For the victim is one and the same, the same now offering by the ministry of priests, who then offered himself on the cross, the manner alone of offering being different . . . If any one saith, that the sacrifice of the mass is only a sacrifice of praise and thanksgiving; or, that it is a bare commemoration of the sacrifice consummated on the cross, but not a propitiatory sacrifice . . . and that it ought not to be offered for the living and the dead for sins, pains, satisfactions, and other necessities: let him be anathema.[19]

Trent teaches that just as Christ was the divine victim and was offered and immolated on the cross as a propitiatory sacrifice for sin, so in the mass, which is a distinct sacrifice in its own right, he is referred to as the divine victim who is again offered and immolated as a propitiatory sacrifice, *just as he was immolated on the cross*. The only difference, according to Trent, between the sacrifice of the mass and the sacrifice of the cross is that one is bloody and the other unbloody.

There are those who object to the charge that what Trent

meant by immolation is a renewed slaying of Christ. Historically, the word immolate had been used by Fathers and theologians of the Church to refer to the eucharist as a commemoration of the once-for-all sacrifice of Christ. Augustine used the word in this way and his definition became normative for centuries afterwards.[20] For example, Peter Lombard in the twelfth century in his *Sentences* expressed the Augustinian view in this way:

> We may briefly reply that what is offered and consecrated by the priest is called a sacrifice and an immolation because it is a memorial and a representation of the true sacrifice and holy immolation made upon the altar of the cross. Christ died once, upon the cross, and there he was immolated in his own person; and yet every day he is immolated sacramentally, because in the sacrament there is a recalling of what was done once.[21]

The meaning of the term as it is expressed here is strictly that of a sacramental commemoration, it was not literal. However, Trent's use of the term added a new dimension of meaning to the word which differs from that of Augustine for he did not view Christ as being physically present in the sacrament, nor the eucharist as a propitiatory sacrifice for sin. Augustine certainly did not teach that the sacrifice of the eucharist was the same as the sacrifice of Calvary.

But in Roman theology the eucharist is not merely the commemoration of a sacrifice, it is itself the same sacrifice as Calvary, and the immolation is literal. In the mass Christ is literally and physically present on the altar. He is referred to as a victim and is literally offered and sacrificed in the same manner as he was offered and sacrificed on the cross as an expiation or satisfaction for sin. One would seem to be justified in concluding that the Council of Trent understood *immolare* to refer to the offering of a victim in sacrifice to God, specifically in death, since this is how Christ was offered on the cross. The teaching of Trent on the nature of the mass is that it is a repetition of the sacrifice of Christ because he is offered again as a propitiation for sin.

While the exact meaning of the term *immolare* as employed by Trent may be disputed, there is no ambiguity about the fact that the Council teaches that the mass is a propitiatory sacrifice for sin. It was at this point that the Reformers universally challenged the Roman teaching. They charged that if the mass were truly a propitiatory sacrifice then Christ must die, which contradicts the clear statement of Scripture that Christ died once for all and can never die again. And on the other hand, if Rome teaches that Christ does not die, its teaching that the mass is propitiatory for sin is false for it is not a true sacrifice. Vatican II says that the mass was instituted in order to perpetuate Christ's sacrifice through time. But if his death was once-for-all it cannot be perpetuated through time. Christ can never die again. Propitiation was accomplished at Calvary.

The propitiatory nature of the eucharist is the official teaching of the Roman Catholic Church and it claims that its interpretation and practice is a fulfilment of the prophecy of Malachi 1:11 that a pure and bloodless sacrifice would be offered throughout the world which was acceptable to God. Once again, however, we find this interpretation disputed by the vast majority of Fathers in the early Church. The Roman Catholic Church would lead us to believe that its particular teaching of the eucharistic sacrifice has been the view universally held in the Church from the very beginning. But, as with the teaching on the Real Presence, there is a parallel situation historically with the concept of the eucharist as a sacrifice. Some of the Fathers approach the Roman Catholic interpretation, but the majority do not. Their writings reveal that they viewed the Lord's Supper as a memorial of thanksgiving and praise in commemoration or remembrance of Christ's once-for-all atoning sacrifice, and not as a propitiatory sacrifice for sin. They referred to the prophecy of Malachi and taught that the eucharist was indeed a partial fulfilment of that prophecy, and even referred to it as a sacrifice, but they did not interpret this in the same way as the Church of Rome has done. As with the term 'tradition', the Roman Church has given the word 'sacrifice' a certain content and meaning and has read that back into the use of the word by the early Church. Because the Fathers use the term sacrifice to refer to the eucharist it does not mean that they accepted the meaning the Roman Church gives to the word, as a brief survey of the writings of the Fathers reveals.

The Eucharist

The *Didache* seems to refer to the eucharist as the *believer's* sacrifice, reflecting the idea of self-giving to the Lord through an offering of praise and thanksgiving for the finished work of Jesus Christ. There is no mention of its being a propitiatory sacrifice. Roman apologists have often appealed to Clement of Rome as a support for their sacrificial interpretation of the eucharist but this is done as a result of a mistranslation. Keating, for example, gives a translation of 1 Clement 44 where Clement mentions those 'from the episcopate who blamelessly and holily have offered its Sacrifices'.[22] The problem with this translation is that Clement does not use the word 'sacrifices' in his original letter but the word 'gifts'. So the appeal to Clement of Rome is an empty one.

Justin Martyr believed the eucharist was a spiritual sacrifice of praise and thanksgiving which commemorated the death of Christ by a Church which now counted Gentiles among its members.[23] Irenaeus also referred to Malachi's prophecy and characterized the eucharist as a thank-offering to God. He maintained that the real sacrifice intended within it was the prayers of true believers, which came from pure hearts wholly yielded to God and undefiled by sin.[24] Similarly, Tertullian argued that the true sacrifices offered to God were not of a carnal, physical kind, but the spiritual sacrifice of a broken and a contrite heart before God.[25] Origen and Clement of Alexandria stressed this same theme: that the real meaning of the eucharistic sacrifice was as a memorial or commemoration of the sacrifice of Christ which demanded the self-surrender of the soul to God. It was a sacrifice because it involved the prayers and praise of God's people; the self-surrender of themselves to God from broken and contrite hearts; and the giving of material offerings to the poor. There is absolutely no mention of the eucharist as the literal and renewed sacrifice of Christ as a propitiatory sin-offering.

Eusebius also explicitly states that the fulfilment of the prophecy of Malachi of a pure and bloodless sacrifice was to be found in the prayers and thanksgiving of true Christians throughout the world from contrite hearts.[26]

But the most influential advocate for this point of view was, once again, Augustine.[27] He was unequivocal in his belief that the Lord's Supper was a sacrifice of praise and thanksgiving, a commemoration of Christ's passion. The eucharist is simply a sacramental way of remembering Christ's once-for-all sacrifice. The sacrament is called a sacrifice only because it is identified with Calvary as a memorial or commemoration of that unique sacrifice.[28] It was not Christ who was offered in this memorial but the Church, who offered herself to God through Christ as a living sacrifice from a broken and a contrite heart. He, too, saw this as the fulfilment of the prophecy of Malachi.[29]

Though the early Church generally viewed the eucharist in spiritual terms, the concept began to emerge of a literal sacrifice in the eucharist. Nearly all historians agree that this change had it beginnings with the third century North African bishop and martyr, Cyprian. The Church at this time was drifting from reliance on God's grace in Jesus Christ to a theology which included the concept of human works to gain merit before God and to atone for sin through penance, asceticism and good works. Thus, the eucharist as a sacrifice began also to be looked upon, by some, as a means of propitiating God for sins committed after baptism. Men began to view the priest and Christian ministry as being parallel to the priesthood and ministry of the Old Testament. And though this analogy had been set forth by earlier Fathers, they always emphasized that the carnal sacrifices of Judaism had been displaced with the spiritual sacrifices of the Church on the basis of the completed sacrifice of Christ. There were no more sacrifices for sin. But the analogy began to lose its strictly spiritual character. Along with a materialistic view of the elements in the eucharist there began to develop through Cyprian, with his view of the sacerdotal nature of the priesthood, the concept of the eucharist as a literal sacrifice. He laid down the axiom:

If Jesus Christ, our Lord and God, is Himself the great High Priest of God the Father, and first offered Himself a Sacrifice to the Father, and commanded this to be done in remembrance of Himself, surely that Priest truly acts in Christ's stead, who imitates that which Christ did; and he then offers a true and full Sacrifice in the Church to God the Father, when he begins to offer it according as he sees Christ Himself offered it.[30]

The Eucharist

In this way Cyprian extended the traditional interpretation of the eucharist to include the concept of a sacramental re-enactment of the original sacrifice of Christ. In his mind, the eucharist was a sacrifice in the sense that it set forth as a memorial the original sacrifice. But given the materializing influences within the Church, it did not take long before the view of the eucharist as a sacramental re-enactment of Christ's sacrifice, in commemoration of him, was extended to the idea that Christ was truly and literally immolated on the altar. Chrysostom, for example, teaches that Christ physically suffers in the eucharistic sacrifice:

The bread which we break, is it not a communion of the Body of Christ?. . . But why adds he also, 'which we break'? For although in the Eucharist one may see this done, yet on the cross not so, but the very contrary. For, 'A bone of Him,' saith one, 'shall not be broken.' But that which He suffered not on the cross, this He suffers in the oblation for thy sake, and submits to be broken, that He may fill all men.[31]

The drama of such a 'real' sacrifice fostered increasingly bizarre 'visions' throughout the Church which were used in turn as proof for the truth of the doctrine. A vivid example of this phenomenon was the defence of the materialist view of the eucharist by Radbertus, the ninth century theologian, by recourse to a succession of 'marvellous stories of the visible appearances of the body and blood of Christ for the removal of doubts or the satisfaction of the pious desire of the saints. The bread on the altar, he reported, was often seen in the shape of a lamb or a little child, and when the priest stretched out his hand to break the bread, an angel descended from heaven with a knife, slaughtered the lamb or the child, and let his blood run into a cup.'[32]

Yet even when the Church was leaning more and more towards the concept of the literal sacrifice of Christ in the eucharist, the old view of the memorial of Christ's sacrifice articulated by Augustine and the early Church Fathers was still widely held. For the first 1200 years of the Church's life there was no unanimity on the nature of the eucharist.

The starting point for both interpretations (material and spiritual) of the eucharist was Scripture. Only in a detailed analysis of what Scripture has to say about the nature of Christ's sacrifice, and how believers are to commemorate this sacrifice, can we come to a definitive understanding.

There is an important Greek word which is used to describe both the death and the sacrifice of Christ: *ephapax*, which means 'once-for-all'. In Romans 6:9-10, Paul clearly states that Christ can never die again because his death was 'once-for-all'. The author of Hebrews insists that Christ cannot be sacrificed daily, that his body is offered 'once-for-all' and that because this once-for-all sacrifice has brought complete forgiveness of sin there is no longer any requirement for an offering or sacrifice for sin.[33] All that the animal sacrifices and human priesthood signified in the Old Testament, Christ has fulfilled. Consequently, God has abolished the priesthood and all sacrifices.

This presents the Roman Catholic Church with a dilemma. Scripture teaches that Christ's body and his sacrifice were offered *once*. Rome teaches that his body and sacrifice are offered *over and over again* in transubstantiation and the repetition of each mass. The Church attempts to get around this problem by claiming that the sacrifice of the mass is not a different sacrifice from that of Calvary but the same sacrifice perpetuated through time. Because God is beyond time the sacrifice of the cross is always present with him, and therefore the sacrifice of the mass is the same sacrifice as that of Calvary. This logic is a semantic smoke-screen: the sacrifice of the cross was an historic space-time event which occurred once and can never be repeated. The application of the Lord's sacrifice goes on through time in terms of the Holy Spirit bringing men to receive the benefits of his finished work, and the commemoration of his sacrifice goes on through time, but the sacrifice *itself* cannot be perpetuated. Indeed, the principal theme of the book of Hebrews is that there are no more sacrifices for sin of any kind whatsoever.

Scripture teaches that the Lord Jesus Christ has not only made a once-for-all-time atonement, but that his historical death on the cross is a complete atonement. He has completely satisfied God's justice: the debt due to man's sin has been fully paid and therefore all those who come to God through Jesus Christ are wholly free from condemnation. No

The Eucharist

further expiation for sin can ever be needed. The biblical view is that cleansing and forgiveness for sin are found in the blood of Jesus Christ alone, and never in the works or sufferings of man, for the law demands death as a penalty for sin. The significance of the reference to blood with respect to the work of Christ is that it signifies his life has been given over in death on our behalf and as a payment for our sin. It is because a full atonement has been made that a full forgiveness can be offered:

The blood of Jesus His Son cleanses us from all sin (*1 John* 1:7).
In Him we have redemption through His blood, the forgiveness of our trespasses, according to the riches of His grace (*Eph.* 1:7).

Scripture nowhere teaches that men must suffer temporal punishment for their own sins to render satisfaction to God, either in this life or in the life to come. All punishment for sin was borne by Christ. This is why the Word of God declares that 'There is therefore now no condemnation for those who are in Christ Jesus' (*Rom.* 8:1). God certainly disciplines believers for sin, but this has nothing to do with making atonement or expiation. In the discipline of his children God's action is remedial, not punitive; it flows from love, not wrath (see *Heb.* 12:4-13).

Scripture does speak of a eucharistic sacrifice. The word 'eucharist' literally means 'thanksgiving' and the New Testament frequently enjoins believers to offer this kind of sacrifice of praise: 'Through Him then, let us continually offer up a sacrifice of praise to God, that is, the fruit of the lips that give thanks to His name' (*Heb.* 13:15). This is the true eucharistic sacrifice. Scripture also speaks of other sacrifices the believer is to offer to God—our goods to meet the needs of others, and ourselves in total surrender to God (*Heb.* 13:16; *Rom.* 12:1). These are all true sacrifices in the New Testament but they have nothing to do with the expiation of sin.

If, as we have seen, there is no more sacrifice for sin—what is the meaning of the Lord's Supper? The Supper was established by the Lord Jesus as a memorial of thanksgiving and praise for his atoning sacrifice by which believers were to commune with him spiritually and also to proclaim his death until he comes again. The bread and wine, as Augustine points out, were given as figures or visible symbols of his body and blood and therefore are figurative expressions of his self-sacrifice. They are visible reminders to his people of what he has done on their behalf. When the Lord says, 'This is my body', he is speaking figuratively and not literally. In fact, in Matthew 26:29, Mark 14:25 and Luke 22:16,18, Christ refers to the wine after consecration as the 'fruit of the vine', indicating that it was still wine. Twice, in 1 Corinthians 11:23-27, Paul refers to the consecrated bread as 'bread'.

When Jesus refers to himself as the bread of life and says that men must eat his flesh and drink his blood, he makes it clear that his words were to be interpreted spiritually and figuratively: 'The flesh profits nothing; the words that I have spoken to you are spirit and are life' (*John* 6:63). This discourse could not refer to the Lord's Supper for Christ had not instituted that ordinance at the time he gave this teaching. He is not speaking here of the eucharist, but of his sacrifice on Calvary. The whole discourse of John 6 is a presentation of Jesus as the atoning sacrifice for the sin of the world in the giving of his flesh and blood, and how men are to appropriate the benefits of that sacrifice. It is those who *believe* who experience the benefits of his work, and so when he likens faith to eating his flesh and drinking his blood he is explaining the nature of saving faith as the appropriation of his person into the believer's heart. The Son of God would have us understand that saving faith is much more than mere intellectual assent to truth. As John Calvin pointed out:

We are quickened by the true partaking of him; and he has therefore designated this partaking by the words 'eating' and 'drinking', in order that no one should think that the life that we receive from him is received by mere knowledge. As it is not the seeing but the eating of bread that suffices to feed the body, so the soul must truly and deeply become partaker of Christ that it may be quickened to spiritual life by his power . . . In this way, the Lord intended, by calling himself 'the bread of life' (*John* 6:51), to teach not only that salvation for us rests on faith in his death and resurrection, but also that, by true partaking of him, his life passes into us and is made ours—just as bread when taken as food imparts vigour to the body.[34]

The Eucharist

Christ often used very vivid language to impress spiritual truth upon men's minds. When speaking with Nicodemus he tells him that he must be 'born again'. He refers to himself as a 'vine' and believers as 'branches'. These references are obviously not to be taken in a literal sense. Again, in Matthew 5:29-30 Jesus says:

And if your right eye makes you stumble, tear it out, and throw it from you; for it is better for you that one of the parts of your body perish, than for your whole body to be thrown into hell. And if your right hand makes you stumble, cut it off, and throw it from you; for it is better for you that one of the parts of your body perish, than for your whole body to go into hell.

Christ is obviously using starkly realistic language to convey an important spiritual truth: the necessity for radical repentance from sin. He speaks in physical terms but we are not meant to take his words in a literal, physical sense. Precisely the same is true with his teaching in John 6 and his words at the institution of the Lord's Supper. To interpret all his words in those passages literally would adopt an interpretation which directly contradicts the teaching of Scripture.

Jesus himself teaches us that the Church is to observe the Supper 'in remembrance of me'. The word remembrance is the Greek word which literally means a memorial. The Supper is no altar of sacrifice, but a table of remembrance, a place of spiritual communion with the Saviour by his Spirit. To teach that Christ has instituted a means whereby his sacrifice can be perpetuated through time is to contradict the plain teaching of Scripture.

This becomes yet clearer from the identification of the Lord's Supper with the Passover memorial of the Old Testament. The Lord's Supper was first celebrated at the time of the Jewish Passover and Jesus specifically identifies it as an equivalent when he says: 'I have earnestly desired to eat this Passover with you before I suffer' (*Luke* 22:15). What exactly was the Passover? It was an annual feast established by God in which the Jews would remember the night in which the angel of death 'passed over' those families which had applied the blood of the lamb to their door-posts (*Exod.* 12:1-13). 'Now this day will be a memorial to you, and you shall celebrate it as a feast to the Lord; throughout your generations you are to celebrate it as a permanent ordinance' (*Exod.* 12:14). This was a 'memorial' to a specific act of God in redeeming his people from bondage and death. The 'memorial' served to bring to remembrance an important event. It did not repeat the event but kept it vivid in the memory through a physical representation.

Just as God instituted a memorial of remembrance of redemption in the Old Testament, he has done the same in the New Testament. 1 Corinthians 5:7 states, 'For Christ our Passover also has been sacrificed.' His death is an accomplished fact. Now we are called, not to a sacrifice, but to a feast: 'Let us therefore celebrate the feast . . . with the unleavened bread of sincerity and truth' (*1 Cor.* 5:8). When Christ states that the bread is to be eaten and the wine drunk in *remembrance* of him, he is employing the same language as that of the Old Testament memorial in reference to the Passover. The Lord's Supper is not a sacrifice, it is the commemoration of a sacrifice.

The Roman Catholic teaching of the eucharist contradicts Scripture and it cannot be validated by the unanimous consent of the Fathers. To teach men to put trust in the eucharist as a sacrificial event is to undermine the gospel of Jesus Christ. It is to deny the sufficiency of his once-for-all sacrifice on the cross of Calvary. To suggest in any way that men must rely upon anything but Christ and his cross as God's means for dealing with sin is to lead men to a false trust and a false gospel.

9

Faith and Justification

The Scriptures teach us that God communicates saving grace to those who believe. Faith is foundational to true Christianity and it involves knowledge, assent, trust and commitment.[1] The object of faith is always God himself and its foundation is the Word of God. For faith to be truly biblical, it must involve more than just the assent of the mind to objective truth about God, Christ and salvation. Knowledge is vital, but it must always lead to trust and commitment to God as a person. This is what Scripture means when it says, 'But as many as received Him, to them He gave the right to become children of God, even to those who believe in His name' (*John* 1:12).

This tells us that salvation is found, not in a Church and its sacraments, but through a personal relationship with Christ himself. Salvation is given directly by Christ to an individual, without the need for any other mediation. To be a Christian means to have personal knowledge of the Son of God, a knowledge which secures commitment to him as Lord and Saviour. More particularly, there will be an implicit trust in the sufficiency of Christ and his work *alone*, and a total repudiation of all attempts to merit or earn forgiveness and eternal life through works of any kind, be they social, moral, religious or sacramental. True biblical faith always repudiates works as a grounds for justification. Genuine faith always involves a turning from sin, self-will and self-rule, and a surrender of the heart to Christ's lordship, with the commitment to live for his will and his glory. Saving faith, in other words, is always accompanied by repentance which means a whole-hearted turning from sin and corresponding surrender of the life to Christ. Where these things are found, there is true saving faith. But for any of these basic elements to be perverted or distorted, is to encourage a 'faith' which is less than saving.

Biblical faith will always produce a life characterized by love, holiness and good works. These works do not save us, but equally, the Epistle of James warns us against a faith which is empty and vain; that is, one that acknowledges the objective facts of God, Christ and salvation to be true but negates or neglects the other essential elements of trust and commitment. The demons believe in that sense, but they perish (*James* 2:19). Intellectual assent alone is empty, James argues. It does not save for it does not bring a person into union with the source of salvation. Where there is true union with Christ there will be a transformed life as evidence of that union; where there is mere intellectual assent divorced from true trust and commitment there may be orthodox belief, but no life of true holiness and love, for the heart has not been sanctified to God and regenerated.

In what sense is the Roman Catholic Church's teaching on faith inconsistent with the biblical teaching? To understand this we must understand the teaching of Thomas Aquinas[2], for it is his conception of faith which has become normative. In his *Summa Theologica*, Aquinas gives an in-depth description of the nature of faith. His conception could be fairly summed up in the following way: Faith means the assent of the intellect to that which is believed.[3] Faith is an assent to truth, by which he understood all the dogmas of the Church. Otherwise faith is lacking. The Scriptures are the foundation, but the Church alone is adequate to determine the correct interpretation of Scripture. Faith for Aquinas, and for the Roman Catholic Church, is thus viewed in purely intellectual terms. While related to the truth of Scripture, it is primarily centred in the Church itself. The major component of commitment and trust in the person of Christ himself is missing—instead, faith is belief in the teachings of the Church.

Yet the early Church did not have this limited conception of faith. In the writings of the Apostolic Fathers[4], for example, the basic biblical elements of faith were emphasized. The object of faith was not truth as an end in itself, nor the Church, but the persons of Father and Son. The trinitarian nature of God, and the human and divine natures of Christ were generally spelled out, and Christ's atonement was emphasized. Faith was opposed to works, and repentance was held to be the necessary complement to faith if one was to appropriate salvation.

However, as the understanding of the work of Christ became distorted, and penance began to replace the biblical concept of repentance, 'faith' was reduced to knowledge and assent to doctrine, especially doctrine related to the Trinity and to Christ. The object of faith was no longer God and Christ *as persons*, but rather the *truths about* God and Christ. Ultimately, with the growing influence of the sacramental view of the Church, saving faith began to be defined as belief in the Church itself and its teachings. This is why the Roman Church calls itself the 'universal sacrament of salvation'. In this theological framework there can be no true union with Christ, for men are taught that the work of Christ is not sufficient to obtain forgiveness for all sin: their own works are necessary to procure God's favour and forgiveness; baptism is the means whereby Christ indwells the heart and the individual is united to him; and the eucharist is the means whereby his presence and this union are sustained in the heart.

The practical result is that the biblical meaning of faith is perverted. There is a false foundation of knowledge to which men are called to assent for the Church and its teachings are held up as the means of salvation. The individual's faith is not directed toward Christ himself so that a person trusts in him alone and commits one's life to him. In effect, it is commitment to and trust in the Church and its sacraments, rather than Christ himself.

This emphasis upon the intellectual aspect of faith, and the corresponding divergence from the biblical standard began in an innocent, subtle way. The need to protect true doctrine against heresy led to growing concerns to demand fealty to creeds or statements of faith. There is nothing innately wrong with creeds. They are useful aids to synthesizing important scriptural truth. The danger comes if men begin to think of Christianity primarily in terms of right belief, and it becomes nothing more than orthodox doctrine. Although the early Fathers such as Irenaeus used the term 'the rule of faith', faith to them was more than belief in a creed; it still included trust in and commitment to the person of Christ. But the doctrinal controversies of the first few centuries on the Trinity and the person of Christ involved a heavy emphasis on philosophical terms, and consequently faith began to be viewed primarily as having right belief about God and Christ. Over time, faith became defined as intellectual assent to the dogmas of the Church as they had been expressed in an orthodox consensus (based on the formulations of the creeds and the opinions of the Fathers as orthodox interpreters of Scripture).

This emphasis on intellectual assent to doctrine as the ground of faith gradually eliminated the other essential elements of commitment and trust in the person and work of the Lord Jesus Christ. Christ's work was slowly subverted by the Church's teaching on purgatory, the eucharist and good works. Penance eventually displaced repentance with the result that salvation was no longer found exclusively in a relationship with Christ alone but in one's relationship with the Church and through one's own works. More and more through time the Church drifted into externalism and religious materialism.

This was a catastrophic loss for the Church, effectively impoverishing it for centuries. Faith in Christ crucified and risen is God's chosen method of justifying his people. This is not to say that an individual is saved *by* faith, but it is *through* faith. It is not faith but Christ who saves and faith is merely the means which God has ordained for appropriating that salvation.

As we have repeatedly seen in different contexts throughout this book, men are justified through faith and not through their own good deeds:[5]

He saved us, not on the basis of deeds which we have done in righteousness, but according to His mercy, by the washing of regeneration and renewing by the Holy Spirit, whom He poured out upon us richly through Jesus Christ our Saviour, that being justified by His grace we might be made heirs according to the hope of eternal life (*Titus* 3:5-7).

To be justified by God's grace does not mean that a believer is so influenced by grace that he or she can do good works and earn justification and eternal life. It means a complete repudiation of works of any kind as a basis for justification. This was reiterated by Paul in his letter of admonition to the Galatian church: 'You have been severed from Christ, you who are seeking to be justified by law; you have fallen from grace' (*Gal.* 5:4). The entire theme of that letter is Paul's reiteration of a crucial principle: to introduce any work, be it a ritual or a work of morality or of holiness, as a supplement to the work of Christ for justification, is to fall from the principle of grace. For those who do so, Paul warns that 'Christ will be of no benefit to you' (*Gal.* 5:2).

The common Roman Catholic interpretation is that the word law refers only to the ceremonial law of the Jews and not to the moral law, the ten commandments. Thus Ludwig Ott writes: 'When St Paul teaches that we are saved by faith without works of the law . . . by the works of the law he means the works of the law of the Old Testament, for example, circumcision.'[6] But this is a misrepresentation of the truth. By the term, law, Paul often refers to the moral law of God. We know this to be the case because in Romans 3:20 Paul tells us that the function of the law is to bring an individual to a knowledge of personal sin and in Romans 7:7-13 he gives us an illustration of how that is accomplished, as well as defining for us what he means by the term 'law':

What shall we say then? Is the law sin? May it never be! On the contrary, I would not have come to know sin except through the law; for I would not have known about coveting if the law had not said, 'You shall not covet.' But sin, taking opportunity through the commandment, produced in me coveting of every kind; for apart from the law sin is dead.

Paul defines the term 'law' here by the command: 'You shall not covet'. That is the tenth commandment and therefore the term 'law', as used by Paul, includes not only the ceremonial law but also the moral law, the ten commandments. It is essential to know this if we are to understand that justification is not based on moral or religious works of any kind.

The word 'justification' is primarily a judicial or legal term. Justification is declarative in nature; it refers to a person's right standing, or status, before God. To 'declare righteous' or 'to justify' are different translations of the same word and they are identical in meaning. Justification is the act of God whereby a sinner is accepted and set free from all judgment and condemnation on the basis of Christ's righteousness which is accounted to him (*Rom.* 5:1, 8:1). The righteousness which saves comes as a gift (*Rom.* 5:17) and is accounted to the believer, making it his own (*2 Cor.* 5:21). This is done because Christ, as the believer's substitute, has fulfilled perfectly every requirement of the law of God on his behalf. Christ has lived a perfect life and has borne the full penalty of God's judgment against sin.

It is this 'righteousness' or obedience of Christ which is imputed as a gift to all who come to him in faith. This is completely independent of the work of man. Righteousness is received by faith and it provides complete acquittal from the guilt of sin and a perfect legal standing before God (*Rom.* 4:1-8; *Phil.* 3:7-9). It is important to point out that when Paul describes the salvation he experienced in Philippians 3 he does not say that he received *grace* by faith which would enable him to work to be justified; he received an objective righteousness as a gift, outside of himself, by which he was justified. Scripture teaches that this righteousness is a completed righteousness because it is Christ's. Apart from our own works, or those of any other, Christ's righteousness is *imputed* to the believer: 'Just as David also speaks of the blessing upon the man to whom God reckons righteousness *apart from works*' (*Rom.* 4:6). Actually, it is a righteousness that is grounded in works, but it is the work of obedience accomplished by Christ and not by us. This righteousness is absolutely essential for an individual to possess because God demands a perfect righteousness for men to be accepted by him. Man's works, even at their very best, and even under the influence of grace, are unacceptable to God as a foundation for salvation, for they are never perfect. Only Christ has accomplished a perfect obedience and has rendered a perfect fulfilment of the law. Justification is a gift that is always related to the work of Christ alone, and never to the work of an individual.

Because justification is totally dependent on the work of Christ, it is perfect and permanent in nature. It is once-for-all. When an individual is justified, therefore, he cannot lose that grace—which is why Scripture speaks with such certainty about the assurance of eternal salvation:

Truly, truly, I say to you, he who hears My word, and believes Him who sent Me, has eternal life, and does not come into judgement, but has passed out of death into life (*John* 5:24).

My sheep hear My voice, and I know them, and they follow Me; and I give eternal life to them, and they shall never perish; and no one shall snatch them out of My hand. My Father, who has given them to Me, is greater than all; and no one is able to snatch them out of the Father's hand (*John* 10:27-29).

Who will bring a charge against God's elect? God is the one who justifies; who is the one who condemns? Christ Jesus is He who died, yes, rather who was raised, who is at the right hand of God, who also intercedes for us. Who shall separate us from the love of Christ? Shall tribulation, or distress, or persecution or famine, or nakedness, or peril, or sword? . . . But in all these things we overwhelmingly conquer through Him who loved us. For I am convinced that neither death, nor life, nor angels, nor principalities, nor things present, nor things to come, nor powers, nor height, nor depth, nor any other created thing, shall be able to separate us from the love of God, which is in Christ Jesus our Lord (*Rom.* 8:33-35, 37-39).

This assurance is also seen in the fact that the words 'justification' and 'salvation' are often used in Scripture with reference to the past, signifying something that is an accomplished fact and not an on-going process that one works to attain.[7]

There are a number of other important benefits of a believer's union with Christ. Salvation is not simply a legal declaration of forgiveness and deliverance from an eternal hell. It is much more. It involves a variety of blessings: the regeneration of the individual so that he becomes a new creation; adoption into the family of God; and the indwelling of the Holy Spirit in the heart empowering him to pursue holiness. Because the individual receives a new heart he has new motivations and desires which manifest themselves in sincere love for God, Christ and men—his life is progressively transformed as he becomes more and more like his Lord and Saviour. This process is known as sanctification and is distinct from, although just as supernatural as, the justification of the believer. Some Roman Catholic apologists have claimed that the two terms are used interchangeably in Scripture but this is simply not the case. The Word of God always presents them as two separate concepts[8]—justification is the name given in the Bible to the changed status, not the changed nature. The same grace which justifies a man eternally in the sight of God is the grace which sanctifies him, but this sanctification is not in any sense part of his justification before God.

Roman apologists are fond of accusing the Reformers and Protestant believers of teaching a false view of salvation. They claim that Luther and Calvin taught that one need only trust in Christ for salvation and that this trust in no way affected the moral life of the individual. In other words, salvation is only a legal declaration of forgiveness which still leaves a man in his sinful condition. But this is a complete misrepresentation of their teaching.[9] The Reformers were concerned to define accurately the true nature of justification as one particular aspect of salvation, but they never taught that salvation could be separated from a life of progressive sanctification. They emphasized the truth of justification because the Scriptures themselves emphasize it and because it had been so perverted.

The Roman Catholic Church's teaching on justification is quite different from that of the Scriptures. It uses biblical terms, but the definition it gives to them corrupts their original biblical meaning.[10] The whole concept of justification has been redefined in Roman Catholic theology in order to harmonise with the rest of the Church's teaching on the work of Christ and the sacraments. Because salvation, according to Roman Catholic theology, is not a completed work and a final forgiveness of sins, it is necessary to participate in the sacraments and the fulfilment of penances and good works. Justification is not a finished act with permanent consequences, but a process in which an individual works to stay in what the Roman Church calls 'a state of grace'. If a person commits a mortal sin, then he loses sanctifying grace and forfeits the state of justification which must be regained through confession and penance, the eucharist and good works. So justification ultimately depends on an individual's own personal works, though the Roman Church claims this is to be attributed solely to the merits of Christ and the grace of God.

Grace, according to the Roman Catholic Church, is an infused quality in the soul of a man, given by God. It enables him to perform righteous acts and thereby to continue on in the process of justification. As a man's sanctification or good works increase, so it is claimed his justification can increase. This infused grace is received with faith and baptism, and continues through participation in the sacraments and by the performance of meritorious works. Faith is not the appropriation of the person of Christ but the assent to truths taught by the Church. It is the sacrament which brings remission of sins, union with Christ, the indwelling of the Spirit, regeneration and adoption into the family of God. The individual is not taught to come to Christ directly in a personal relationship and to trust him completely for salvation, but to receive his grace through the sacraments of the Church. Those who are baptized as infants are told that in baptism all of the things mentioned above occurred to them and now they are responsible for maintaining the grace received through good works and the sacraments. There is no need to come to Christ for they have already been baptized.

In Roman Catholic theology sanctification is merged into justification and becomes part of the basis for our gaining and maintaining forgiveness and acceptance with God. Justification, in the Roman view, is not a legal declarative act of God based upon the imputed righteousness of Christ, but a process related to imparted grace by which a man, who has received grace to be justified, works to continue to be justified.

According to Roman Catholic theology justification is

merited by human works. Roman Catholic theologian, Ludwig Ott, states:

> The Council of Trent teaches that for the justified eternal life is both a gift or grace promised by God and a reward for his own good works and merits. As God's grace is the presupposition and foundation of good works, by which man merits eternal life, so salutary works are, at the same time gifts of God and meritorious acts of man . . . Blessedness in heaven is the reward for good works performed on this earth, and rewards and merit are correlative concepts . . . A just man merits for himself through each good work . . . eternal life (if he dies in a state of grace).[11]

Even though the Roman Church speaks of grace which alone can enable an individual to perform righteous acts, by adding human merit to grace in justification, it completely nullifies the biblical concept of grace as Romans 11:6 makes very clear: 'But if it is by grace, it is no longer on the basis of works, otherwise grace is no longer grace.' The Roman Catholic teaching of grace and justification is a perversion of the biblical teaching. For all its talk about grace, Rome, in the name of grace, has perverted and overthrown its true meaning.

The Roman Catholic Church characteristically defends its position by interpreting passages of Scripture which relate solely to sanctification as if they were speaking about justification. Philippians 2:12-13 provides an example: 'So then, my beloved, just as you have always obeyed, not as in my presence only, but now much more in my absence, work out your salvation with fear and trembling, for it is God who is at work in you, both to will and to work for His good pleasure.' We are told specifically here to 'work out' our salvation. But Paul is writing to men and women who have already experienced *justification*; he is exhorting them to a life of *sanctification*. He is not telling them to work *for* their salvation, but to work *out* what God has already worked in—'for it is God who is at work in you, to will and to do for his good pleasure'. Not only does the logic of the passage refute the Roman Catholic interpretation, but to accept the view that Paul is instructing the believers in Philippi to ensure their justification through their good works would make the apostle a liar, because else-

Faith and Justification

where he told Titus and the believers in Ephesus, Galatia and Rome as well as these same brothers and sisters in Philippi that justification is not by works but by faith (*Titus* 3:5; *Eph.* 2:8-9; *Gal.* 2:16; *Rom.* 3:19-20; *Phil.* 3:3-9).

To teach that a man is justified in any way by works is legalism which is condemned in the Word of God. But to teach that a man can be saved or justified without his life manifesting the grace of sanctification is antinomianism, which is also condemned in Scripture. Justification and sanctification must both be emphasized as parts of salvation. But the works of sanctification are never the *basis* upon which a person is justified. The true believer will walk in holiness for the express reason that he is justified. Paul brings these two concepts together:

> For by grace you have been saved through faith; and that not of yourselves, it is the gift of God; not as a result of works, that no one should boast. For we are His workmanship, created in Christ Jesus for good works, which God prepared beforehand, that we should walk in them (*Eph.* 2:8-10).

We are justified through faith and not through our own good works, but when we are made a new creation in Christ, we will then live a life of good works. The Word of God never makes sanctification the grounds for justification, and we must be careful to maintain the same distinction. The righteousness by which we are justified is not the righteousness of sanctification but the imputed righteousness of Christ which is received as a gift.

To shift the basis of justification from the imputed righteousness of Christ to a human righteousness is to pervert the gospel of Jesus Christ. It is the very thing condemned by Paul in his epistle to the Galatians. It deceives men as to the nature of true salvation, for rather than being an exclusive work of God which men receive through faith as a gift by grace, it becomes a work of man. Man's work ultimately displaces the work of Jesus Christ. 'The praise of the glory of his grace' (*Eph.* 1:6) is silenced. The Church of Rome would do well to heed the warning of the apostle:

> I am amazed that you are so quickly deserting Him who called you by the grace of Christ, for another gospel; which is really not

another; only there are some who are disturbing you, and want to distort the gospel of Christ. But even though we, or an angel from heaven, should preach to you a gospel contrary to that which we have preached to you, let him be accursed . . . Nevertheless knowing that a man is not justified by the works of the Law but through faith in Christ Jesus, even we have believed in Christ Jesus . . . since by the works of the Law shall no flesh be justified (*Gal.* 1:6-8; 2:16).

10

Truth: The Defining Issue

The Roman Catholic Church makes certain claims for its tradition which it says can be validated by Scripture and the facts of history. It states that it alone is the one true Church which has faithfully preserved the apostolic teaching of the gospel received from Jesus Christ, either orally or in writing. The case we have sought to set out in these pages is that these assertions are false. When the Lord Jesus began to preach and teach the Word of God he was opposed by the religious leaders of the Church of his day, who claimed that he did not follow the Jewish tradition. Jesus' response was to condemn their tradition because much of its teaching invalidated the Word of God. Tragically, just as traditional practices corrupted and superseded God's Word in the minds of the Jewish people before Jesus was born, the same thing happened in his Church after he ascended into heaven.

In *The Life and Times of Jesus the Messiah*, Alfred Edersheim documents the development of a body of tradition within Judaism known as the 'tradition of the elders'. He points out that the Jews possessed the Scriptures in the Old Testament, but they also believed there had been an oral tradition given by God to Moses which was faithfully passed down through the Jewish fathers. And over time a body of scriptural interpretation by the most revered fathers and rabbis developed which became as authoritative as Scripture itself. The Old Testament, within Judaism, was acknowledged to be authoritative and inspired, but for all practical purposes the real authority in the life of the nation was its tradition.

The parallel in the development of a tradition within the

Roman Catholic Church is astonishing. Scripture is acknowledged to be inspired and authoritative but, as with Judaism, it is argued that God's Word has been supplemented by an oral tradition handed down by the apostles from Christ, faithfully preserved by the Fathers and bishops, and eventually viewed as equally authoritative as the Scriptures themselves. Although the claim is made that Rome's tradition is apostolic, it is, in reality a tradition which has embraced many of the same corruptions which characterized the Jewish tradition.

The New Testament is full of warnings against traditionalism, sacramentalism, legalism, asceticism and human philosophy, for these were the specific errors of Judaism. Yet the Church failed to heed these warnings and began to repeat the same errors:

> The Jews adhered to a body of tradition which invalidated the Word of God. Likewise, the Roman Catholic Church promotes a tradition, the teachings of which also invalidate the Word of God.
>
> The Jews taught sacramentalism by teaching that circumcision was a rite which guaranteed the individual's inheritance as part of the Jewish nation. Similarly, the Roman Catholic Church embraced sacramentalism in its teaching that a man is saved through baptism and being a part of the Roman Catholic Church.
>
> The Jews taught legalism through their identification of repentance with penance, good works and asceticism to merit God's forgiveness and favour, as is clear from Christ's many criticisms of the religious leaders. In the same way, Rome promotes legalism through its identification of repentance with penance, good works and asceticism.
>
> Christ condemned the practice of mechanical praying, that is, simply repeating the same words over and over again in a set form, a practice he described as vain or meaningless repetition. The Roman Catholic Church has repeated this error in its promotion of the rosary and other form prayers.
>
> The Jewish leadership was condemned by Christ for its

spirit of greed in using the temple and spiritual duties to enrich themselves and the treasury. The papacy's historic use of indulgences for its own enrichment is a direct parallel.

Judaisers taught that one must become a Jew to experience salvation. The Roman Catholic Church teaches that one must become a Roman Catholic to be saved.

The parallels are only too plain. In effect, in the name of Christ the Roman Catholic Church has perverted the gospel of Christ.

All this has direct bearing on how one defines the nature of the Church. The Roman Catholic Church claims that it alone is the Church which is truly catholic and apostolic. But the Church of Rome has redefined the biblical concept of the Church so that it is identified with an outward, visible organization, while the Scriptures teach that the Church is first spiritual in nature. It is comprised of all who are united to Jesus Christ and indwelt by the Holy Spirit. Such persons will normally be members of churches, but one can be part of the visible organization and not be united to Jesus Christ.

The claims to apostolic authority and catholicity are undermined by the Roman Catholic tradition. Such claims cannot be supported by alleged apostolic succession and papal authority; they have to be proved by conformity to apostolic teaching as recorded in Scripture. Truth, and especially the truth of the gospel, is the foundation and absolute essential to the nature of the true Church. In its breadth this gospel transcends all denominational and visible church organizations.

The New Testament makes it abundantly clear that a particular church can only be regarded as such as long as it is true to the truth. Churches exist for the gospel and without the gospel they are no churches at all. So Paul writes of 'the household of God, which is the church of the living God, the pillar and support of the truth' (*1 Tim.* 3:15). Roman apologists have long insisted that this verse teaches that the Church is the foundation to the Scriptures and is therefore the ultimate authority. But the verse actually tells us that the

Church is to support the truth, not determine what it is. The Church's business is to uphold the truth of God by guarding (*2 Tim.* 1:14), defending (*Jude* 3), proclaiming (*2 Tim.* 4:2) and holding it fast (*Phil.* 2:16).

The truth of the gospel is the real cornerstone and foundation to the whole issue of unity. The Roman Catholic Church is very fond of contrasting its supposed unity with what it characterizes as the rampant disunity of the Protestant Church. But this argument is empty on two counts. First of all the appearance of unity within the Roman Catholic Church is very misleading. Do all Roman Catholics agree on every single point of doctrine defined by the Council of Trent and Vatican I? Do all Roman Catholics agree with the anathemas of these Councils against anyone who disagrees with their teachings? Do all the bishops and priests agree on every point of doctrine authoritatively decreed by the Roman Church? The answer, obviously, is no. There is a vast array of subjects upon which one will find large scale disagreement among Roman Catholics. There are multitudes of Roman Catholics who do not take seriously the dogmatic teachings of their own Church. But for the sake of argument let us assume that there is complete unanimity of opinion in the Roman Church and a perfect unity. That proves nothing. Unity is not the issue. Truth is the issue. The Jews and the false prophets in Elijah's day were solidly unified. Does their unity make them right? The question is, Is the unity based on truth? To be unified around falsehood may prove that we are unified; it does not prove that we have true biblical unity.

Then there is the question of the Protestant Church. Is it really as disunified as the Roman Church would have us believe? The Protestant Church is made up of a number of main-line denominations which in turn consist of many subgroups if you will. These denominations do not agree on every point of doctrine, it is true. But generally speaking, the disagreements centre around issues that are peripheral to the fundamental issues of the faith. When it comes to the essentials and the basics of the faith, as set forth in their confessional statements, they are generally in agreement. The creed of the Protestant Church, as a whole, is in complete agreement with the content of the apostolic tradition described by Irenaeus. Multitudes of Protestant churches are true to their creed and fully embrace the teaching of the Trinity, the authority of Scripture, the redeeming work of Christ, his resurrection, ascension and second coming, justification by faith, heaven and hell and the judgment to come. There is unity in the belief that there are two sacraments: the Lord's Supper and baptism. There is unity in the rejection of the Roman Catholic teachings on the papacy and Mary. The fact is, to embrace unity with the Roman Catholic Church of today is to embrace disunity with the truly catholic Church of the early centuries. The Protestant Reformation was not heretical or schismatic; it was rather a return to historic Christianity and a reaffirmation of the biblical gospel. It is the Roman Church which is the true promoter of schism and heresy as over the centuries it has departed from the truth and demanded submission to falsehood.

There are of course Protestant denominations which have departed from the basics of the faith as defined by the Scriptures and the Protestant Reformers. They are no longer truly Protestant, they are apostate. And there are many disagreements between Protestants which are based on personalities and sinful attitudes. This is wrong and must be censured from Scripture as strongly as errors in belief are to be censured. But the existence of sin and unbelief does not invalidate the truth around which the Reformation was focused. What unites Protestants is far greater than what divides them. The gospel which united men and women to Christ is still the same gospel which makes them essentially one. The ecumenical movement would have us downplay the importance of truth and would seek a unity that compromises the gospel. But uniformity is not unity. True spiritual unity can only be attained by adherence to truth.

It is, then, at the point of truth, both biblical and historical, that the Roman Catholic Church's claim to be truly apostolic and catholic is found to be spurious. While it affirms much teaching that is certainly catholic and apostolic, it undermines the truth by adding teachings which contradict the Scriptures and the truth of the gospel. The Roman system is no more the friend of Christ than was Judaism.

The Roman Catholic Church has distorted the truth by

elevating man and man's authority and works to the central place which belongs to Christ and God alone in the crucial issues of authority and salvation. Through its legalistic teachings it has invalidated the work of Christ in salvation. By elevating Mary to the position of mediatrix and queen, and the pope as visible head of the Church, it has set aside the biblical teaching that Christ is the only head and sovereign over the church. By encouraging the worship of Mary it has promoted idolatry. By its teachings on the sacraments and the priesthood it has undermined the sufficiency of the atonement of Jesus Christ and his unique and exclusive role as mediator and priest. In its teaching on grace and justification it has shifted the foundation for salvation from the imputed righteousness of Christ to imparted grace which enables a man to merit heaven by his own works thereby perverting the biblical meaning of grace and centring salvation in a work of man. Through its teaching on asceticism and purgatory it has embraced the influences of pagan philosophy in Gnosticism, Stoicism and Platonism. In short, by elevating the teachings of men in its tradition to a place of authority equal to the Scriptures, it has displaced God's authority with its own.

* * *

From the historical standpoint, the Roman Catholic Church claims that the content of its tradition can be traced back two thousand years through a unanimous consent of the Fathers in unbroken succession to the apostles and the Lord Jesus Christ himself. As we have seen, this unanimous consent never existed. The facts demonstrate that not only is there no unanimous consent among the Fathers for the Roman tradition, but that many of the teachings now promoted by Rome were either contradicted, opposed or repudiated by the *magisterium* of the early Church.

The tradition of Roman Catholicism simply is not true, either biblically or historically. The Church of Rome responds to this judgment by appealing to papal infallibility as a guarantee of the impossibility of such a defection. But the theory of infallibility is equally opposed by the facts of history and the truth of Scripture. As Scripture itself warns,

Gentile churches are no more promised preservation from unbelief and error than were the Jews: 'they were broken off for their unbelief, and you stand *only* by your faith. Do not be conceited, but fear' (*Rom.* 11:20).[1] No such words would have been necessary if the Roman interpretation of Scripture that Christ would grant the Church infallibility and immunity from error were true. The facts of history prove it is not true. The Roman Catholic Church *has* erred in its teaching and cloaking itself in a humanly engineered shroud of infallibility will not change that reality. The tragic results of such a teaching are that it insulates those who accept it from being able to hear the voice of the Spirit of God who desires to bring the Church to repentance. The same thing happened to the Jews in Jesus' day. Their false presuppositions regarding their religious status and their relationship to God led them to refuse to listen to the Son of God as he criticised their tradition. And like the Jews, the Roman Church is leading multitudes astray by its false teaching.

Christ called the Jews of his day back to the final authority of the Word of God and to an abandonment of those traditional teachings which had invalidated Scripture for so long. For Christ, Scripture is the ultimate authority, and he is still calling men back to a submission to the final authority of Scripture and its message of salvation. For those who will heed, the message is clear: salvation is not found in a Church and sacraments and human works but in coming to the person of Jesus Christ, personally and directly, by repudiating all works—sacramental, moral and social—and committing one's life unreservedly to him and trusting in him and his work alone as the source of salvation. Christianity is not a matter of being a Roman Catholic *or* even a Protestant in the formal sense. It is not a matter of being associated with a certain Church. We must hear the truth of the gospel, understand that truth and then respond to it in repentance and faith. We enter the kingdom of God by being personally and directly united to the person of Christ through the power of the Holy Spirit.

Scripture teaches us that Christianity is Christ, not a Church. It is knowing Christ, being submitted to Christ, committed to Christ, trusting in Christ, serving Christ, worshipping Christ, obeying Christ, loving Christ, walking with Christ, and following Christ—exclusively.

In the issues of authority and salvation we are pointed by Scripture to Christ as the only rock and head of the Church; to Christ as the only mediator, sacrifice and priest; to Christ as the only Saviour; to Christ *alone* who is received by faith *alone*. Christianity is Christ!

* * *

In order to come to Christ, then, every one who truly desires salvation must look to Scripture to reveal the way to God. And where Scripture proves contrary to church tradition or any religious system, the truth seeker must willingly turn from all else to follow Christ according to the divinely inspired Word of God. Scripture calls us to commitment to the person of Christ, not a Church. There are Catholics within the Roman system who have seen this and have come into a genuine experience of salvation by the grace of God. They have rejected the dogmatic teachings of the Church and have trusted in Christ alone. I do not want to be misunderstood as saying that all Roman Catholics are lost. That simply is not the case. But such individuals are confronted with a very difficult and inescapable decision. A commitment to Christ means a commitment to truth, especially the truth of the gospel. Paul makes it clear in Galatians 1:6-8 that to be identified with a perverted gospel is to desert the person of Christ himself. But the gospel taught by the Church of Rome is a perversion of the gospel of grace. Therefore to stay within Roman Catholicism is to be identified with a system that denies the sufficiency of the work of Christ alone. One cannot be true to Christ and remain in a system that is so fundamentally opposed to him in teaching and practice.

I would plead with those within Roman Catholicism who are struggling with the implications of true faith in Christ to come out and be fully identified with truth. And I would plead with Roman Catholics whose trust and commitment is centred in the Church—dear reader—heed the Word of God and look at history. Turn from error and embrace truth. Come to Christ in true biblical faith and be saved!

APPENDICES

1

The Fathers on the Meaning of Tradition and its Relationship to Scripture

Irenaeus (140–202 A.D.)
We have learned from none others the plan of our salvation, than from those through whom the gospel has come down to us, which they did at one time proclaim in public, and, at a later period, by the will of God, handed down to us in the Scriptures, to be the ground and pillar of our faith.[1]

Since, therefore, the tradition from the apostles does thus exist in the church, and is permanent among us, let us revert to the scriptural proof furnished by those apostles who did also write the Gospel, in which they recorded the doctrine regarding God.[2]

Tertullian (155/160–240/250 A.D.)
Let them, then, prove to us that those angels derived their flesh from the stars. If they do not prove it because it is not written, neither will the flesh of Christ get its origin therefrom, for which they borrow the precedent of the angels . . . But there is no evidence of this, because Scripture says nothing.[3]

The Scriptures . . . indeed furnish us with our Rule of faith.[4]

On the whole, then, if that is evidently more true which is earlier, if that is earlier which is from the beginning, if that is from the beginning which has the apostles for its authors, then it will certainly be quite as evident, that that comes down from the apostles, which has been kept as a sacred deposit in the churches of the apostles. Let us see what milk the Corinthians drank from Paul; to what rule of faith the Galatians were brought for correction; what the Philippians, the Thessalonians, the Ephesians read by it; what utterance also the Romans give, so very near to the apostles . . . We have also St. John's foster churches. For although Marcion rejects his Apocalypse, the order of the bishops (thereof), when traced up to their origin, will rest on John as their author . . . I say . . . that the Gospel of Luke . . . has stood its ground from its very first publication . . . The same authority of the apostolic churches will afford evidence to the other Gospels also, which we possess equally through their means, and according to their usage—I mean the Gospels of John and Matthew— whilst that which Mark published may be affirmed to be Peter's whose interpreter Mark was.[5]

Hippolytus (d. 235 A.D.)
There is, brethren, one God, the knowledge of whom we gain from the Holy Scriptures, and from no other source. For just as a man if he wishes to be skilled in the wisdom of this world, will find himself unable to get at it in any other way than by mastering the dogmas of philosophers, so all of us who wish to practise piety will be unable to learn its practice from any other quarter than the oracles of God. Whatever things then the Holy Scriptures declare, at these let us look; and whatsoever things they teach these let us learn.[6]

Cyprian (200/210–258 A.D.)
'Be there no innovation,' he says, 'beyond what has been handed down to us.' Whence is that tradition? Whether does it descend from the authority of the Lord and the Gospel, or does it come from the injunctions and Epistles of the Apostles? For that we are to do what is written, God testifieth and admonisheth, saying to Joshua: 'The book of this law shall not depart out of thy mouth; but thou shalt meditate therein day and night, that thou mayest observe to do accord-

ing to all that is written therein.' Likewise the Lord, sending His Apostles, directs that the nations should be baptized and taught to observe all things whatsoever He had commanded. If then it is commanded in the Gospel, or is contained in the Epistles or Acts of the Apostles, that 'such as come from any heresy whatsoever should not be baptized, but hands only laid on them in order to repentance'; then be this divine and holy tradition observed.[7]

Clement of Alexandria (c.150–211/216 A.D.)
But those who are ready to toil in the most excellent pursuits, will not desist from the search after truth, till they get the demonstration from the Scriptures themselves.

He, who has spurned the ecclesiastical tradition, and darted off to the opinion of heretical men, has ceased to be a man of God and to remain faithful to the Lord. But he who has returned from this deception, on hearing the Scriptures, and turned his life to the truth, is, as it were, from being a man made a god. For we have, as the source of teaching, the Lord, both by the prophets, the Gospel, and the blessed apostles, 'in divers manners and at sundry times', leading from the beginning of knowledge to the end. But if one should suppose that another origin was required, then no longer truly could an origin be preserved. He, then, who of himself believes the Scripture and voice of the Lord, which by the Lord acts to the benefiting of men, is rightly [regarded] faithful. Certainly we use it as a criterion in the discovery of things. What is subjected to criticism is not believed till it is so subjected; so that what needs criticism cannot be a first principle . . . and receiving in abundance, from the first principle itself, demonstrations in reference to the first principle, we are by the voice of the Lord trained up to the knowledge of the truth.[8]

Origen (c.185–253/254 A.D.)
But that we may not appear to build our assertions on subjects of such importance and difficulty on the ground of

inference alone, or to require the assent of our hearers to what is only conjectural, let us see whether we can obtain any declarations from holy Scripture, by the authority of which these positions may be more credibly maintained.[9]

In proof of all words which we advance in matters of doctrine, we ought to set forth the sense of Scripture as confirming the meaning which we are proposing. For as all gold which was outside of the temple was not sanctified, so every sense which is outside of the divine Scripture, however admirable it may appear to some, is not sacred because it is not limited by the sense of Scripture. Therefore we should not take our own ideas for the confirmation of doctrine, unless someone shows that they are holy because they are contained in the divine Scriptures as in the temples of God.[10]

Cyril of Jerusalem (315–386 A.D.)
For concerning the divine and sacred Mysteries of the Faith, we ought not to deliver even the most casual remark without the Holy Scriptures: nor be drawn aside by mere probabilities and the artifices of argument. Do not then believe me because I tell thee these things, unless thou receive from the Holy Scriptures the proof of what is set forth: for this salvation, which is of our faith, is not by ingenious reasonings, but by proof from the Holy Scriptures.[11]

Let us then speak nothing concerning the Holy Ghost but what is written; and if any thing be not written, let us not busy ourselves about it. The Holy Ghost Himself spake the Scriptures; He has also spoken concerning Himself as much as He pleased, or as much as we could receive. Be those things therefore spoken, which He has said; for whatsoever He has not said, we dare not say.[12]

Chrysostom (344/354–407 A.D.)
These then are the reasons; but it is necessary to establish them all from the Scriptures, and to show with exactness that all that has been said on this subject is not an invention of human reasoning, but the very sentence of the Scriptures.[13]

All Scripture is given by inspiration of God, and is profitable for doctrine, for reproof, for correction, for instruction in righteousness . . . For doctrine. For thence we shall know, whether we ought to learn or be ignorant of any thing. And thence we may disprove what is false, thence we may be corrected and brought to a right mind, may be comforted and consoled, and if any thing is deficient, we may have it added to us. That the man of God may be perfect. For this is the exhortation of the Scripture given, that the man of God may be rendered perfect by it; without this therefore he cannot be perfect. Thou hast the Scriptures, he says, in place of me. If thou wouldest learn any thing, thou mayest learn it from them. And if he thus wrote to Timothy, who was filled with the Spirit, how much more to us![14]

Hilary of Poitiers (315–367/368 A.D.)
We believe in accordance with evangelical and apostolic tradition in one God the Father Almighty, the Creator, Maker and Disposer of all things that are, and from whom are all things. And in one Lord Jesus Christ, His Only-begotten Son . . . And in the Holy Ghost . . . Having therefore held this faith from the beginning, and being resolved to hold it to the end in the sight of God and Christ, we say anathema to every heretical and perverted sect, and if any man teaches contrary to the wholesome and right faith of the Scriptures . . . let him be anathema . . . For all those things which are written in the divine Scriptures by Prophets and by Apostles we believe and follow truly and with fear.[15]

Augustine (354–430 A.D.)
What more shall I teach you than what we read in the apostle? For Holy Scripture fixes the rule for our doctrine, lest we dare be wiser than we ought. Therefore I should not teach you anything else except to expound to you the words of the Teacher.[16]

Let those things be removed from our midst which we quote against each other not from divine canonical books but from elsewhere. Someone may perhaps ask: Why do you want to remove these things from the midst? Because I do not want the holy church proved by human documents but by divine oracles.[17]

Jerome (347–420 A.D.)
What the Saviour says was written down was certainly written down. Where is it written down? The Septuagint does not have it, and the Church does not recognize the Apocrypha. Therefore we must go back to the book of the Hebrews, which is the source of the statements quoted by the Lord, as well as the example cited by the disciples.[18]

As then the Church reads Judith, Tobit and the books of Maccabees, but does not admit them among the canonical Scriptures, so let it read these two volumes (Wisdom of Solomon and Ecclesiasticus) for the edification of the people, not to give authority to doctrines of the Church.[19]

Eusebius (263–340 A.D.)
For they say that all the early teachers and the apostles received and taught what they now declare, and that the truth of the Gospel was preserved until the times of Victor . . . but that from his successor, Zephryrinus, the truth had been corrupted. And what they say might seem plausible, if first of all the Divine Scriptures did not contradict them.[20]

And I rejoiced over the constancy, sincerity, docility, and intelligence of the brethren, as we considered in order and with moderation the questions and the difficulties and the points of agreement. And we abstained from defending in every manner and contentiously the opinions which we had once held, unless they appeared to be correct. Nor did we evade objections, but we endeavoured as far as possible to hold to and confirm the things which lay before us, and if the reason given satisfied us, we were not ashamed to change our opinions and agree with others; but on the contrary, conscientiously and sincerely, and with hearts laid open before God, we accepted whatever was established by the proofs and teachings of the Holy Scriptures.[21]

The Fathers on Tradition and Scripture

Athanasius (295–375 A.D.)
For the true and pious faith in the Lord has become manifest to all, being both 'known and read' from the Divine Scriptures.[22]

But our faith is right and starts from the teaching of the Apostles and the tradition of the fathers, being confirmed both by the New Testament and the Old . . . While the Apostolic tradition teaches in the words of blessed Peter, 'Forasmuch then as Christ suffered for us in the Flesh'; and in what Paul writes, 'Looking for the blessed hope and appearing of our great God and Saviour Jesus Christ, Who gave Himself for us that He might redeem us from all iniquity, and purify unto Himself a people for His own possession, and zealous of good works.'[23]

John of Damascus (645–749 A.D.)
Moreover, by the Law and the Prophets in former times, and afterwards by His Only-begotten Son, our Lord and God and Saviour Jesus Christ, He disclosed to us the knowledge of Himself as that was possible for us. All things, therefore, that have been delivered to us by Law and Prophets and Apostles and Evangelists we receive, and know, and honour, seeking for nothing beyond these . . . As knowing all things, therefore, and providing for what is profitable for each, He revealed that which it was to our profit to know; but what we were unable to bear He kept secret. With these things let us be satisfied, and let us abide by them, not removing everlasting boundaries, nor overpassing the divine tradition.[24]

2

Vatican I and Vatican II on Papal Infallibility

VATICAN I

Moreover, that the supreme power of teaching is also included in the Apostolic primacy, which the Roman Pontiff, as the successor of Peter, Prince of the Apostles, possesses over the whole Church, this Holy See has always held, the perpetual practice of the Church confirms, and ecumenical councils also have declared, especially those in which the East with the West met in the union of faith and charity...

This gift, then, of truth and never-failing faith was conferred by heaven upon Peter and his successors in this chair, that they might perform their high office for the salvation of all; that the whole flock of Christ, kept away by them from the poisonous food of error, might be nourished with the pasture of heavenly doctrine; that the occasion of schism being removed, the whole Church might be kept one, and, resting on its foundation, might stand firm against the gates of hell.

But since in this very age, in which the salutary efficacy of the Apostolic office is most of all required, not a few are found who take away from its authority, we judge it altogether necessary solemnly to assert the prerogative which the only-begotten Son of God vouchsafed to join with the supreme pastoral office.

Therefore faithfully adhering to the tradition received from the beginning of the Christian faith, for the glory of God our Saviour, the exaltation of the Christian religion, and the salvation of Christian people, the sacred Council approving, we teach and define that it is a dogma divinely revealed: that the Roman Pontiff, when he speaks ex cathedra, that is, when in discharge of the office of pastor and doctor of all Christians, by virtue of his supreme Apostolic authority, he defines a doctrine regarding faith and morals to be held by the universal Church, by the divine assistance promised to him in blessed Peter, is possessed of that infallibility with which the divine Redeemer willed that his Church should be endowed for defining doctrine regarding faith or morals; and that therefore such definitions of the Roman Pontiff are irreformable of themselves, and not from the consent of the Church.

But if any one—which may God avert—presume to contradict this our definition: let him be anathema.[1]

VATICAN II

Bishops, teaching in communion with the Roman Pontiff, are to be respected by all as witnesses to divine and Catholic truth. In matters of faith and morals, the bishops speak in the name of Christ and the faithful are to accept their teaching and adhere to it with a religious assent of soul. This religious submission of will and mind must be shown in a special way to the authentic teaching authority of the Roman Pontiff, even when he is not speaking ex cathedra. That is, it must be shown in such a way that his supreme magisterium is acknowledged with reverence, the judgments made by him are sincerely adhered to, according to his manifest mind and will. His mind and will in the matter may be known chiefly either from the character of the documents, from his frequent repetition of the same doctrine, or from his manner of speaking.

Although the individual bishops do not enjoy the prerogative of infallibility, they can nevertheless proclaim Christ's doctrine infallibly . . . This infallibility with which the divine Redeemer willed His Church to be endowed in defining a doctrine of faith and morals extends as far as extends the deposit of divine revelation, which must be religiously guarded and faithfully expounded. This is the infallibility which the Roman Pontiff, the head of the college of bishops, enjoys in virtue of his office, when, as the supreme shepherd and teacher of all the faithful, who confirms his brethren in their faith (cf. *Luke* 22:32), he proclaims by a definitive act some doctrine of faith or morals. Therefore his definitions, of themselves, are not from the consent of the Church, are justly styled irreformable, for they are pronounced with the assistance of the Holy Spirit, an assistance promised to him in blessed Peter. Therefore they need no approval of others, nor do they allow an appeal to any other judgment. For then the Roman Pontiff is not pronouncing judgment as a private person. Rather, as the supreme teacher of the universal Church, as one in whom the charism of the infallibility of the Church herself is individually present, he is expounding or defending a doctrine of Catholic faith.[2]

3

The Bull Unam Sanctam
by Boniface VIII

Boniface, Bishop, Servant of the servants of God. For perpetual remembrance:

Urged on by our faith, we are obliged to believe and hold that there is one holy, catholic, and apostolic Church. And we firmly believe and profess that outside of her there is no salvation nor remission of sins, as the bridegroom declares in the Canticles, 'My dove, my undefiled, is but one; she is the only one of her mother; she is the choice one of her that bare her.' And this represents the one mystical body of Christ, and of this body Christ is the head, and God is the head of Christ. In it there is one Lord, one faith, one baptism. For in the time of the Flood there was the single ark of Noah, which prefigures the one Church, and it was finished according to the measure of one cubit and had one Noah for pilot and captain, and outside of it every living creature on the earth, as we read, was destroyed. And this Church we revere as the only one, even as the Lord saith by the prophet, 'Deliver my soul from the sword, my darling from the power of the dog.' He prayed for his soul, that is, for himself, head and body. And this body he called one body, that is, the Church, because of the single bridegroom, the unity of the faith, the sacraments, and the love of the Church. She is that seamless shirt of the Lord which was not rent but was allotted by the casting of lots. Therefore, this one and single Church has one head and not two heads,—for had she two heads, she would be a monster,—that is, Christ and Christ's vicar, Peter and

Peter's successor. For the Lord said unto Peter, 'Feed my sheep.' 'My,' he said, speaking generally and not particularly, 'these and those,' by which it is to be understood that all the sheep are committed unto him. So, when the Greeks and others say that they were not committed to the care of Peter and his successors, they must confess that they are not of Christ's sheep, even as the Lord says in John, 'There is one fold and one shepherd.'

That in her and within her power are two swords, we are taught in the Gospels, namely, the spiritual sword and the temporal sword. For when the Apostles said, 'Lo, here,'—that is, in the Church,—are two swords, the Lord did not reply to the Apostles 'it is too much,' but 'it is enough.' It is certain that whoever denies that the temporal sword is in the power of Peter hearkens ill to the words of the Lord which he spake, 'Put up thy sword into its sheath.' Therefore, both are in the power of the Church, namely, the spiritual sword and the temporal sword; the latter is to be used for the Church, the former by the Church; the former by the hand of the priest, the latter by the hand of princes and kings, but at the nod and sufferance of the priest. The one sword must of necessity be subject to the other, and the temporal authority to the spiritual. For the Apostle said, 'There is no power but of God, and the powers that be are ordained of God'; and they would not have been ordained unless one sword had been made subject to the other, and even as the lower is subjected to the other for higher things. For, according to Dionysius, it is a divine law that the lowest things are made by mediocre things to attain to the highest. For it is not according to the law of the universe that all things in an equal way and immediately should reach their end, but the lowest through the mediocre and the lower through their higher. But that the spiritual power excels the earthly power in dignity and worth, we will the more clearly acknowledge just in proportion as the spiritual is higher than the temporal. And this we perceive quite distinctly from the donation of the tithe and functions of benediction and sanctification, from the mode in which the power was received, and the government of the subjected realms. For truth being the witness, the spiritual power has the functions of establishing the temporal power and sitting in judgment on it if it should prove to be not good. And to the Church and the Church's power the prophecy of Jeremiah attests: 'See, I have set thee this day over the nations and kingdoms to pluck up and to break down and to destroy and to overthrow, to build and to plant.'

And if the earthly power deviate from the right path, it is judged by the spiritual power; but if a minor spiritual power deviate from the right path, the lower in rank is judged by its superior; but if the supreme power [the papacy] deviate, it can be judged not by man, but by God alone. And so the Apostle testifies, 'He which is spiritual judges all things, but he himself is judged by no man.' But this authority, although it be given to a man, and though it be exercised by a man, is not a human but a divine power given by divine word of mouth to Peter and confirmed to Peter and to his successors by Christ himself, whom Peter confessed, even him whom Christ called the Rock. For the Lord said to Peter himself, 'Whatsoever thou shalt bind on earth,' etc. Whoever, therefore, resists this power so ordained by God, resists the ordinance of God, unless perchance he imagines two principles to exist, as did Manichaeus, which we pronounce false and heretical. For Moses testified that God created heaven and earth not in the beginnings but 'in the beginning'.

Furthermore, that every human creature is subject to the Roman pontiff,—this we declare, say, define, and pronounce to be altogether necessary to salvation.[1]

4

Vatican I and Vatican II on Papal Primacy

VATICAN I

Chapter I: Of the Institution of the Apostolic Primacy in blessed Peter.

We therefore teach and declare that, according to the testimony of the Gospel, the primacy of jurisdiction over the universal Church of God was immediately and directly promised and given to blessed Peter the Apostle by Christ the Lord. For it was to Simon alone, to whom he had already said: 'Thou shalt be called Cephas,' that the Lord after the confession made by him, saying: 'Thou art the Christ, the Son of the living God,' addressed these solemn words: 'Blessed art thou, Simon Bar-Jona, because flesh and blood have not revealed it to thee, but my Father who is in heaven. And I say to thee that thou art Peter; and upon this rock I will build my Church, and the gates of hell shall not prevail against it. And I will give to thee the keys of the kingdom of heaven. And whatsoever thou shalt bind on earth, it shall be bound also in heaven; and whatsoever thou shalt loose on earth, it shall be loosed also in heaven.' And it was upon Simon alone that Jesus after his resurrection bestowed the jurisdiction of chief pastor and ruler over all his fold in the words: 'Feed my lambs; feed my sheep.' At open variance with this clear doctrine of Holy Scripture as it has been ever understood by the Catholic Church are the perverse opinions of those who, while they distort the form of government established by Christ the Lord in his Church, deny that Peter in his single person, preferably to all the other Apostles, whether taken separately or together, was endowed by Christ with a true and proper primacy of jurisdiction; or of those who assert that the same primacy was not bestowed immediately and directly upon blessed Peter himself, but upon the Church, and through the Church on Peter as her minister.

If anyone, therefore, shall say that blessed Peter the Apostle was not appointed the Prince of all the Apostles and the visible Head of the whole Church Militant; or that the same directly and immediately received from the same our Lord Jesus Christ a primacy of honor only, and not of true and proper jurisdiction: let him be anathema.

Chapter II: On the Perpetuity of the Primacy of blessed Peter in the Roman Pontiffs.

That which the Prince of Shepherds and great Shepherd of the sheep, Jesus Christ our Lord, established in the person of the blessed Apostle Peter to secure the perpetual welfare and lasting good of the Church, must, by the same institution, necessarily remain unceasingly in the Church; which, being founded upon the Rock, will stand firm to the end of the world. For none can doubt, and it is known to all ages, that the holy and blessed Peter, the Prince and Chief of the Apostles, the pillar of the faith and foundation of the Catholic Church, received the keys of the kingdom from our Lord Jesus Christ, the Saviour and Redeemer of mankind, and lives, presides, and judges, to this day and always, in his successors the Bishops of the Holy See of Rome, which was founded by him and consecrated by his blood. Whence, whosoever succeeds to Peter in this See, does by the institution of Christ himself obtain the Primacy of Peter over the whole Church. The disposition made by Incarnate Truth therefore remains, and blessed Peter, abiding through the strength of the Rock in the power that he received, has not abandoned the direction of the Church. Wherefore it has at all times been necessary that every particular Church—that is to say, the faithful throughout the world—should agree with the Roman Church, on account of the greater authority of the princedom which this has received; that all being associated in the unity of that See whence the rights of communion spread to all, might grow together as members of one Head in the compact unity of the body.

If, then, any should deny that it is by institution of Christ the Lord, or by divine right, that blessed Peter should have a perpetual line of successors in the Primacy over the universal Church, or that the Roman Pontiff is the successor of blessed Peter in this primacy: let him be anathema.

Chapter III: On the Power and Nature of the Primacy of the Roman Pontiff.

Wherefore, resting on plain testimonies of the Sacred Writings, and adhering to the plain and express decrees both of our predecessors, the Roman Pontiffs, and of the General Councils, we renew the definition of the ecumenical Council of Florence, in virtue of which all the faithful of Christ must believe that the holy Apostolic See and the Roman Pontiff possesses the primacy over the whole world, and that the Roman Pontiff is the successor of blessed Peter, Prince of the Apostles, and is true vicar of Christ, and head of the whole Church, and father and teacher of all Christians; and that full power was given to him in blessed Peter to rule, feed, and govern the universal Church by Jesus Christ our Lord; as is also contained in the acts of the General Councils and in the sacred Canons.

Hence we teach and declare that by the appointment of our Lord the Roman Church possesses a superiority of ordinary power over all other churches, and that this power of jurisdiction of the Roman Pontiff, which is truly episcopal, is immediate; to which all, of whatever right and dignity, both pastors and faithful, both individually and collectively, are bound, by their duty of hierarchial subordination and true obedience, to submit not only in matters which belong to faith and morals, but also in those which appertain to the discipline and government of the Church throughout the world, so that the Church of Christ may be one flock under one supreme pastor through the preservation of unity both of communion and of profession of the same faith with the Roman Pontiff. This is the teaching of Catholic truth, from which no one can deviate without loss of faith and salvation. But so far is this power of the Supreme Pontiff from being any prejudice to the ordinary and immediate power of episcopal jurisdiction, by which Bishops, who have been set by the Holy Ghost to succeed and hold the place of the Apostles, feed and govern, each his own flock, as true pastors, that this their episcopal authority is really asserted, strengthened, and protected by the supreme and universal Pastor; in accordance with the words of St. Gregory the Great: 'My honor is the honor of the whole Church. My honor is the firm strength of my brethren. I am truly honored when the honor due to each and all is not withheld.'

Further, from this supreme power possessed by the Roman Pontiff of governing the universal Church, it follows that he has the right of free communication with the pastors of the whole Church, and with their flocks, that these might be taught and ruled by him in the way of salvation. Wherefore we condemn and reject the opinions of those who hold that the communication between this supreme head and the pastors and their flocks can lawfully be impeded; or who make this communication subject to the will of the secular power, so as to maintain that whatever is done by the Apostolic See, or by its authority, for the government of the Church, can not have force or value unless it be confirmed by the assent of the secular power.

And since by the divine right of Apostolic primacy the Roman Pontiff is placed over the universal Church, we further teach and declare that he is the supreme judge of the faithful, and that in all causes, the decision of which belongs to the Church, recourse may be had to his tribunal, and that none may re-open the judgment of the Apostolic See, than whose authority there is no greater, nor can any lawfully review its judgment. Wherefore they err from the right course who assert that it is lawful to appeal from the judgments of the Roman Pontiffs to an ecumenical Council, as to an authority higher than that of the Roman Pontiff.

If, then, any shall say that the Roman Pontiff has the office merely of inspection or direction, and not full and supreme power of jurisdiction over the universal Church, not only in things which belong to faith and morals, but also in those which relate to the discipline and government of the Church spread throughout the world; or assert that he possesses merely the principal part, and not all the fulness of this supreme power; or that this power which he enjoys is not ordinary and immediate, both over each and all the churches, and over each and all the pastors and the faithful: let him be anathema.[1]

VATICAN II

In order that the episcopate itself might be one and undivided, He [Jesus Christ] placed blessed Peter over the other apostles, and instituted in him a permanent and visible source and foundation of unity of faith and fellowship. And all this teaching about the institution, the perpetuity, the force and reason for the sacred primacy of the Roman Pontiff and of his infallible teaching authority, this sacred Synod again proposes to be firmly believed by all the faithful. Continuing in the same task of clarification begun by Vatican I, this Council has decided to declare and proclaim before all men its teaching concerning bishops, the successors of the apostles, who together with the successor of Peter, the Vicar of Christ and the visible Head of the whole Church, govern the house of the living God . . . These apostles (cf. *Luke* 6:13) He formed after the manner of a college or a fixed group, over which He placed Peter, chosen from among them (cf. *John* 21:15-17) . . . Just as the role that the Lord gave individually to Peter, the first among the apostles, is permanent and was meant to be transmitted to his successors, so also the apostles' office of nurturing the Church is permanent, and was meant to be exercised without interruption by the sacred order of bishops.

But the college or body of bishops has no authority unless it is simultaneously conceived of in terms of its head, the Roman Pontiff, Peter's successor, and without any lessening of his power of primacy over all, pastors as well as general faithful. For in virtue of his office, that is, as Vicar of Christ and pastor of the whole Church, the Roman Pontiff has full, supreme and universal power over the Church. And he can always exercise this power freely . . . Together with its head, the Roman Pontiff, and never without this head, the episcopal order is the subject of supreme and full power over the universal Church. But this power can be exercised only with the consent of the Roman Pontiff. For our Lord made Simon Peter alone the rock and keybearer of the Church (cf. M*att.* 16:18-19), and appointed him shepherd of the whole flock (cf. *John* 21:15 ff) . . . The Roman Pontiff, as the successor of Peter, is the perpetual and visible source and foundation of the unity of the bishops and of the multitude of the faithful.[2]

5

Writings of the Fathers on the Meaning of the Rock and Keys of Matthew

Hilary of Poitiers (315–367/368 A.D.)
A belief that the Son of God is Son in name only, and not in nature, is not the faith of the Gospels and of the Apostles . . . whence I ask, was it that the blessed Simon Bar-Jona confessed to Him, Thou art the Christ, the Son of the living God? . . . And this is the rock of confession whereon the Church is built . . . that Christ must be not only named, but believed, the Son of God . . . This faith it is which is the foundation of the Church; through this faith the gates of hell cannot prevail against her . . . This is the Father's revelation, this the foundation of the Church, this the assurance of her permanence.[1]

Origen (c.185–253/254 A.D.)
And if we too have said like Peter, 'Thou art the Christ, the Son of the living God,' not as if flesh and blood had revealed it unto us, but by light from the Father in heaven having shone in our heart, we become a Peter, and to us there might be said by the Word, 'Thou art Peter,' etc. For a rock is every disciple of Christ of whom those drank who drank of the spiritual rock which followed them, and upon every such rock is built every word of the church, and the polity in accordance with it; for in each of the perfect, who have the combination of words and deeds and thoughts which fill up the blessedness, is the church built by God.

But if you suppose that upon the one Peter only the whole church is built by God, what would you say about John the son of thunder or each one of the Apostles? Shall we otherwise dare to say, that against Peter in particular the gates of Hades shall not prevail, but that they shall prevail against the other Apostles and the perfect? Does not the saying previously made, 'The gates of Hades shall not prevail against it,' hold in regard to all and in the case of each of them? And also the saying, 'Upon this rock I will build My church'? Are the keys of the kingdom of heaven given by the Lord to Peter only, and will no other of the blessed receive them? But if this promise, 'I will give unto thee the keys of the kingdom of heaven,' be common to others, how shall not all things previously spoken of, and the things which are subjoined as having been addressed to Peter, be common to them?[2]

Cyril of Alexandria (d. 444 A.D.)
For Christ is the foundation and unshakeable base of all things—Christ who restrains and holds together all things, that they may be very firm. Upon him also we all are built, a spiritual household, put together by the Holy Spirit into a holy temple in which he himself dwells; for by our faith he lives in our hearts. But the next foundations, those nearer to us, can be understood to be the apostles and evangelists, those eyewitnesses and ministers of the word who have arisen for the strengthening of the faith. For when we recognize that their own traditions must be followed, we serve a faith which is true and does not deviate from Christ. For when he wisely and blamelessly confessed his faith to Jesus saying, 'You are Christ, Son of the living God,' Jesus said to divine Peter: 'You are Peter and upon this rock I will build my Church.' Now by the word 'rock', Jesus indicated, I think, the immoveable faith of the disciple.[3]

The Church is unshaken, and 'the gates of hell shall not prevail against it', according to the voice of the Saviour, for it has Him for a foundation.[4]

Eusebius (263–340 A.D.)
By 'the foundations of the world', we shall understand the strength of God's wisdom, by which, first, the order of the

universe was established, and then, the world itself was founded—a world which will not be shaken. Yet you will not in any way err from the scope of the truth if you suppose that 'the world' is actually the Church of God, and that its 'foundation' is in the first place, that unspeakably solid rock on which it is founded, as Scripture says: 'Upon this rock I will build my Church, and the gates of hell shall not prevail against it'; and elsewhere: 'The rock, moreover, was Christ.' For, as the Apostle indicates with these words: 'No other foundation can anyone lay than that which is laid, which is Christ Jesus.' Then, too, after the Savior himself, you may rightly judge the foundations of the Church to be the words of the prophets and apostles, in accordance with the statement of the Apostle: 'Built upon the foundation of the apostles and the prophets, Christ Jesus himself being the cornerstone.'[5]

Jerome (347–420 A.D.)
The one foundation which the apostolic architect laid is our Lord Jesus Christ. Upon this stable and firm foundation, which has itself been laid on solid ground, the Church of Christ is built . . . For the Church was founded upon a rock . . . upon this rock the Lord established his Church; and the apostle Peter received his name from this rock (*Matt.* 16:18).[6]

She, that with a firm root is founded upon the rock, Christ, the Catholic Church, is the one dove; she stands the perfect one, and near to His right hand, and has nothing sinister in her.[7]

The rock is Christ, Who gave to His apostles, that they also should be called rocks, 'Thou art Peter, and upon this rock I will build My Church.'[8]

Was there no other province in the whole world to receive the gospel of pleasure, and into which the serpent might insinuate itself, except that which was founded by the teaching of Peter upon the rock Christ.[9]

But you say, the Church was founded upon Peter: although

elsewhere the same is attributed to all the Apostles, and they all receive the keys of the kingdom of heaven, and the strength of the Church depends upon them all alike, yet one among the twelve is chosen so that when a head has been appointed, there may be no occasion for schism.[10]

Gregory of Nazianzen (330–389 A.D.)
Shall I bring forth another and laudable example of order and discipline—one great and laudable, especially worthy of our present commemoration and calling to mind? Notice how out of the disciples of Christ—all great and lofty, all worthy of Christ's selection—only one is called a rock and receives for his faith the founding of the Church. And another is loved more earnestly, and rests upon the breast of Jesus; yet the other disciples accept it with a calm spirit that these should be preferred to themselves. Now when Christ made his ascent up the mountain to be transfigured and to lay open his divinity and to lay that bare which was covered by the flesh, who, pray, went up together with him—for not all were admitted to the sight of this miracle? Peter, James and John who were esteemed above the others.[11]

Gregory of Nyssa (335–394 A.D.)
But what effort is required of us to exert ourselves in such a way that our commemoration may be worthy of the virtue of the apostles? The warmth of our praises does not extend to Simon insofar as he was a catcher of fish; rather it extends to his firm faith, which is at the same time the foundation of the whole Church.[12]

Athanasius (295–375 A.D.)
But ye are blessed, who by faith are in the Church, dwell upon the foundations of the faith, and have full satisfaction, even the highest degree of faith which remains among you unshaken. For it has come down to you from Apostolic tradition, and frequently has accursed envy wished to unsettle it, but has not been able. On the contrary, they have rather been cut off from their attempts to do so. For thus it

is written, 'Thou art the Son of the Living God,' Peter confessing it by revelation of the Father, and being told, 'Blessed art thou, Simon Barjona, for flesh and blood did not reveal it to thee, but My Father Who is in heaven,' and the rest. No one therefore will ever prevail against your Faith, most beloved brethren.[13]

And so the works of the Jews are undone, for they were a shadow; but the Church is firmly established; it is founded on the rock, and the gates of hell shall not prevail against it. Theirs it was to say, Why dost Thou, being a man, make Thyself God? and their disciple is the Samosatene; whence to his followers with reason does he teach his heresy. But we have not so learned Christ, if so be that we have heard Him, and have learned from Him.[14]

Ambrosiaster (works dated 366–384 A.D.)
(Verse 20). 'Built upon the foundation of the apostles and prophets, Christ Jesus himself being the cornerstone.' The above puts together New and Old Testaments. For the apostles proclaimed what the prophets said would be, although Paul says to the Corinthians: 'God placed the apostles first, the prophets second' (*1 Cor.* 12:28). But this refers to other prophets, for in 1 Corinthians Paul writes about ecclesiastical orders; here he is concerned with the foundation of the Church. The prophets prepared, the apostles laid the foundations. Wherefore the Lord says to Peter: 'Upon this rock I shall build my Church,' that is, upon this confession of the catholic faith I shall establish the faithful in life.[15]

Paul of Emesa (d. *c.*445 A.D.)
Upon this faith the Church of God has been founded. With this expectation, upon this rock the Lord God placed the foundations of the Church. When then the Lord Christ was going to Jerusalem, He asked the disciples, saying, 'Whom do men say that the Son of Man is?' The apostles say, 'Some Elias, others Jeremias, or one of the prophets.' And He says, but you, that is, My elect, you who have followed Me for three

years, and have seen My power, and miracles, and beheld Me walking on the sea, who have shared My table, 'Whom do you say that I am?' Instantly, the Coryphaeus of the apostles, the mouth of the disciples, Peter, replied, 'Thou art the Christ, the Son of the living God.'[17]

Epiphanius (315–403 A.D.)
The same applies to the chief of the apostles, Peter, who once denied the Lord. Peter stands forth for us in the likeness of a solid rock upon which the Church has been fully erected, and upon which, as upon a foundation, our faith in the Lord rests. Among the foremost in faith, Peter confessed that Christ was the son of the living God, and in return he heard: 'Upon this rock' of solid faith 'I shall build my Church.'[18]

Aphraates (280–345 A.D.)
But before all things I desire that thou wouldst write and instruct me concerning this that straitens me, namely concerning our faith; how it is, and what its foundation is, and on what structure it rises, and on what it rests, and in what way is its fulfilment and consummation, and what are the works required for it.

Faith . . . is like a building that is built up of many pieces of workmanship and so its edifice rises to the top. And know, my beloved, that in the foundations of the building stones are laid, and so resting upon stones the whole edifice rises until it is perfected. Thus also the true Stone, our Lord Jesus Christ is the foundation of all faith. And on Him, on (this) Stone faith is based. And resting on faith all the structure rises until it is completed. For it is the foundation that is the beginning of all the building. For when anyone is brought nigh unto faith, it is laid for him upon the Stone, that is our Lord Jesus Christ. And His building cannot be shaken by the waves, nor can it be injured by the winds. By the stormy blasts it does not fall, because its structure is reared upon the rock of the true Stone. And in that I have called Christ the Stone, I have not spoken my own thought, but the Prophets beforehand called Him the Stone.[19]

Theodoret (393–466 A.D.)
Let no one then foolishly suppose that the Christ is any other than the only begotten Son. Let us not imagine ourselves wiser than the gift of the Spirit. Let us hear the words of the great Peter, 'Thou art the Christ, the Son of the living God.' Let us hear the Lord Christ confirming this confession, for 'On this rock,' He says, 'I will build my church and the gates of Hell shall not prevail against it.' Wherefore too the wise Paul, most excellent master builder of the churches, fixed no other foundation than this. 'I,' he says, 'as a wise master builder have laid the foundation, and another buildeth thereon. But let every man take heed how he buildeth thereon. For other foundation can no man lay than that is laid, which is Jesus Christ.' How then can they think of any other foundation, when they are bidden not to fix a foundation, but to build on that which is laid? The divine writer recognises Christ as the foundation, and glories in this title.[20]

Wherefore our Lord Jesus Christ permitted the first of the apostles, whose confession He had fixed as a kind of groundwork and foundation of the Church, to waver to and fro, and to deny Him, and then raised him up again.[21]

Surely he is calling pious faith and true confession a 'rock.' For when the Lord asked his disciples who the people said he was, blessed Peter spoke up, saying 'You are Christ, the Son of the living God.' To which the Lord answered: 'Truly, truly I say to you, you are Peter and upon this rock I shall build my Church, and the gates of hell shall not prevail against it.'[22]

Gregory the Great (540–604 A.D.)
For since the truth shines forth from the Church Catholic alone, the Lord says that there is a place by Him, from which He is to be seen. Moses is placed on a rock, to behold the form of God, because if any one maintains not the firmness of Faith, he discerns not the Divine presence. Of which firmness the Lord says, 'Upon this rock I shall build my Church.'[23]

The Fathers on the Rock and Keys of Matthew

Cassiodorus (490–583 A.D.)
'It will not be moved' is said about the Church to which alone that promise has been given: 'You are Peter and upon this rock I shall build my Church and the gates of Hell shall not prevail against it.' For the Church cannot be moved because it is known to have been founded on that most solid rock, namely, Christ the Lord . . . [24]

The Church's foundation is Christ the Lord, who thus holds his Church together, so that it can by no shaking collapse, just as the Apostle says: 'For no other foundation can any one lay than that which is laid, which is Christ Jesus' (*1 Cor.* 3:11).[25]

Palladius of Helenopolis (363–431 A.D.)
'You, however, who do you say I am?' Not all responded, but Peter only, interpreting the mind of all: 'You are Christ, Son of the living God.' The Saviour, approving the correctness of this response, spoke, saying: 'You are Peter, and upon this rock'—that is, upon this confession—'I shall build my Church, and the gates of Hell shall not prevail against it.'[26]

Basil of Seleucia (d. *c.*468 A.D.)
'You are Christ, Son of the living God.' Jesus confirmed this statement with his approbation, thereby instructing all: 'Blessed are you Simon Bar-Jonah, for flesh and blood have not revealed this to you, but my Father who is in Heaven.' He called Peter blessed, so that Peter might join faith to his statement, just as he praised the response because of its meaning . . . Now Christ called this confession a rock, and he named the one who confessed it 'Peter', perceiving the appellation which was suitable to the author of this confession. For this is the solemn rock of religion, this the basis of salvation, this the wall of faith and the foundation of truth: 'For no other foundation can anyone lay than that which is laid, which is Christ Jesus.' To whom be glory and power forever.[27]

Nilus of Ancyra (d. *c.*430 A.D.)
If, moreover, a man of the Lord is meant, the first to be compared to gold would be Cephas, whose name is interpreted 'rock.' This is the highest of the apostles, Peter, also called Cephas, who furnished in his confession of faith the foundation for the building of the Church.[28]

Isidore of Seville (560–636 A.D.)
Peter bears the character of the Church, which has the power to forgive sins and to lead men from Hades to the heavenly kingdom . . . All the apostles also bear the type of the whole Church, since they also have received a like power of forgiving sins. They bear also the character of the patriarchs, who by the word of preaching spiritually brought forth God's people in the whole world . . . The wise man who built his house upon the rock signifies the faithful teacher, who has established the foundations of his doctrine and life upon Christ.[29]

Moreover, Christ is called a 'foundation' because faith is established in him, and because the catholic Church is built upon him.[30]

John of Damascus (645–749 A.D.)
At Caesarea Philippi . . . where his disciples were assembled, on the spur of the moment the Rock of Life himself excavated a seat from a certain rock. Then he asked his disciples who the people were saying the Son of Man was. He did not seek this information because he was unaware of the ignorance of men; for Jesus requires no investigation . . . . As a man he posed a probing question, but as God he brought him out of the dark who first had been called and first had followed. This was the man whom Christ in his foreknowledge had predestined to be a worthy overseer of the Church. As God, Jesus inspired this man and spoke through him. What was the question? 'But who do you say I am?' And Peter, fired by a burning zeal and prompted by the Holy Spirit replied: 'You are Christ, Son of the living God.' Oh

The Fathers on the Rock and Keys of Matthew

blessed mouth! Perfectly blessed lips! Oh theological soul! ... This is that firm and immoveable faith upon which, as upon the rock whose surname you bear, the Church is founded. Against this the gates of hell, the mouths of heretics, the machines of demons—for they will attack—will not prevail. They will take up arms but they will not conquer.[31]

This rock was Christ, the incarnate Word of God, the Lord, for Paul clearly teaches us: 'The rock was Christ' (*1 Cor. 10:4*).[32]

6

Letter of Gregory the Great to John of Constantinople Objecting to his Adoption of the Title Universal Bishop

Gregory to John, Bishop of Constantinople.

... I beg you, I beseech you, and with all the sweetness in my power demand of you, that your Fraternity gainsay all who flatter you and offer you this name of error, nor foolishly consent to be called by the proud title.

Consider, I pray thee, that in this rash presumption the peace of the whole Church is disturbed, and that it is in contradiction to the grace that is poured out on all in common ... And thou wilt become by so much the greater as thou restrainest thyself from the usurpation of a proud and foolish title: and thou wilt make advance in proportion as thou art not bent on arrogation by derogation of thy brethren. Wherefore, dearest brother, with all thy heart love humility, through which the concord of all the brethren and the unity of the holy universal Church may be preserved.

Certainly the apostle Paul, when he heard some say, I am of Paul, I of Apollos, but I of Christ (*1 Cor.* 1:13), regarded with the utmost horror such dilaceration of the Lord's body, whereby they were joining themselves, as it were, to other heads, and exclaimed, saying, Was Paul crucified for you? or were ye baptized in the name of Paul (*1 Cor.* 1:13)? If then he shunned the subjecting of the members of Christ partially to certain heads, as if beside Christ, though this were to the apostles themselves, what wilt thou say to Christ, who is the Head of the universal Church, in the scrutiny of the last judgment, having attempted to put all his members under thyself by the appellation of Universal? Who, I ask, is proposed for imitation in his wrongful title but he who, despising the legions of angels constituted socially with himself, attempted to start up to an eminence of singularity, that he might seem to be under none and to be alone above all? Who even said, I will ascend into heaven, I will exalt my throne above the stars of heaven; I will sit upon the mount of the testament, in the sides of the North: I will ascend above the heights of the clouds; I will be like the most High (*Isa.* 14:13).

For what are all thy brethren, the bishops of the universal Church, but stars of heaven, whose life and discourse shine together amid the sins and errors of men, as if amid the shades of night? And when thou desirest to put thyself above them by this proud title, and to tread down their name in comparison with thine, what else dost thou say but I will ascend into heaven; I will exalt my throne above the stars of heaven? Are not all the bishops together clouds, who both rain in the words of preaching, and glitter in the light of good works? And when your Fraternity despises them, and you would fain press them down under yourself, what else say you but what is said by the ancient foe, I will ascend above the heights of the clouds?

This most holy man the lord John, of so great abstinence and humility, has, through the seduction of familiar tongues, broken out into such a pitch of pride as to attempt, in his coveting of that wrongful name, to be like him who, while proudly wishing to be like God, lost even the grace of the likeness granted him, and because he sought false glory, thereby forfeited true blessedness.

Certainly Peter, the first of the apostles, himself a member of the holy and universal Church, Paul, Andrew, John—what were they but heads of particular communities? And yet all were members under one Head. And (to bind all together in a short girth of speech) the saints before the law, the saints under the law, the saints under grace, all these making up the Lord's Body, were constituted as members of the Church, and not one of them has wished himself to be called universal. Now let your Holiness acknowledge to what extent you swell within yourself in desiring to be called by that name by which no one presumed to be called who was truly holy.

Was it not the case, as your Fraternity knows, that the prelates of this Apostolic See, which by the providence of God I serve, had the honour offered them of being called universal by the venerable Council of Chalcedon. But yet not one of them has ever wished to be called by such a title, or seized upon this ill-advised name, lest if, in virtue of the rank of the pontificate, he took to himself the glory of singularity, he might seem to have denied it to all his brethren . . . What, then, can we bishops say for ourselves, who have received a place of honour from the humility of our Redeemer, and yet imitate the pride of the enemy himself? . . . What, then, dearest brother, wilt thou say in that terrible scrutiny of the coming judgment, if thou covetest to be called in the world not only father, but even general father? . . . Lo, by reason of this execrable title of pride the Church is rent asunder, the hearts of all the brethren are provoked to offence . . . And thou attemptest to take the honour away from all which thou desirest unlawfully to usurp to thyself singularly.

I therefore have once and again through my representatives taken care to reprove in humble words this sin against the whole Church; and now I write myself.[1]

7

The Official Teaching of the Roman Catholic Church on the Person of Mary

THE DECREE OF POPE PIUS IX ON THE IMMACULATE CONCEPTION OF MARY FROM THE BULL *INEFFABILIS DEUS* (1854).

Since we have never ceased in humility and fasting to offer up our prayers and those of the Church to God the Father through his Son, that he might deign to direct and confirm our mind by the power of the Holy Ghost, after imploring the protection of the whole celestial court, and after invoking on our knees the Holy Ghost the Paraclete, under his inspiration we PRONOUNCE, DECLARE, AND DEFINE, unto the glory of the Holy and Indivisible Trinity, the honour and ornament of the holy Virgin the Mother of God, for the exaltation of the Catholic faith and increase of the Christian religion, by the authority of our Lord Jesus Christ and the blessed Apostles Peter and Paul, and in our own authority, that the doctrine which holds the blessed Virgin Mary to have been, from the first instant of her conception, by a singular grace and privilege of Almighty God, in view of the merits of Christ Jesus the Saviour of mankind, preserved free from all stain of original sin, was revealed by God, and is, therefore, to be firmly and constantly believed by all the faithful. Therefore, if some should presume to think in their hearts otherwise than we have defined (which God forbid), they shall know and thoroughly understand that they are by their own judgment condemned, have made shipwreck concerning the faith, and fallen away from the unity of the Church; and, moreover, that they, by this very act, subject themselves to the penalties ordained by law, if, by word or writing, or any other external means, they dare to signify what they think in their hearts.[1]

VATICAN II ON THE IMMACULATE CONCEPTION OF MARY
It is no wonder, then, that the usage prevailed among the holy Fathers whereby they called the Mother of God entirely holy and free from all stain of sin, fashioned by the Holy Spirit into a kind of new substance and new creature. Adorned from the first instance of her conception with the splendours of an entirely unique holiness, the Virgin of Nazareth is, on God's command, greeted by an angel messenger as 'full of grace' (cf. *Luke* 1:28) . . . Embracing God's saving will with a full heart and impeded by no sin, she devoted herself totally as a handmaid of the Lord to the person and work of her Son . . . Finally, preserved free from all guilt of original sin, the Immaculate Virgin was taken up body and soul into heavenly glory upon the completion of her earthly sojourn.[2]

THE DECREE OF POPE PIUS XII ON THE ASSUMPTION OF MARY FROM THE BULL *MUNIFICENTISSIMUS DEUS*.
All these proofs and considerations of the holy Fathers and the theologians are based upon the Sacred Writings as their ultimate foundation. These set the loving Mother of God as it were before our very eyes as most intimately joined to her divine Son and as always sharing His lot. Consequently it seems impossible to think of her, the one who conceived Christ, brought Him forth, nursed Him with her milk, held Him in her arms, and clasped Him to her breast, as being apart from Him in body, even though not in soul, after this earthly life. Since our Redeemer is the Son of Mary, He could not do otherwise, as the perfect observer of God's law, than to honour, not only His eternal Father, but also His most beloved Mother. And, since it was within His power to grant her this great honour, to preserve her from the corruption of the tomb, we must believe that He really acted in this way.

Hence the revered Mother of God, from all eternity joined in a hidden way with Jesus Christ in one and the same decree of predestination, immaculate in her conception, a most perfect virgin in her divine motherhood, the noble associate of the divine Redeemer who has won a complete triumph over sin and its consequences, finally obtained, as the supreme culmination of her privileges, that she should be preserved free from the corruption of the tomb and that, like her own Son, having overcome death, she might be taken up body and soul to the glory of heaven where, as Queen, she sits in splendor at the right hand of her Son, the immortal King of the Ages.

For which reason, after we have poured forth prayers of supplication again and again to God, and have invoked the light of the Spirit of Truth, for the glory of Almighty God Who has lavished His special affection upon the Virgin Mary, for the honour of her Son, the immortal King of the Ages and the Victor over sin and death, for the increase of the glory of that same august Mother, and for the joy and exultation of the entire Church; by the authority of our Lord Jesus Christ, of the blessed Apostles Peter and Paul, and by Our own authority, We pronounce, declare, and define it to be a divinely revealed dogma: that the Immaculate Mother of God, the ever Virgin Mary, having completed the course of her earthly life, was assumed body and soul into heavenly glory.

Hence, if anyone, which God forbid, should dare wilfully to deny or call into doubt that which we have defined, let him know that he has fallen away completely from the divine and Catholic faith . . . It is forbidden to any man to change this, Our declaration, pronouncement, and definition or, by rash attempt, to oppose and counter it. If any man should presume to make such an attempt, let him know that he will incur the wrath of Almighty God and of the Blessed Apostles Peter and Paul.[3]

VATICAN II ON THE ASSUMPTION OF MARY
Finally, preserved free from all guilt of original sin, the Immaculate Virgin was taken up body and soul into heavenly glory upon the completion of her earthly sojourn . . . For, taken up into heaven, she did not lay aside this saving role,

but by her manifold acts of intercession continues to win for us gifts of eternal salvation . . . Therefore the Blessed Virgin is invoked by the Church under the titles of Advocate, Auxiliatrix, Adjutrix, and Mediatrix . . . As the most holy Mother of God she was, after her Son, exalted by divine grace above all angels and men. Hence the Church appropriately honours her with special reverence . . . In all perils and needs, the faithful have fled prayerfully to her protection.[4]

8

The Fathers on the Real Presence and the Eucharist

The Didache (written between 70 and 140 A.D.)
But as touching the eucharistic thanksgiving give ye thanks thus. First, as regards the cup: We give Thee thanks, O our Father, for the holy vine of Thy son David, which Thou madest known unto us through Thy Son Jesus; Thine is the glory for ever and ever. Then as regards the broken bread: We give Thee thanks, O our Father, for the life and knowledge which Thou didst make known unto us through Thy Son Jesus; Thine is the glory for ever and ever. As this broken bread was scattered upon the mountains and being gathered together from the ends of the earth into Thy kingdom; for Thine is the glory and the power through Jesus Christ for ever and ever. But let no one eat or drink of this eucharistic thanksgiving, but they that have been baptized into the name of the Lord; for concerning this also the Lord hath said: Give not that which is holy to dogs.
And after ye are satisfied thus give ye thanks: We give Thee thanks, Holy Father, for Thy holy name, which Thou hast made to tabernacle in our hearts, and for the knowledge and faith and immortality, which Thou hast made known unto us through Thy Son Jesus; Thine is the glory for ever and ever. Thou, Almighty Master, didst create all things for Thy name's sake, and didst give food and drink unto men for enjoyment, that they might render thanks to Thee; but didst bestow upon us spiritual food and drink and eternal life through Thy Son. Before all things we give Thee thanks that Thou art powerful; Thine is the glory for ever and ever.[1]

Justin Martyr (100/110–165 A.D.)
It is quite evident that this prophecy also alludes to the bread which our Christ gave us to offer in remembrance of the Body which He assumed for the sake of those who believe in Him, for whom He also suffered, and also to the cup which He taught us to offer in the Eucharist, in commemoration of His blood.[2]

Theophilus of Antioch (d. *c.*185–191 A.D.)
For though yourself prudent, you endure fools gladly. Otherwise you would not have been moved by senseless men to yield yourself to empty words, and to give credit to the prevalent rumour wherewith godless lips falsely accuse us, who are worshippers of God, and are called Christians . . . that we eat human flesh.[3]

Clement of Alexandria (*c.*150–211/216 A.D.)
The Scripture, accordingly, has named wine the symbol of the sacred blood.[4]

Cyprian (200/210–258 A.D.)
But when the blood of grapes is mentioned, what else is shewn than the wine of the Cup of the Blood of the Lord? . . . I marvel much whence this practice has arisen, that in some places, contrary to Evangelical and Apostolic discipline, water is offered in the Cup of the Lord, which alone cannot *represent* the Blood of Christ . . . For that waters signify peoples, Holy Scripture declares in the Revelations, saying, The waters which thou sawest, on which the whore sitteth, are peoples and multitudes and nations and tongues. This too we perceive is contained in the Mystery of the Cup. For because Christ loves us all in that He bore our sins also, we see that in the water the people are intended, but that in the wine is shewn the Blood of Christ. But in the Cup water is mingled with wine, His people are united to Christ, and the multitude of believers are united and conjoined with Him in Whom they believe.[5]

Eusebius (263–340 A.D.)
For by means of the wine, which was the symbol . . . of His

blood, He cleanses from their former sins those who are baptised into His death and have believed on His blood, 'Take, drink, this is My blood which is poured out for you for the remission of sins; do this for My memorial'; and that the words 'His teeth whiter than milk' signify the brightness and purity of the mystic food. For again He gave to His disciples the symbols . . . of the divine dispensation, bidding them make the image . . . of His own body.[6]

Athanasius (295–375 A.D.)
Here also He has used both terms about Himself, namely flesh and spirit; and He distinguished the spirit from what relates to the flesh in order that they might believe not only in what was visible in Him but also in what was invisible, and might thereby learn that what He says is not fleshly but spiritual. For how many would the body suffice for eating, that it should become the food for the whole world? But for this reason He made mention of the ascension of the Son of Man into heaven, in order that He might draw them away from the bodily notion, and that from henceforth they might learn that the aforesaid flesh was heavenly eating from above and spiritual food given by Him. For, He says, what I have spoken unto you is spirit and life, as much as to say, That which is manifested, and is given for the salvation of the world, is the flesh which I wear. But this and its blood shall be given to you by Me spiritually as food, so that this may be imparted . . . spiritually to each one, and may become to all a preservative for resurrection to eternal life.[7]

Augustine (354–430 A.D.)
1. Augustine teaches that the Sacraments, including the eucharist, are signs and figures which represent or symbolize spiritual realities:

He committed and delivered to His disciples the figure of His Body and Blood.[8]

A sacrifice, therefore, is the visible sacrament or sacred sign of an invisible sacrifice . . . for that which in common speech is called sacrifice is only the symbol of the true sacrifice.[9]

In fine, He Himself, when He says, 'He that eateth my flesh and drinketh my blood, dwelleth in me, and I in him,' shows what it is in reality, and not sacramentally to eat His body and drink His blood; for this is to dwell in Christ, that He also may dwell in us.[10]

For these have eaten the body of Christ, not only sacramentally but really, being incorporated into His body[11]...

But this is what belongs to the virtue of the sacrament, not to the visible sacrament; he that eateth within, not without; who eateth in his heart, not who presses with his teeth ... Just as we are made better by participation of the Son, through the unity of His body and blood, which thing that eating and drinking signifies. We live then by Him, by eating Him, that is, by receiving Him as the eternal life, which we did not have from ourselves.[12]

2. Secondly, because Christ is physically in heaven Augustine interprets the discourse in John 6 of eating Christ's flesh and drinking his blood figuratively. If a person partakes of the sacrament but does not abide in Christ, he does not eat the flesh of Christ or drink his blood:

We have heard the True Master, the Divine Redeemer, the human Saviour, commending to us our Ransom, His Blood. For He spake to us of His Body and Blood; He called His Body Meat, His Blood Drink ... When therefore commending such Meat and such Drink He said, 'Except ye shall eat My Flesh and drink My Blood, ye shall have no life in you;' ... His disciples were offended ... What then did He answer? 'Doth this offend you? ... Do ye imagine that I am about to make divisions of this My Body which ye see; and to cut up My Members, and give them to you? What then if ye shall see the Son of Man ascend up where He was before?' Assuredly, He who could ascend Whole could not be consumed ... That drinking, what is it but to live? Eat Life, drink Life; thou shalt have life, and the Life is Entire. But then this shall be, that is, the Body and the Blood of Christ shall be each man's Life; if what is taken in the Sacrament visibly is in the truth itself eaten spiritually, drunk spiritually. For we have heard the

Lord Himself saying, 'It is the Spirit that quickeneth, but the flesh profiteth nothing. The words that I have spoken unto you, are Spirit and Life.[13]

Who is the Bread of the kingdom of God, but He who saith, 'I am the living Bread which came down from heaven'? Do not get thy mouth ready, but thine heart. On this occasion it was that the parable of this supper was set forth. Lo, we believe in Christ, we receive Him with faith. In receiving Him we know what to think of. We receive but little, and we are nourished in heart. It is not then what is seen, but what is believed, that feeds us. Therefore we too have not sought for that outward sense.[14]

This is then to eat the meat, not that which perisheth, but that which endureth unto eternal life. To what purpose dost thou make ready teeth and stomach? Believe, and thou hast eaten already.[15]

He now explains how that which He speaks of comes to pass, and what it is to eat His body and to drink His blood. 'He that eateth my flesh, and drinketh my blood, dwelleth in me, and I in him.' This it is, therefore, for a man to eat that meat and to drink that drink, to dwell in Christ, and to have Christ dwelling in him. Consequently, he that dwelleth not in Christ, and in whom Christ dwelleth not, doubtless neither eateth His flesh (spiritually) nor drinketh His blood (although he may press the sacrament of the body and blood of Christ carnally and visibly with his teeth . . . Just as we are made better by participation of the Son, through the unity of His body and blood, which thing that eating and drinking signifies. We live then by Him, by eating Him, that is, by receiving Himself as the eternal life, which we did not have from ourselves.[16]

'Except ye eat the flesh of the Son of man,' says Christ, 'and drink His blood, ye have no life in you.' This seems to enjoin a crime or a vice; it is therefore a figure, enjoining that we should have a share in the sufferings of our Lord, and that we should retain a sweet and profitable memory of the fact that His flesh was wounded and crucified for us.[17]

9

The Fathers on the Eucharistic Sacrifice as not being Propitiatory in Nature but a Memorial of Thanksgiving and Praise

The Didache (written between 70 and 140 A.D.)
And on the Lord's own day gather yourselves together and break bread and give thanks, first confessing your transgressions, that your sacrifice may be pure. And let no man, having his dispute with his fellow, join your assembly until they have been reconciled, that your sacrifice may not be defiled; for this sacrifice it is that was spoken of by the Lord; In every place and at every time offer Me a pure sacrifice; for I am a great king, saith the Lord, and My name is wonderful among the nations.[1]

Justin Martyr (100/110–165 A.D.)
It is quite evident that this prophecy also alludes to the bread which our Christ gave us to offer in remembrance of the Body which He assumed for the sake of those who believe in Him, for whom He also suffered, and also to the cup which He taught us to offer in the Eucharist, in commemoration of His Blood.

'Likewise,' I continued, 'the offering of flour, my friends, which was ordered to be presented for those cleansed from leprosy, was a prototype of the Eucharistic Bread, which our Lord Jesus Christ commanded us to offer in remembrance [for a memorial] of the Passion He endured for all those souls who are cleansed from sin . . . Now, I also admit that prayers and thanksgivings, offered by worthy persons, are the only perfect and acceptable sacrifices to God. For Christians were instructed to offer only such prayers, even at their thanksgiving for their food, both liquid and solid, whereby the Passion which the Son of God endured for us is commemorated.'[2]

Origen (*c.*185–253/254 A.D.)
And that man truly celebrates a feast who does his duty and prays always, offering up continually bloodless sacrifices in prayer to God.[3]

Eusebius (263–340 A.D.)
Having then received the memory of this sacrifice to celebrate upon the Table by means of the symbols of His body and His saving blood, according to the laws of the new covenant, we are again taught by the prophet David to say: 'Thou hast prepared a table before me in the sight of mine adversaries, Thou hast anointed my head with oil; and Thy cup cheering me, how good it is.' Plainly then are here signified the mystic Christ and the solemn sacrifices of the Table of Christ, through which in our happy sacrificial rites . . . we have been taught to offer all life long bloodless and reasonable and acceptable sacrifices to the supreme God through His High priest, who is over all . . . these spiritual sacrifices . . . again the words of the prophet proclaim, saying in a certain place: 'Sacrifice to God the sacrifice of praise; and pay thy vows to the Most High: And call upon Me in the day of trouble; and I will deliver thee, and thou shalt glorify Me.' And again, 'The lifting up of my hands the evening sacrifice.' And again, 'A sacrifice to God is a contrite spirit.'

We then both sacrifice and burn incense, celebrating the memory of the great sacrifice in the mysteries which He has delivered to us and bringing to God our thanksgiving for our salvation . . . by means of pious hymns and prayers, and also wholly dedicating ourselves to Him and to His High Priest, the Word Himself, making our offering . . . in body and soul. Our Saviour Jesus, the Christ of God, after the manner of Melchizedek still even now accomplishes by means of His ministers the rites of His priestly work among men. For as that priest of the Gentiles never seems to have used bodily sacrifices, but only wine and bread when He blessed Abraham, so our Saviour and Lord Himself first, and then all the priests who in succession from Him are throughout all the nations, celebrating the spiritual priestly work in accordance with the laws of the Church, represent . . . with wine and bread the mysteries of His body and saving blood.[4]

Chrysostom (344/354–407 A.D.)
What then? Do we not offer every day? We offer indeed, but making a remembrance of His death, and this [remembrance] is one and not many. How is it one, and not many? Inasmuch as that [Sacrifice] was once for all offered, [and] carried into the Holy of Holies. This is a figure of that [sacrifice] and this remembrance of that . . . This is done in remembrance of what was then done. For (saith He) 'do this in remembrance of Me.' (*Luke* 22:19.) It is not another sacrifice, as the High Priest, but we offer always the same, or rather we perform a remembrance of a Sacrifice.[5]

Our High Priest is on high . . . we have our victim on high, our priest on high, our sacrifice on high: let us bring such sacrifices as can be offered on that altar, no longer sheep and oxen, no longer blood and fat. All these things have been done away; and there has been brought in their stead 'the reasonable service' (*Rom.* 12:1). But what is 'the reasonable service'? The [offerings made] through the soul; those made through the spirit. ('God,' it is said, 'is a Spirit, and they that worship Him must worship in spirit and in truth'—*John* 4:24); things which have no need of a body, no need of instruments, nor of special places, whereof each one is himself the Priest, such as, moderation, temperance, mercifulness, enduring ill-treatment, long-suffering, humbleness of mind.[6]

Augustine (354–430 A.D.)
While we consider it no longer a duty to offer sacrifices, we recognize sacrifices as part of the mysteries of Revelation, by which the things prophesied were foreshadowed. For they were our examples, and in many and various ways they all pointed to the one sacrifice which we now commemorate. Now that this sacrifice has been revealed, and has been offered in due time, sacrifice is no longer binding as an act of

worship, while it retains its symbolical authority.[7]

The Hebrews, again, in their animal sacrifices, which they offered to God in many varied forms, suitably to the significance of the institution, typified the sacrifice offered by Christ. This sacrifice is also commemorated by Christians, in the sacred offering and participation of the body and blood of Christ.[8]

'He that offereth the sacrifice of praise glorifieth me, and in this way will I show him my salvation.' Before the coming of Christ, the flesh and blood of this sacrifice were foreshadowed in the animals slain; in the passion of Christ the types were fulfilled by the true sacrifice; after the ascension of Christ, this sacrifice is commemorated in the sacrament.[9]

10

Thomas Aquinas
on the Nature of Faith

Accordingly if we consider, in faith, the formal aspect of the object, it is nothing else than the First Truth. For the faith of which we are speaking does not assent to anything, except because it is revealed by God. Hence the mean on which faith is based is the Divine Truth. If, however, we consider materially the things to which faith assents, they include not only God, but also many other things . . . Things concerning Christ's human nature, and the sacraments of the Church, or any creatures whatever, come under faith, in so far as by them we are directed to God, and in as much as we assent to them on account of the Divine Truth.

Faith implies assent of the intellect to that which is believed.

Now, since the chief object of faith consists in those things which we hope to see, according to Hebrews 11:1: Faith is the substance of things to be hoped for, it follows that those things are in themselves of faith, which order us directly to eternal life. Such are the Trinity of Persons in Almighty God, the mystery of Christ's Incarnation, and the like: and these are distinct articles of faith.

Now the act of believing is an act of the intellect assenting to the Divine truth at the command of the will moved by the grace of God, so that it is subject to the free-will in relation to God; and consequently the act of faith can be meritorious.

Now the act of faith is to believe . . . which is an act of the intellect determinate to one object by the will's command.

To believe is an act of the intellect, inasmuch as the will moves it to assent . . . Now to believe is immediately an act of the intellect, because the object of that act is the true, which pertains properly to the intellect. Consequently, faith, which is the proper principle of that act, must needs reside in the intellect.

Now the formal object of faith is the First Truth, as manifested in Holy Writ and the teachings of the Church, which proceeds from the First Truth. Consequently whoever does not adhere, as to an infallible and Divine rule, to the teaching of the Church, which proceeds from the First Truth manifested in Holy Writ, has not the habit of faith, but holds that which is of faith otherwise than by faith . . . Now it is manifest that he who adheres to the teaching of the Church, as to an infallible rule, assents to whatever the Church teaches; otherwise, if, of the things taught by the Church, he holds what he chooses to hold, and rejects what he chooses to reject, he no longer adheres to the teaching of the Church as to an infallible rule, but to his own will . . . Faith adheres to all the articles of faith by reason of one mean, viz. on account of the First Truth proposed to us in the Scriptures, according to the teaching of the Church who has the right understanding of them. Hence whoever abandons this mean is altogether lacking in faith.[1]

11

Martin Luther and John Calvin on the Relationship Between Justification and Good Works

MARTIN LUTHER
True, then, are these two sayings: 'Good works do not make a man good, but a good man does good works; bad works do not make a bad man, but a bad man does bad works.' Thus it is always necessary that the substance or person should be good before any good works can be done, and that good works should follow and proceed from a good person. As Christ says, 'A good tree cannot bring forth evil fruit, neither can a corrupt tree bring forth good fruit' (*Matt.* 7:18). Now it is clear that the fruit does not bear the tree, nor does the tree grow on the fruit; but, on the contrary, the trees bear the fruit, and the fruit grows on the trees. As then trees must exist before their fruit, and as the fruit does not make the tree either good or bad, but, on the contrary, a tree of either kind produces fruit of the same kind, so must first the person of the man be good or bad before he can do either a good or a bad work; and his works do not make him bad or good, but he himself makes his works either bad or good.

Since then works justify no man, but a man must be justified before he can do any good work, it is most evident that it is faith alone which, by the mere mercy of God through Christ, and by means of His word, can worthily and sufficiently justify and save the person; and that a Christian man needs no work, no law, for his salvation; for by faith he is free from all law, and in perfect freedom does gratuitously all that he does, seeking nothing either of profit or of salvation—since by the grace of God he is already saved and rich in all things through his faith—but solely that which is well-pleasing to God.

From all this it is easy to perceive on what principle good works are to be cast aside or embraced, and by what rule all teachings put forth concerning works are to be understood. For if works are brought forward as grounds of justification, and are done under the false persuasion that we can pretend to be justified by them, they lay on us the yoke of necessity, and extinguish liberty along with faith, and by this very addition to their use they become no longer good, but really worthy of condemnation. For such works are not free, but blaspheme the grace of God, to which alone it belongs to justify and save through faith. Works cannot accomplish this, and yet, with impious presumption, through our folly, they take it on themselves to do so; and thus break in with violence upon the office and glory of grace.

We do not then reject good works; nay, we embrace them and teach them in the highest degree. It is not on their own account that we condemn them, but on account of this impious addition to them and the perverse notion of seeking justification by them.

It is not from works that we are set free by the faith of Christ, but from the belief in works, that is from foolishly presuming to seek justification through works. Faith redeems our consciences, makes them upright, and preserves them, since by it we recognise the truth that justification does not depend on our works, although good works neither can nor ought to be absent, just as we cannot exist without food and drink and all the functions of this mortal body.[1]

JOHN CALVIN
This, in one word, is enough to refute the shamelessness of certain impious persons who slanderously charge us with abolishing good works, and with seducing men from the

pursuit of them, when we say that men are not justified by works and do not merit salvation by them; and again, charge us with making the path to righteousness too easy when we teach that justification lies in free remission of sins; and, by this enticement, with luring into sin men who are already too much inclined to it of their own accord.

We dream neither of a faith devoid of good works nor of a justification that stands without them. This alone is of importance: having admitted that faith and good works must cleave together, we still lodge justification in faith, not in works.

Why, then, are we justified by faith? Because by faith we grasp Christ's righteousness, by which alone we are reconciled to God. Yet you could not grasp this without at the same time grasping sanctification also. For he 'is given unto us for righteousness, wisdom, sanctification, and redemption' (*1 Cor.* 1:30). Therefore Christ justifies no one whom he does not at the same time sanctify. These benefits are joined together by an everlasting and indissoluble bond, so that those whom he illumines by his wisdom, he redeems; those whom he redeems, he justifies; those whom he justifies, he sanctifies.

It is as if he (James) said: 'Those who by true faith are righteous prove their righteousness by obedience and good works, not by a bare and imaginary mask of faith.' To sum up, he is not discussing in what manner we are justified but demanding of believers a righteousness fruitful in good works. And as Paul contends that we are justified apart from the help of works, so James does not allow those who lack good works to be reckoned righteous.[2]

12

Comments of the Fathers on the Nature of Justification

Clement (flourished c.80–101 A.D.)
In love the Master took us unto Himself; for the love which He had toward us, Jesus Christ our Lord hath given His blood for us by the will of God, and His flesh for our flesh and His life for our lives . . . They all therefore were glorified and magnified, not through themselves or their own works or the righteous doing which they wrought, but through His will. And so we, having been called through His will in Christ Jesus, are not justified through ourselves or through our own wisdom or understanding or piety or works which we wrought in holiness of heart, but through faith, whereby Almighty God justified all men that have been from the beginning; to whom be the glory for ever and ever.[1]

Polycarp (69–155/156 A.D.)
Forasmuch as ye know that it is by grace ye are saved, not of works, but by the will of God through Jesus Christ.[2]

Ignatius (d. c.110 A.D.)
Ye are not living after men but after Jesus Christ, who died for us, that believing on His death ye might escape death . . . But as for me, my charter is Jesus Christ, the inviolable character is His cross and His death and resurrection, and faith through Him . . . Yea, and we love the prophets also, because they too pointed to the Gospel in their preaching and set their hope on Him and awaited Him; in whom also having faith they were saved in the unity of Jesus Christ, being

worthy of all love and admiration as holy men, approved of Jesus Christ and numbered together in the Gospel of our common hope.[3]

Justin Martyr (100/110–165 A.D.)
After this He was crucified, in order that the rest of the prophecy be verified, for the words, 'washing His robe in the blood of the grape', were a forewarning of the passion He was to endure, purifying with His blood those who believe in Him . . . Indeed, Isaias did not send you to the bath to wash away murder and other sins which all the water of the ocean could not cleanse, but, as expected, it was of old that bath of salvation which he mentioned and which was for the repentant, who are no longer made pure by the blood of goats and sheep, or by the ashes of a heifer, or by the offerings of fine flour, but by faith through the blood and death of Christ who suffered death for this precise purpose . . . Indeed, when Abraham himself was still uncircumcised, he was justified and blessed by God because of his faith in Him, as the Scriptures tell us . . . We pray, also, that you may believe in Jesus Christ, and thus at His second triumphant coming you will be saved and not be condemned by Him to the fire of hell . . . Abraham, indeed, was considered just, not by reason of his circumcision, but because of his faith. For, before his circumcision it was said of him: 'Abraham believed God, and it was reputed to him unto justice.' We also, therefore, because of our belief in God through Christ, even though we are uncircumcised in the flesh, have the salutary circumcision, namely, that of the heart, and we thereby hope to be just and pleasing to God, since we have already obtained this testimony from Him through the words of the Prophets.[4]

Irenaeus (140–202 A.D.)
Men can be saved in no other way from the old wound of the serpent than by believing in him who, in the likeness of sinful flesh, is lifted up from the earth upon the tree of martyrdom, and draws all things to Himself, and vivifies the dead . . . For Abraham, according to his faith, followed the command of the word of God, and with a ready mind delivered up, as a sacrifice to God, his only-begotten and beloved son,

The Fathers on the Nature of Justification

in order that God also might be pleased to offer up for all his seed His own beloved and only-begotten Son, as a sacrifice for our redemption. Since, therefore, Abraham was a prophet, and saw in the Spirit the day of the Lord's coming, and the dispensation of His suffering, through whom both he himself and all who following the example of his faith, trust in God, should be saved, he rejoiced exceedingly. The Lord, therefore was not unknown to Abraham, whose day he desired to see; nor, again, was the Lord's Father, for he had learned from the Word of the Lord, and believed Him; wherefore it was accounted to him by the Lord for righteousness. For faith towards God justifies a man . . . For the Lord is the good man of the house, who rules the entire house of His Father; and who delivers a law suited both for slaves and those who are as yet undisciplined; and gives fitting precepts to those that are free, and have been justified by faith. . . . Wherefore, then, in all things, and through all things, there is one God, the Father, and one Word, and one Son, and one Spirit, and one salvation to all who believe in Him.[5]

13

The Teaching of the Council of Trent on Justification

The Synod furthermore declares, that, in adults, the beginning of the said Justification is to be derived from the prevenient grace of God, through Jesus Christ, that is to say, from his vocation, whereby, without any merits existing on their parts, they are called; that so they, who by sins were alienated from God, may be disposed through his quickening and assisting grace, to convert themselves to their own justification, by freely assenting to and co-operating with that said grace: in such sort that, while God touches the heart of man by the illumination of the Holy Ghost, neither is man himself utterly inactive while he receives that inspiration, forasmuch as he is also able to reject it; yet is he not able, by his own free will, without the grace of God, to move himself unto justice in his sight.

Now they (adults) are disposed unto the said justice, when, excited and assisted by divine grace, conceiving faith by hearing, they are freely moved towards God, believing those things to be true which God has revealed and promised—and this especially, that God justifies the impious by his grace, through the redemption that is in Christ Jesus; and when, understanding themselves to be sinners, they, by turning themselves, from the fear of divine justice whereby they are profitably agitated, to consider the mercy of God, are raised unto hope, confiding that God will be propitious to them for Christ's sake; and they begin to love him as the fountain of all justice; and are therefore moved against sins by a certain hatred and detestation, to wit, by that penitence which must be performed before baptism: lastly, when they purpose to receive baptism, to begin a new life, and to keep the commandments of God. Concerning this disposition it is written: He that cometh to God must believe that he is, and is a rewarder to them that seek him; and, Be of good faith, son, thy sins are forgiven thee; and, The fear of the Lord driveth out sin; and, Do penance, and be baptized every one of you in the name of Jesus Christ, for the remission of your sins, and you shall receive the gift of the Holy Ghost; and, Going, therefore, teach ye all nations, baptizing them in the name of the Father, and of the Son, and of the Holy Ghost; finally, Prepare your hearts unto the Lord.

This disposition, or preparation, is followed by Justification itself, which is not the remission of sins merely, but also the sanctification and renewal of the inward man, through the voluntary reception of the grace, and of the gifts, whereby man of unjust becomes just, and of an enemy a friend, so that he may be an heir according to the hope of life everlasting. Of this Justification the causes are these: the final cause indeed is the glory of God and of Jesus Christ, and life everlasting; while the efficient cause is a merciful God who washes and sanctifies gratuitously, signing, and anointing with the holy Spirit of promise, who is the pledge of our inheritance; but the meritorious cause is his most beloved only-begotten, our Lord Jesus Christ, who, when we were enemies, for the exceeding charity wherewith he loved us, merited Justification for us by his most holy Passion on the wood of the cross, and made satisfaction for us unto God the Father; the instrumental cause is the sacrament of baptism, which is the sacrament of faith, without which (faith) no man was ever justified; lastly, the alone formal cause is the justice of God, not that whereby he himself is just, but that whereby he maketh us just, that, to wit, with which we, being endowed by him, are renewed in the spirit of our mind, and we are not only reputed, but are truly called, and are just, receiving justice within us, each one according to his own measure, which the Holy Ghost distributes to everyone as he wills, and according to each one's proper disposition and co-operation. For, although no one can be just, but he to whom the merits of the Passion of our Lord Jesus Christ are communicated, yet is this done in the said justification of the impious, when by the merit of that same most holy Passion, the charity of God is poured forth by the Holy Spirit, in the hearts of those that are justified, and is inherent therein: whence, man, through Jesus Christ, in whom he is ingrafted, receives, in the said justification, together with the remission of sins, all these (gifts) infused at once, faith, hope and charity.

For faith, unless hope and charity be added thereto, neither unites man perfectly with Christ, nor makes him a living member of his body. For which reason it is most truly said, that Faith without works is dead and profitless; and, In Christ Jesus neither circumcision availeth any thing nor uncircumcision, but faith which worketh by charity. This faith, Catechumens beg of the Church—agreeably to a tradition of the apostles—previously to the sacrament of Baptism; when they beg for the faith which bestows life everlasting, which, without hope and charity, faith can not bestow: whence also do they immediately hear that word of Christ: If thou wilt enter into life, keep the commandments. Wherefore, when receiving true and Christian justice, they are bidden, immediately on being born again, to preserve it pure and spotless, as the first robe given them through Jesus Christ in lieu of that which Adam, by his disobedience, lost for himself and for us, that so they may bear it before the judgment-seat of our Lord Jesus Christ, and may have life eternal.

Having, therefore, been thus justified, and made the friends and domestics of God, advancing from virtue to virtue, they are renewed, as the apostle says, day by day; that is, by mortifying the members of their own flesh, and by presenting them as instruments of justice unto sanctification, they, through the observance of the commandments of God and of the Church, faith co-operating with good works, increase in that justice which they have received through the grace of Christ, and are still further justified, as it is written: He that is just, let him be justified still; and again, Be not afraid to be justified even to death; and also, Do you see that by works a man is justified, and not by faith only. And this increase of justification holy Church begs, when she prays, 'Give unto us, O Lord, increase of faith, hope, and charity.'

As regards those who, by sin, have fallen from the received

grace of Justification, they may be again justified, when, God exciting them, through the sacrament of Penance they shall have attained to the recovery, by the merit of Christ, of the grace lost: for this manner of Justification is of the fallen the reparation: which the holy Fathers have aptly called a second plank after the shipwreck of grace lost. For, on behalf of those who fall into sins after baptism, Christ Jesus instituted the sacrament of Penance, when he said, Receive ye the Holy Ghost, whose sins you shall forgive, they are forgiven them, and whose sins you shall retain, they are retained. Whence it is to be taught, that the penitence of a Christian, after his fall, is very different from that at (his) baptism; and that therein are included not only a cessation from sins, and a detestation thereof, or, a contrite and humble heart, but also the sacramental confession of the said sins,—at least in desire, and to be made in its season,—and sacerdotal absolution; and likewise satisfaction by fasts, alms, prayers, and the other pious exercises of the spiritual life; not indeed for the eternal punishment,—which is, together with the guilt, remitted, either by the sacrament, or by desire of the sacrament,—but for the temporal punishment, which, as the sacred writings teach, is not always wholly remitted, as is done in baptism, to those who, ungrateful to the grace of God which they have received, have grieved the Holy Spirit, and have not feared to violate the temple of God. Concerning which penitence is written: Be mindful whence thou art fallen; do penance, and do the first works. And again: The sorrow that is according to God worketh penance steadfast unto salvation. And again: Do penance, and bring forth fruits worthy of penance . . .

It is to be maintained, that the received grace of Justification is lost, not only by infidelity whereby even faith itself is lost, but also by any other mortal sin whatever, though faith be not lost; thus defending the doctrine of the divine law, which excludes from the kingdom of God not only the unbelieving, but the faithful also (who are) fornicators, adulterers, effeminate, liars with mankind, thieves, covetous, drunkards, railers, extortioners, and all others who commit deadly sins; from which, with the help of divine grace, they can refrain, and on account of which they are separated from the grace of Christ . . .

And, for this cause, life eternal is to be proposed to those working well unto the end, and hoping in God, both as a grace mercifully promised to the sons of God through Jesus Christ, and as a reward which is according to the promise of God himself, to be faithfully rendered to their good works and merits. For this is that crown of justice which the apostle declared was, after his fight and course, laid up for him, to be rendered to him by the just Judge, and not only to him, but alas to all that love his coming. For, whereas Jesus Christ himself continually infuses his virtue into the said justified,—as the head into the members, and the vine into the branches,— and this virtue always precedes and accompanies and follows their good works, which without it could not in any wise be pleasing and meritorious before God—we must believe that nothing further is wanting to the justified, to prevent their being accounted to have, by those very works which have been done in God, fully satisfied the divine law according to the state of this life, and to have truly merited eternal life, to be obtained also in its (due) time, if so be, however, that they depart in grace: seeing that Christ, our Saviour, saith: If any one shall drink of the water that I will give him, he shall not thirst forever; but it shall become in him a fountain of water springing up unto life everlasting.

Trent then goes on to list a number of Canons related to justification:

Canon X. If any one saith, that men are just without the justice of Christ, whereby he merited for us to be justified; or that it is by that justice itself that they are formally just: let him be anathema.

Canon XI. If any one saith, that men are justified, either by the sole imputation of the justice of Christ, or by the sole remission of sins, to the exclusion of the grace and the charity which is poured forth in their hearts by the Holy Ghost, and is inherent in them; or even that the grace, whereby we are justified is only the favour of God: let him be anathema.

Canon XXIV. If any one saith, that the justice received is not preserved and also increased before God through good

Teaching of the Council of Trent on Justification

works; but that the said works are merely the fruits and signs of Justification obtained, but not a cause of the increase thereof: let him be anathema.

Canon XXIX. If any one saith, that he who has fallen after baptism is not able by the grace of God to rise again; or, that he is able indeed to recover the justice which he has lost, but by faith alone without the sacrament of Penance, contrary to what the holy Roman and universal Church—instructed by Christ and his Apostles—has hitherto professed, observed, and taught: let him be anathema.

Canon XXX. If any one saith, that, after the grace of Justification has been received, to every penitent sinner the guilt is remitted, and the debt of eternal punishment is blotted out in such wise that there remains not any debt of temporal punishment to be discharged either in this world, or in the next in Purgatory, before the entrance into the kingdom of heaven can be opened (to him): let him be anathema.

Canon XXXII. If any one saith, that the good works of one that is justified are in such manner the gifts of God, that they are not also the good merits of him that is justified; or, that the said justified, by the good works which he performs through the grace of God and the merit of Jesus Christ, whose living member he is, does not truly merit increase of grace, eternal life, and the attainment of eternal life,—if so be, however, that he depart in grace,—and also an increase of glory: let him be anathema.[1]

Notes

1. The Authority of Scripture

1. The same point is made in Hebrews 1:1, where the writer says, 'God, after He spoke long ago to the fathers in the prophets in many portions and in many ways . . .' God spoke in the Old Testament in and through his prophets, in their preaching and in their writings.
2. The Greek word is *ophelimos*, which can mean either profitable or useful.
3. Origen, *Commentary in Matthew*. 28. Cited by B. F. Westcott, *A General Survey of the History of the Canon of the New Testament* (New York: Macmillan, 1889), p. 510.
4. William Whiston, Trans., *Josephus* (Grand Rapids, Kregel, 1960), *Against Apion* 1.8, p. 609.
5. *New Catholic Encyclopedia*, vol. II, 'Canon, Biblical' (Washington D.C.: Catholic University, 1967), p. 29.
6. Philip Schaff and Henry Wace, *Nicene and Post-Nicene Fathers*, vol. VII, Cyril of Jerusalem, *Catechetical Lectures* IV.33–36 (Grand Rapids: Eerdmans, 1955), pp. 26–28.
7. Philip Schaff and Henry Wace, *Nicene and Post-Nicene Fathers*, Second Series, vol. I, Eusebius, *Church History* IV.26.13–14 (Grand Rapids: Eerdmans, 1952), p. 206.
8. Philip Schaff and Henry Wace, *Nicene and Post-Nicene Fathers*, Second Series, vol. I, Eusebius, *Church History* VI.25.1–2 (Grand Rapids: Eerdmans, 1952), p. 272.
9. *The Panarion of Epiphanius*, Book I, Section I.6, 1. Nag Hammadi Studies, Martin Krause, James Robinson, Frederick Wisse, ed., (Leiden: Brill, 1987).
10. *Philocalia*, c. 3, Paris edition 1618, p. 63. Cited by John Cosin, *A Scholastical History of the Canon of the Holy Scripture*, vol. III (Oxford: Parker, 1849), p. 83.
11. Cited by John Cosin, *A Scholastical History of the Canon of the Holy Scripture*, vol. III (Oxford: Parker, 1849), p. 85.
12. Cited by John Cosin, *A Scholastical History of the Canon of the Holy Scripture*, vol. III (Oxford: Parker, 1849), pp. 62–63.
13. Philip Schaff and Henry Wace, *Nicene and Post-Nicene Fathers*, Second Series, vol. IV, St. Athanasius, *Letter* 39.6 (Grand Rapids: Eerdmans, 1953), p. 552.
14. Ibid., *Letter* 39.7, p. 552.
15. Philip Schaff and Henry Wace, *Nicene and Post-Nicene Fathers*, Second

Series, vol. III, Rufinus, *A Commentary on the Apostles' Creed* 36–38 (Grand Rapids: Eerdmans, 1953), pp. 557–58.
16. Philip Schaff and Henry Wace, *Nicene and Post-Nicene Fathers*, Second Series, vol. VI, St. Jerome, *Prefaces to Jerome's Works, Proverbs, Ecclesiastes and the Song of Songs, Daniel* (Grand Rapids: Eerdmans, 1954), pp. 492–93.
17. *Library of the Fathers of the Holy Catholic Church,* Gregory the Great, *Morals on the Book of Job*, vol. II, Parts III and IV, Book XIX.34 (Oxford: Parker, 1845), p. 424.
18. Taken from his comments on the final chapter of Esther, cited in *A Disputation on Holy Scripture* by William Whitaker (Cambridge: Parker Society, 1849), p. 48. (See also John Cosin, *A Scholastical History of the Canon of the Holy Scripture*, vol. III, ch. XVII, pp. 257–258 and B. F. Westcott, *A General Survey of the Canon of the New Testament*, p. 475).
19. Philip Schaff, *Nicene and Post-Nicene Fathers*, vol. II, St. Augustin's The City of God and On Christian Doctrine II.8.12 (Grand Rapids: Eerdmans, 1956), pp. 538–39.
20. Philip Schaff, *Nicene and Post-Nicene Fathers*, vol. II, St Augustin's City of God and Christian Doctrine, *The City of God* XVIII.26,36 (Grand Rapids: Eerdmans, 1956), pp. 374, 382.
21. *Contra Epistolam Gaudentii Donatistae*, ch. 23. Cited by William Henry Green, *General Introduction to the Old Testament; The Canon* (London: Murray, 1899), p. 172.
22. *New Catholic Encyclopedia*, vol. I (Washington D.C.: Catholic University, 1967), p. 390.

2. Scripture and Tradition

1. Thayer defines the word as: 'A giving over which is done by word of mouth or in writing, i.e. tradition by instruction, narrative, precept, etc. . . . hence instruction . . . objectively what is delivered, the substance of the teaching'. Joseph Henry Thayer, *The New Greek-English Lexicon of the New Testament* (Lafayette: APQA, 1979), p. 481.
2. Karl Keating, *Catholicism and Fundamentalism* (San Francisco: Ignatius, 1988), pp. 137–38.
3. For another example, see Romans 4:1–8.
4. See Romans 3:19–20, 3:27–28, 4:1–6, 10:1–4, 11:6; Galatians 2:16, 21; Ephesians 2:8–9; Philippians 3:8; Titus 3:5.
5. See Romans 11:6.
6. See Galatians 5:19–21; Ephesians 5:3–6; 1 Corinthians 6:9–10.

3. Tradition and Roman Catholicism

1. J.N.D. Kelly, *Early Christian Doctrines* (San Francisco: Harper & Row, 1978), p. 46.
2. Alexander Roberts and W. H. Rambaut, trans., *The Writings of Irenaeus, Against Heresies,* 3.1.1 (Edinburgh: T. & T. Clark, 1874), p. 258.
3. For comments by the early Fathers on the content of the tradition

and its relationship to Scripture see Appendix 1.
4. Alexander Roberts and W. H. Rambaut, trans., *The Writings of Irenaeus, Against Heresies* I.10.1–2 (Edinburgh: T. & T. Clark, 1874), pp. 42–43; Alexander Roberts and James Donaldson, *The Ante-Nicene Fathers*, vol. III, Latin Christianity: Its Founder, Tertullian, *On Prescription Against Heretics* 13 (Grand Rapids: Eerdmans, 1951), p. 249.
5. *De Bono Viduitatis*, ch. 2. Cited in *An Examination of the Council of Trent* by Martin Chemnitz, vol. I (St. Louis: Concordia, 1971), p. 15
6. Philip Schaff, *Nicene and Post-Nicene Fathers*, vol. II, St. Augustin's *The City of God*, Book XIX, ch. 1 (Grand Rapids: Eerdmans, 1956), p. 413.
7. Ibid., vol. II, St. Augustin's The City of God and On Christian Doctrine, Book II, ch. 9, p. 539.
8. *Contra Cresconium*, Book II, ch. 31, 32. Cited in *An Examination of the Council of Trent*, by Martin Chemnitz, vol. I (St. Louis: Concordia, 1971), p. 174.
9. *A Library of the Fathers of the Holy Catholic Church, The Catechetical Lectures of St Cyril* 4.17, (Oxford: Parker, 1845), p. 42.
10. This is fully documented in Heiko Oberman, *The Harvest of Medieval Theology: Gabriel Biel and Late Medieval Nominalism* (Grand Rapids: Harvard University, 1963) and Brian Tierney, *Origins of Papal Infallibility, 1150–1350* (Leiden: Brill, 1972).
11. Heiko Oberman, *The Harvest of Medieval Theology: Gabriel Biel and Late Medieval Nominalism* (Grand Rapids: Harvard University, 1963) pp. 373–97.
12. Alexander Roberts and James Donaldson, trans., The *Ante-Nicene Fathers*, vol. III, Latin Christianity: Its Founder, Tertullian, *On Prescription Against Heretics*, ch. 19 (Grand Rapids: Eerdmans, 1951), pp. 251–52.
13. Heiko Oberman, *The Harvest of Medieval Theology: Gabriel Biel and Late Medieval Nominalism* (Grand Rapids: Harvard University, 1963), p. 369.
14. Philip Schaff and Henry Wace, *Nicene and Post-Nicene Fathers,* vol. VIII, St. Basil: Letters and Select Works, *On the Holy Spirit* 27.65 (Grand Rapids: Eerdmans, 1955), p. 40.
15. Ibid., *Letter* 189.3, p. 229.
16. Philip Schaff and Henry Wace, *Nicene and Post-Nicene Fathers*, vol. XI, Vincent of Lérins, *A Commonitory*, 2.4.6 (Grand Rapids: Eerdmans, 1955), p. 132.
17. Universality: 'The universal Church, moreover, through the whole world, has received this tradition from the apostles.' Alexander Roberts and W. H. Rambaut, *The Writings of Irenaeus, Against Heresies* II.9.1 (Edinburgh: T. & T. Clark, 1874), p. 143.
Consent: 'The preaching of the church is everywhere consistent and continues in an even course and receives testimony from the prophets, the apostles, and all the disciples.' (Ibid., III.24.1), p. 369.
Antiquity: 'True knowledge is that which consists in the doctrine of the apostles and the ancient constitution of the church throughout all the world, and the distinctive manifestation of the body of Christ according to the succession of bishops by which they

have handed down that church which exists in every place, and has come even unto us, being guarded and preserved without any forging of Scriptures, by a very complete system of doctrine, and neither receiving addition, nor suffering curtailment in the truths which she believes.' (Ibid., IV.33.8), p. 11.
18. *The Council of Trent,* Fourth Session, The Canonical Scriptures (Rockford: Tan, 1978), pp. 18–19.
19. *Dogmatic Decrees of the Vatican Council,* as found in *The Creeds of Christendom* vol. II by Philip Schaff (New York: Harper, 1877), p. 242.
20. Boniface Ramsey, *Beginning to Read the Fathers* (London: Darton, Longman and Todd, 1986), p. 6.

4. The Papacy and the 'Rock' of Matthew 16

1. For the decrees of Vatican I and II on Papal Primacy and Infallibility see Appendix 4.
2. In addition to the primary word *luo*, there are a number of derivatives which show that the word 'loose' when dealing with the kingdom of God refers primarily to release from bondage to sin and Satan.
   Apoluo, which means to release; to set free; to send away; to loose from; to dismiss; to forgive.
   Lutron means a ransom or the price for redeeming. So that it refers to a loosing that can take place, a setting at liberty that can be effected, where a ransom has been paid. The significance of this can be seen immediately in the fact that the Greek word for redemption in the New Testament is the word *apolutrosis*. This is a form of the word *lutron* which goes back to the word *luo* or loose as its primary root.
   Apolutrosis means 'a releasing effected by payment of a ransom; redemption, deliverance, liberation procured by the payment of a ransom'. Joseph Henry Thayer, *The New Greek-English Lexicon of the New Testament* (Lafayette: APQA, 1979). This word is used in the New Testament to describe deliverance from Satan and forgiveness of sin based on the atoning work of Christ in shedding his blood and giving his life as a payment for sin. Note this relationship in Colossians 1:13–14; Ephesians 1:7; Romans 3:24–25.
3. James White, *Pros Apologian,* Papal Pretensions (Phoenix: Alpha and Omega Ministries, 1991), pp. 2–3.
4. There is, of course, no evidence that *any* church of the New Testament era was ruled by a single *presbuteros* (elder/bishop).
5. Richard P. McBrien, *Catholicism,* vol. II (Minneapolis: Winston, 1980), pp. 831–32.
6. For comments by the Fathers on the interpretations of the Rock of Matthew 16:18 see Appendix 5.
7. 'Of all the Fathers who interpret these passages in the Gospels (*Matt.* 16.18, *John* 21.17), not a single one applies them to the Roman bishops as Peter's successors. How many Fathers have busied

themselves with these texts, yet not one of them whose commentaries we possess—Origen, Chrysostom, Hilary, Augustine, Cyril, Theodoret, and those whose interpretations are collected in catenas—has dropped the faintest hint that the primacy of Rome is the consequence of the commission and promise to Peter!' Janus (Johann Joseph Ignaz von Döllinger), *The Pope and the Council* (Boston: Roberts, 1869), p. 74.

8. Philip Schaff, *Nicene and Post-Nicene Fathers*, vol. VI, Saint Augustin, *Sermons on New Testament Lessons*, Sermon 26.1–2 (Grand Rapids: Eerdmans, 1956), p. 340.

9. 'On thee,' He says, 'I will build My Church'; and 'I will give to thee the keys', not to the Church; and 'Whatsoever thou shalt have loosed or bound', not 'what they shall have loosed or bound'. For so withal the result teaches. In [Peter] himself the Church was reared; that is through [Peter] himself; [Peter] himself essayed the key; you see what [key]: 'Men of Israel, let what I say sink into your ears: Jesus the Nazarene, a man destined by God for you,' and so forth. [Peter] himself, therefore, was the first to unbar, in Christ's baptism, the entrance to the heavenly kingdom, in which (kingdom) are 'loosed' the sins that were beforetime 'bound' . . . Alexander Roberts and James Donaldson, *The Ante-Nicene Fathers*, vol. IV, Tertullian, *On Modesty*, ch. 21 (Grand Rapids: Eerdmans, 1951), p. 99.

10. *A Library of the Fathers of the Holy Catholic Church*, Treatise V, *On the Unity of the Church*, ch. 3 (Oxford: Parker, 1842), p. 134.

11. Michael Winter, *St. Peter and the Popes* (Westport: Greenwood, 1960), pp. 47–48.

12. *A Library of the Fathers of the Holy Catholic Church*, The Epistles of S. Cyprian, *Epistle* 43.4 (Oxford: Parker, 1844), p. 96.

13. Robert Eno, *The Rise of the Papacy* (Wilmington: Michael Glazier, 1990), p. 58.

14. W. A. Jurgens, *The Faith of the Early Fathers*, vol. II, St. Ambrose, *On the Twelve Psalms*, Number 1261 (Collegeville: Liturgical, 1979), p. 150.

15. 'He, then, who before was silent, to teach us that we ought not to repeat the words of the impious, this one, I say, when he heard, "But who do you say I am?" immediately, not unmindful of his station, exercised his primacy, that is the primacy of his confession, not of honour; the primacy of belief, not of rank. This, then, is Peter who has replied for the rest of the Apostles; rather before the rest of men. And so he is called the foundation, because he knows how to preserve not only his own but the common foundation . . . Faith, then, is the foundation of the Church, for it was not said of Peter's flesh, but of his faith, that "the gates of hell shall not prevail against it". But his confession of faith conquered hell. And this confession did not shut out one heresy, for, since the Church like a good ship is often buffeted by many waves, the foundation of the Church should prevail against all heresies.' *The Fathers of the Church*, Saint Ambrose, *The Sacrament of the Incarnation of Our Lord*, IV.32–V.34

(Washington D.C: Catholic University, 1963), pp. 230–31.
16. 'He speaks from this time lowly things, on His way to His passion, that He might show His humanity. For He that hath built His Church upon Peter's confession, and has so fortified it, that ten thousand dangers and deaths are not to prevail over it . . . And I say unto thee, Thou art Peter, and upon this rock I will build My Church; that is, on the faith of his confession.' *Homilies on the Gospel of Matthew* 82.3, 54.3. See Philip Schaff, *Nicene and Post-Nicene Fathers*, First Series, vol. X (Grand Rapids: Eerdmans, 1956), pp. 494, 333.
17. *On the Inscription of Acts*, II. Cited by E. Giles, ed., *Documents Illustrating Papal Authority* (London: SPCK, 1952), p. 168.
18. Cited by John Bigane, *Faith, Christ or Peter: Matthew 16:18 in Sixteenth-Century Roman Catholic Exegesis* (Washington D.C.: University Press, 1981), pp. 31–32.
19. John Meyendorff, *St. Peter in Byzantine Theology*. Found in *The Primacy of Peter* (London: Faith, 1963), p. 11.
20. Karlfried Froehlich, *Saint Peter, Papal Primacy, and Exegetical Tradition, 1150–1300*, pp. 3–4. Taken from *The Religious Roles of the Papacy: Ideals and Realities, 1150–1300*, Christopher Ryan, ed., Papers in Medieval Studies 8 (Toronto: Pontifical Institute of Medieval Studies, 1989).
21. John Bigane, *Faith, Christ or Peter: Matthew 16:18 in Sixteenth Century Roman Catholic Exegesis* (Washington D.C.: University Press, 1981) pp. 1–203.
22. Oscar Cullmann, *Peter: Disciple, Apostle, Martyr* (Westminster: Philadelphia, 1953), p. 162.

5. *Papal Authority and Infallibility: The Test of History*

1. Robert Eno, *The Rise of the Papacy* (Wilmington: Glazier, 1990), p. 39.
2. *A Library of the Fathers of the Holy Catholic Church, The Epistles of S. Cyprian*, *Epistle* 67 (Parker Society: Oxford, 1844), p. 208.
3. Ibid., The judgments of eighty-seven bishops in the Council of Carthage on the question of baptizing heretics, pp. 286–87.
4. The ecumenical councils were called by the Roman emperors. Only the first seven of these, between 325 and 787 A.D. are recognized by both the Western and Eastern churches.
5. Janus (Johann Joseph Ignaz von Dollinger), *The Pope and the Council* (Boston: Roberts, 1869), pp. 63–64. See n.7 p. 219.
6. Council of Nicea: Canon 6; Synod of Antioch: Canon 9; Council of Constantinople: Canons 2 and 3; Council of Chalcedon: Canon 28. Charles Joseph Hefele, *A History of the Councils of the Church*, vol. II (Edinburgh: T. & T. Clark, 1883), pp. 69, 355, 357; vol. III, pp. 389, 411–12.
7. For the letter of Gregory the Great to John of Constantinople refer to Appendix 6.
8. Philip Schaff and Henry Wace, *Nicene and Post-Nicene Fathers*, Second Series, vol. XII, Leo the Great, Gregory the Great, *Epistles of St*

NOTES FOR PAGES 62–67

    Gregory the Great, Book VII, *Epistle* 33 (Grand Rapids: Eerdmans, 1956), p. 226.
9. Karl Keating, *Catholicism and Fundamentalism* (San Francisco: Ignatius, 1988), p. 219.
10. Pelagius denied that Adam's fall transmitted guilt or corruption to all mankind and claimed that Christians could live lives of perfect holiness and fulfilment of the will of God.
11. Charles Joseph Hefele, *A History of the Councils of the Church*, vol. II (Edinburgh: T. & T. Clark, 1883), pp. 456–57.
12. Karl Keating refers to Augustine, who he claims affirmed his belief in papal infallibility during the Pelagian controversy. He gives a quote from one of Augustine's sermons in which he refers to Pope Innocent's judgment on Pelagius. He quotes him as saying, 'Rome has spoken; the case is closed.' But such an assertion is a total distortion of Augustine's true position. It is to give a quote out of the context of the historical situation and the rest of his writings to arrive at a false perspective of what he really means. Augustine never endorsed such a teaching. That should be obvious in that the next pope, Zosimus, also spoke, but his judgment was rejected and opposed by Augustine and the North African Church. Döllinger makes these comments in correcting the false impression subsequently repeated by Keating and others:
'Innocent I, when invoked by the Africans, after five years of disputing, had sanctioned the decrees of their two Synods of Milevis and Carthage (417), and pronounced a work of Pelagius heretical, so that St. Augustine said, in a sermon, 'The matter is now ended.' But he deceived himself, for the strife was only fairly begun, and it was not ended till many years later, by the decision of the Ecumenical Council of Ephesus in 431.
But St. Augustine's saying . . . has been alleged in proof of his accepting Papal infallibility, which, in dealing with the baptismal controversy, he so often and so pointedly repudiates. Such a notion was utterly foreign to his mind. The Pelagian system was in his eyes so manifest and deadly an error . . . there seemed to him no need even of a Synod to condemn it. The two African Synods, and the Pope's assent to their decrees, appeared to him more than enough, and so the matter might be regarded at an end. That a Roman judgment in itself was not conclusive, but that a '*Concilium plenarium*' was necessary for that purpose, he had himself emphatically maintained; and the conduct of Pope Zosimus could only confirm his opinion.
Janus (Johann Joseph Ignaz von Döllinger), *The Pope and the Council* (Boston: Roberts, 1870), pp. 57–58.
13. Charles Joseph Hefele, *A History of the Councils of the Church*, vol. IV (Edinburgh: T. & T. Clark, 1895), pp. 322–23.
14. The orthodox position is that Christ, though one person, possesses both a human and a divine will, because both human and divine natures are united in his one person.

15. The Council declared that the letters of Honorius: 'were quite foreign . . . to the apostolic dogmas, and to the declarations of the holy Councils and to all the accepted Fathers, and that they follow the false teachings of the heretics; therefore we entirely reject them, and execrate them as hurtful to the soul . . . And with these we define that there shall be expelled from the holy Church of God and anathematised Honorius who was some time Pope of old Rome, because of what we found written by him to Sergius.' Philip Schaff and Henry Wace, *Nicene and Post-Nicene Fathers,* Second Series, vol. XIV, *The Seven Ecumenical Councils* (Grand Rapids: Eerdmans, 1956), p. 344.
16. Janus (Johann Joseph Ignaz von Döllinger), *The Pope and the Council* (Boston: Roberts, 1870), p. 61.
17. For the bull *Unam Sanctam* by Boniface VIII see Appendix 3.
18. The decree of the Council of Constance states: 'This holy Council of Constance . . . declares, first that it is lawfully assembled in the Holy Spirit, that it constitutes a General Council, representing the Catholic Church, and therefore it has its authority immediately from Christ; and that all men, of every rank and condition, including the Pope himself, is bound to obey it in matters concerning the Faith . . . Secondly it declares that any one, of any rank and condition, who shall contumaciously refuse to obey the orders, decrees, statutes or instructions, made or to be made by this holy Council, or by any other lawfully assembled general council . . . shall, unless he comes to a right frame of mind, be subjected to fitting penance and punished appropriately: and, if need be, recourse shall be had to the other sanctions of the law.' Henry Bettenson, ed., *Documents of the Christian Church,* The Decree of the Council of Constance, '*Sacrosancta*' (London: Oxford University, 1963), p. 135.
19. George Salmon, *The Infallibility of the Church* (London: Murray, 1914), p 252.

6. Marian Dogmas

1. For documentation on the authoritative teachings of the Roman Catholic Church on the person of Mary see Appendix 7.
2. Karl Keating, *Catholicism and Fundamentalism* (San Francisco: Ignatius, 1988), pp. 269–70.
3. Juniper B. Carol, O.F.M., ed., *Mariology,* vol. I (Milwaukee: Bruce, 1955), p. 147.
4. 'Who ever originated a heresy that did not first dissever himself from the consentient agreement of the universality and antiquity of the Catholic Church? That this is so is demonstrated in the clearest way by examples. For who ever before the profane Pelagius attributed so much antecedent strength to Free-will, as to deny the necessity of God's grace to aid it towards good in every single act? Who ever before his monstrous disciple Celestius denied that the whole human race is involved in the guilt of Adam's sin?' *A Commonitory* 24.62, in Philip Schaff and Henry Wace, *Nicene and Post-Nicene*

Fathers, Second Series, vol. XI, Sulpitius Severus, Vincent of Lérins, John Cassian (Grand Rapids: Eerdmans, 1955), pp. 149–50.

5. Whitney Oates, *The Basic Writings of Augustine*, vol. I, *On Original Sin*, ch. 47 (New York: Random House, 1948), p. 654.
6. Eamon Duffy, *What Catholics Believe About Mary* (London: Catholic Truth Society, 1989), p. 21.
7. For documentation on the Roman Catholic dogma of the Assumption of Mary see Appendix 7.
8. Eamon Duffy, *What Catholics Believe About Mary* (London: Catholic Truth Society, 1989), p. 17.
9. 'But if some think us mistaken, let them search the Scriptures. They will not find Mary's death; they will not find whether she died or did not die; they will not find whether she was buried or was not buried ... Scripture is absolutely silent [on the end of Mary] ... For my own part, I do not dare to speak, but I keep my own thoughts and I practice silence ... The fact is, Scripture has outstripped the human mind and left [this matter] uncertain ... Did she die, we do not know ... Either the holy Virgin died and was buried ... Or she was killed ... Or she remained alive, since nothing is impossible with God and He can do whatever He desires; *for her end no-one knows.*' Epiphanius, *Panarion*, Haer. 78.10–11, 23. Cited by Juniper Carol, O.F.M. ed., Mariology, vol. II (Milwaukee: Bruce, 1957), pp. 139–40.
10. Juniper B. Carol, O.F.M., ed., *Mariology*, vol. I (Milwaukee: Bruce, 1955), p. 154.
11. Ibid., vol. I, p. 149.
12. Ibid., vol. II, p. 147.
13. *New Testament Apocrypha*, William Schneemelcher, ed. (Cambridge: James Clarke, 1991), p. 38.
14. Pope Gelasius I, *Epistle 42*, Migne Series, M.P.L. vol. 59, Col. 162.
15. Henry Denzinger, *The Sources of Catholic Dogma* (London: Herder, 1954), pp. 69–70.
16. Henry Denzinger, *The Sources of Catholic Dogma* (London: Herder, 1954), pp. 66–69.
    W. A. Jurgens, *The Faith of the Early Fathers*, vol. I (Collegeville: Liturgical, 1970), p. 404.
    New Catholic Encyclopedia, vol. VII (Washington D.C.: Catholic University, 1967), p. 434.
    Hefele, *A History of the Councils of the Church* (Edinburgh: T. & T. Clark, 1895), vol. IV, pp. 43–44.
17. Alexander Roberts and James Donaldson, *The Ante-Nicene Fathers*, vol. III, Latin Christianity: Its Founder, Tertullian, *Against Praxeas*, ch. X and XI (Grand Rapids: Eerdmans, 1951), p. 605.
18. In Alphonsus de Liguori's, *The Glories of Mary* (Rockford: Tan, 1977, originally published in 1750) the following are just some of the terms used to describe or to praise her: Mediatrix, Mediatress, Advocate of Sinners, Source of Salvation, Source of Grace, Queen of Mercy, Refuge of Sinners, Medicine of Sinners, Possessor of the Keys of the Kingdom of Heaven, Mother of Divine Grace, Protector, Guide,

Appeaser of God's Wrath, Intercessor, Reconciler of God with Man, Mother of Grace, Source of Love, Source of Light, Help in Temptation, Strength in Weakness, Succour of Sinners, Protector against Satan, Deliverer in Temptation, Peacemaker between God and Man, Trust for Salvation, Deliverer from Condemnation, Purifier of the Soul, Gate of Heaven, Ladder of Heaven.

19. Karl Keating, *Catholicism and Fundamentalism* (San Francisco: Ignatius, 1988), p. 279.
20. *Jucunda semper* (1894). Cited by Juniper B. Carol, O.F.M., ed., *Mariology*, vol. I (Milwaukee: Bruce, 1955), p. 383.
21. *Miserentissimus Redemptor* (1928), Cited by Juniper B. Carol, O.F.M., ed., *Mariology*, vol. I (Milwaukee: Bruce, 1955), p. 37.
22. *De Corredemptione*, Cited by Juniper B. Carol, O.F.M., ed., *Mariology*, vol. I (Milwaukee: Bruce, 1955), p. 37.
23. *De Corredemptione*, Cited by Juniper B. Carol, O.F.M., ed., *Mariology*, vol. I (Milwaukee: Bruce, 1955), p. 39.

7. Salvation and the Sacramental System

1. *The Canons and Decrees of the Council of Trent*, in Philip Schaff, *The Creeds of Christendom*, vol. II, Session VII, On the Sacraments in General (Harper: New York, 1877), p. 120.
2. Philip Hughes, *A Commentary on the Epistle to the Hebrews* (Grand Rapids: Eerdmans, 1977) p. 268.
3. For example, Acts 20:17, 28.
4. G.W.H. Lampe's *A Patristic Greek Lexicon* (Oxford: University, 1961) mentions such fathers as Didymus the Blind, Basil, Chrysostom, Theodoret, Gregory Nazianzen, Cyril of Alexandria and Gregory of Nyssa as those who used the term.
5. Richard McBrien, *Catholicism*, vol. III (Minneapolis: Winston, 1980), p. 802.
6. Ibid., vol. II, pp. 12–127.
7. The following are the teachings of the Council of Trent:
   'Canon IX: If any one saith, that the sacramental absolution of the priest is not a judicial act, but a bare ministry of pronouncing and declaring sins to be forgiven to him who confesses; provided only he believe himself to be absolved, or (even though) the priest absolve not in earnest, but in joke; or saith, that the confession of the penitent is not required, in order that the priest may be able to absolve him: let him be anathema.
   'Canon XII: If any one saith, that God always remits the whole punishment together with the guilt, and that the satisfaction of penitents is no other than the faith whereby they apprehend that Christ has satisfied for them: let him be anathema.
   'Canon XIII: If any one saith, that the satisfaction for sins, as to their temporal punishment, is nowise made to God, through the merits of Jesus Christ, by the punishments inflicted by him, and patiently borne, or by those enjoined by the priest, nor even by those voluntarily

undertaken, as by fastings, prayers, alms-deeds, or by other works also of piety; and that, therefore, the best penance is merely a new life: let him be anathema.

'Canon XIV: If any man saith, that the satisfactions, by which penitents redeem their sins through Jesus Christ, are not a worship of God, but traditions of men, which obscure the doctrine of grace, and the true worship of God, and the benefit itself of the death of Christ: let him be anathema.'

The Canons and Decrees of the Council of Trent, in Philip Schaff, *The Creeds of Christendom*, vol. II, On the Most Holy Sacrament of Penance (Harper: New York, 1877), pp. 167–69.

8. Kirsopp Lake, *The Apostolic Fathers*, 1 Clement 32.3–4 (New York: Macmillan, 1912), p. 63.
9. *A Library of the Fathers of the Holy Catholic Church, The Epistles of Cyprian, Epistle* 75.4 (Oxford: Parker, 1844), p. 271
10. Writing in the middle of the fourth century Basil the Great, the Bishop of Caesarea, describes in great detail the different classes of penitents and the type and length of penance one must undergo for committing any form of sexual sin, murder or apostasy. The following is but one example of many that are given in his writings: 'The intentional homicide, who has afterwards repented, will be excommunicated from the sacrament for twenty years. The twenty years will be appointed for him as follows: for four he ought to weep, standing outside the door of the house of prayer, beseeching the faithful as they enter in to offer prayer on his behalf, and confessing his own sin. After four years he will be admitted among the hearers, and during five years will go out with them. During seven years he will go out with the kneelers, praying. During four years he will only stand with the faithful, and will not take part in the oblation. On the completion of this period he will be admitted to the sacrament.' Philip Schaff and Henry Wace, *Nicene and Post-Nicene Fathers*, vol. VIII, St. Basil, *Letter* 217, *Canon* LVI, (Grand Rapids: Eerdmans, 1955), p. 256.
11. Charles Joseph Hefele, *A History of the Councils of the Church*, vol. IV (Edinburgh, T. & T. Clark, 1895), pp. 419–20.
12. John McNeill and Helena Gamer, *Medieval Handbooks of Penance* (New York: Octagon, 1985), pp. 6, 29.
13. Reinhold Seeberg in his *Text-Book of the History of Doctrines*, vol. 1 (Grand Rapids: Baker, 1952), pp. 132–34, quotes Tertullian to show his pattern of thinking: 'Thou hast offended, but thou mayest yet be reconciled. Thou hast one to whom thou mayest render satisfaction, and he, too, is willing.'... It is necessary 'to satisfy the offended Lord' ... 'in order that I may reconcile myself to God, whom by sinning I have offended.'... This is done by repentance: 'by repentance God is appeased'... 'But repentance consists of heartfelt sorrow... and confession... which embraces a purpose of satisfaction... The sinner humbles himself by confession... he sighs, weeps, fasts, and thus atones for his transgression. He makes satisfaction to God and earns for himself forgiveness... He even brings a sin-offering to God

       . . . and thus satisfaction is rendered to God. Since man thus punishes himself, he frees himself from eternal punishment.'
14. John Hardon S.J., *The Question and Answer Catholic Catechism* (Garden City: Image, 1981), Questions 1318, 1320, 1390, 1392, 1395, 1400.
15. Philip Schaff, *A History of the Christian Church,* vol. V (Grand Rapids: Charles Scribner's, 1910), pp. 732, 734–35.
16. Philip Schaff, *A History of the Christian Church,* vol. V (Grand Rapids: Eerdmans, 1907), pp. 740–42.
17. *The Jerusalem Bible* (Garden City: Doubleday, 1970), pp. 623–24.
18. 'But whoever blasphemes against the Holy Spirit never has forgiveness, but is guilty of an eternal sin.' (*Mark* 3:29).
19. Richard McBrien, *Catholicism*, vol. II, (Minneapolis: Winston, 1980), p. 1143.
20. See, for instance, Jacques Le Goff, *The Birth of Purgatory* (Chicago: University of Chicago, 1981), pp. 46–47.
21. Ibid., pp. 50–51.
22. Ibid., pp. 30–37.

8. *The Eucharist*

1. For comments by the Fathers on the Eucharist and the Real Presence see Appendix 8.
2. 'We call this food the Eucharist . . . Not as ordinary bread or as ordinary drink do we partake of them, but just as, through the word of God, our Saviour Jesus Christ became incarnate and took upon Himself flesh and blood for our salvation, so we have been taught, the food which has been made the Eucharist by the prayer of His word, and which nourishes our flesh and blood by assimilation, is both the flesh and blood of that Jesus who was made flesh.' Thomas B. Falls, *The Fathers of the Church, Saint Justin Martyr, First Apology* 65–66 (Washington D.C.: Catholic University, 1948), pp. 105–06.
3. It is quite evident that this prophecy also alludes to the bread which our Christ gave us to offer in remembrance of the Body which He assumed for the sake of those who believe in Him, for whom He also suffered, and also to the cup which He taught us to offer in the Eucharist, in commemoration of His blood (Ibid., *Dialogue with Trypho* 70, p. 262).
4. Alexander Roberts and W. H. Rambaut, trans., *The Writings of Irenaeus, Against Heresies,* 5.2.2 (Edinburgh: T. & T. Clark, 1874), p. 59.
5. Ibid., *Against Heresies* 4.18.4–5, pp. 434–35.
6. Alexander Roberts and James Donaldson, *The Ante-Nicene Fathers,* vol. III, Latin Christianity: Its Founder, Tertullian, *On the Resurrection of the Flesh,* ch. 37 (Grand Rapids: Eerdmans, 1951), p. 572.
7. Ibid., Tertullian, *On the Resurrection of the Flesh,* ch. 37, p. 572.
8. Alexander Roberts and James Donaldson, *The Ante-Nicene Fathers, vol.* II, Clement of Alexandria, *The Instructor,* Book I, ch. VI (Grand Rapids: Eerdmans, 1951), pp. 215–22.

9. Eusebius of Caesarea, *On the Theology of the Church* iii.11,12. Taken from Darwell Stone, *A History of the Doctrine of the Holy Eucharist*, vol. I (New York: Longmans, Green, 1909), pp. 85–89.
10. *A Library of the Fathers of the Holy Catholic Church, The Catechetical Lectures of Cyril of Jerusalem*, XXII.1–2, XXIII.7 (Oxford: Parker, 1842), pp. 270, 275.
11. Pope Gelasius, I *On the Two Natures in Christ*. Taken from Darwell Stone, *A History of the Doctrine of the Holy Eucharist*, vol. I (London: Longmans, Green, 1909), p. 102.
12. J.N.D. Kelly, *Early Christian Doctrines* (San Francisco: Harper & Row, 1978), pp. 440–41, 445–46.
13. For comments by Augustine on the nature of the Eucharist and the Real Presence refer to Appendix 8.
14. 'If the sentence ... seems to enjoin a crime or vice ... it is figurative. "Except ye eat the flesh of the Son of man," says Christ, "and drink His blood, ye have no life in you." This seems to enjoin a crime or a vice; it is therefore a figure, enjoining that we should have a share in the sufferings of our Lord, and that we should retain a sweet and profitable memory of the fact that His flesh was wounded and crucified for us.' Philip Schaff, *Nicene and Post-Nicene Fathers*, vol. II, St. Augustin: The City of God and On Christian Doctrine, *On Christian Doctrine* 3.16.2 (Grand Rapids: Eerdmans, 1956), p. 563.
15. 'In respect of the presence of the Majesty we have Christ always; in respect of the presence of the flesh, it was rightly said to the disciples, But Me ye will not always have. For the Church had Him in respect of the presence of the flesh, for a few days; now, by faith it holds, not with eyes beholds Him.' *A Library of the Fathers of the Holy Catholic Church, Homilies on the Gospel According to St. John by S. Augustine*, Homily 92.1, p. 873; Homily 50.13 (Oxford: Parker, 1849), pp. 677–78.
16. Philip Schaff, *Nicene and Post-Nicene Fathers, vol.* VII, St Augustin, *Homilies on the Gospel of John*, Tractate XXVi.I (Grand Rapids: Eerdmans, 1956), p. 168.
17. For instance: Theologians such as Duns Scotus, Biel, Occam & Wessel. See Seeberg, vol. 2, pp. 203ff. for details
18. Karl Keating, *Catholicism and Fundamentalism* (San Francisco: Ignatius, 1988), p. 238.
19. Philip Schaff, *The Creeds of Christendom*, vol. II, *The Canons and Decrees of the Council of Trent* (New York: Harper, 1877), pp. 179, 184–85.
20. Philip Schaff, *Nicene and Post-Nicene Fathers*, vol. I, *The Confessions and Letters of St Augustin*, Letter 98.9, *Ad Boniface* (Grand Rapids: Eerdmans, 1956), p. 410.
21. Sentences, book IV, dist. 12, cap. 5. Taken from Francis Clark, *Eucharistic Sacrifice and the Reformation* (Oxford: Basil Blackwell, 1967), p. 407.
22. Karl Keating, *Catholicism and Fundamentalism* (San Francisco: Ignatius, 1988), p. 255.
23. 'God has therefore announced in advance that all the sacrifices

offered in His name, which Jesus Christ commanded to be offered, that is, the Eucharist of the Bread and of the Chalice, which is offered by us Christians in every part of the world, are pleasing to Him... Now, I also admit that prayers and thanksgivings, offered by worthy persons, are the only perfect and acceptable sacrifices to God.' Thomas Falls, *Saint Justin Martyr,* Dialogue with Trypho 117, (Washington D.C.: Catholic University, 1948), p. 328.

24. Alexander Roberts and W. H. Rambaut, *The Writings of Irenaeus, Against Heresies* IV.17.5–6, 18.1–4 (Edinburgh: T. & T. Clark, 1874), pp. 430–35.
25. Alexander Roberts and James Donaldson, *The Ante-Nicene Fathers,* vol. III, Latin Christianity: Its Founder, Tertullian, *An Answer to the Jews,* ch. 5 (Grand Rapids: Eerdmans, 1951), pp. 156–57.
26. Eusebius, *Dem. Evang.* I.x.28–38. Taken from Darwell Stone, *A History of the Doctrine of the Holy Eucharist,* vol. I (New York: Longmans, Green, 1909), pp. 110–11.
27. For a detailed documentation of the teachings of the Fathers and Augustine on the nature of the eucharistic sacrifice see Appendix 9.
28. 'While we consider it no longer a duty to offer sacrifices, we recognise sacrifices as part of the mysteries of Revelation, by which the things prophesied were foreshadowed. For they were our examples, and in many and various ways they pointed to the one sacrifice which we now commemorate. Now that this sacrifice has been revealed, and has been offered in due time, sacrifice is no longer binding as an act of worship, while it retains its symbolic authority... Before the coming of Christ, the flesh and blood of this sacrifice were foreshadowed in the animals slain; in the passion of Christ the types were fulfilled by the true sacrifice; after the ascension of Christ, this sacrifice is commemorated in the sacrament.' Philip Schaff, *Nicene and Post-Nicene Fathers,* vol. IV, St. Augustin: The Writings Against the Manicheans and Against the Donatists, *Reply to Faustus the Manichean* 6.5, 20.21 (New York: Longmans, Green, 1909), pp. 169, 262.
29. 'For, as we have many members in one body, and all members have not the same office, so we, being many, are one body in Christ... This is the sacrifice of Christians: we being many, are one body in Christ. And this also is the sacrifice which the Church continually celebrates in the sacrament of the altar, known to the faithful, in which she teaches that she herself is offered in the offering she makes to God... For we ourselves, who are His own city, are His most noble and worthy sacrifice, and it is this mystery we celebrate in our sacrifices, which are well known to the faithful... For through the prophets the oracles of God declared that the sacrifices which the Jews offered as a shadow of that which was to be would cease, and that the nations, from the rising to the setting of the sun, would offer one sacrifice.' Philip Schaff, *Nicene and Post-Nicene Fathers,* vol. II, p. 230–31. St. Augustin: The City of God and On Christian Doctrine, *The City of God* Book 10, ch. 6; Book 19, ch. 23 (Grand Rapids: Eerdmans, 1956), pp. 184, 418.

30. *A Library of the Fathers of the Holy Catholic Church,* Epistle 63.11 (Oxford: Parker, 1844), p. 192.
31. Philip Schaff, *Nicene and Post-Nicene Fathers,* vol. XII, Saint Chrysostom, *Homilies on the Epistles of Paul to the Corinthians,* Homily 24.4–5 (Grand Rapids: Eerdmans, 1956), pp. 139–40.
32. Philip Schaff, *History of the Christian Church,* vol. 4 (Grand Rapids: Eerdmans, 1910), p. 548.
33. See Hebrews: 7:27, 10:10–14, 10:18.
34. *The Library of Christian Classics,* John McNeill, ed., vol. XXI, *Calvin: Institutes of the Christian Religion,* vol. II, Book IV, ch. 17 (Philadelphia: Westminster, 1960), p. 1365.

9. Faith and Justification

1. See Romans 5:1; John 5:24; Romans 3:28; Ephesians 2:8–9.
2. For documentation of the teachings of Thomas Aquinas on the nature of faith see Appendix 10 .
3. Thomas Aquinas, *Summa Theologica of St. Thomas Aquinas,* vol. 3 (Westminster: Christian Classics, 1981), p. 1165.
4. For comments by the Fathers on the nature of faith and justification see Appendix 12.
5. See also Galatians 2:16–21; Ephesians 2:8–9; Titus 3:5; Romans 3:19–28, 4:13–14, 11:6.
6. Ludwig Ott, *Fundamentals of Catholic Dogma* (Rockford: Tan, 1974), p. 254. This interpretation is expressly denied by Augustine, *On the Spirit and the Letter* 14, Philip Schaff, *Nicene and Post-Nicene Fathers,* vol. V, Saint Augustin: *Anti-Pelagian Writings* (Grand Rapids: Eerdmans, 1956), p. 88.
7. See Romans 5:1; Ephesians 2:8–9; Titus 3:5.
8. For example, Paul wrote in his first epistle to the Corinthians: 'But by His doing you are in Christ Jesus, who became to us wisdom from God, and righteousness and sanctification, and redemption' (*1 Cor.* 1:30).
9. For comments by Luther and Calvin on the relationship between justification and good works see Appendix 11.
10 . The following is a summary of the official teaching of the Council of Trent regarding justification:
1) All men are born in sin and have need of prevenient grace to respond to the call of God.
2) Jesus Christ, by his passion, merited salvation for man.
3) Justification must be preceded by faith which is assent to what has been divinely revealed and promised, and repentance which means a hatred of sin and the performing of penance, and the resolve to begin a new life and keep the commandments of God.
4) Justification is received through baptism which is called the sacrament of faith.
5) Justification is not only a remission of sins but also the sanctification and renewal of the inward man through the reception of grace.

6) The righteousness given in justification is not the righteousness of God himself but that by which he 'makes' a person righteous. It is the reception of grace by which he renews the inward man.
7) The faith that saves is a faith that works by hope and love.
8) A man is justified by faith in the sense that faith is the beginning of salvation.
9) It is a vain and ungodly presumption to say that a man can be assured of complete forgiveness of sins or to teach that a man who has been justified will persevere in a life of holiness.
10) Through the exercise of faith, obedience to the commandments of God and by good works an individual maintains and increases in justification.
11) The grace of justification can be lost through mortal sin by which one is cut off and severed from Christ and is subject once again to eternal damnation.
12) The grace of justification can be regained only through a repentance of the sin from the heart, sacramental confession and absolution, and the performance of deeds of satisfaction such as fasts, alms, prayers and other devout exercises.
13) The works which an individual does in the state of grace, which are empowered by Jesus Christ, fully satisfy the divine law and merit eternal life.
The Canons and Decrees of the Council of Trent, Decree on Justification, chs. 1-16, Canons 1-33. Taken from Philip Schaff, *The Creeds of Christendom* (New York: Harper & Brothers, 1877), pp. 89-118. For further details, see the documentation in Appendix 13.

11. Ludwig Ott, *Fundamentals of Catholic Dogma* (Rockford: Tan, 1974), pp. 264, 267.

10. *Truth: The Defining Issue*

1. As the *Westminster Confession* says (xxv:v) 'The purest churches under heaven are subject both to mixture and error; and some have so degenerated as to become no churches of Christ, but synagogues of Satan.'

Appendix 1

1. Alexander Roberts and W. H. Rambaut, trans., *The Writings of Irenaeus, Against Heresies*, 3.1.1 (Edinburgh: T. & T. Clark, 1874), p. 258.
2. Ibid., 3.5.1., p. 266.
3. Alexander Roberts and James Donaldson, *The Ante-Nicene Fathers*, vol. III, Latin Christianity: Its Founder, Tertullian, *On the Flesh of Christ*, ch. 6 (Grand Rapids: Eerdmans, 1951), p. 527.
4. Ibid., *Against Praxeas*, ch. 11, p. 606.
5. Ibid., *Against Marcion*, Book IV, ch. 5, p. 349-50.
6. Alexander Roberts and James Donaldson, *The Ante-Nicene Fathers*,

vol. V, Hippolytus, *Against the Heresy of One Noetus* 9 (Grand Rapids: Eerdmans, 1951), p. 227.
7. *A Library of the Fathers of the Holy Catholic Church, The Epistles of S. Cyprian, Epistle* 74.1–2, (Oxford: London, 1844), p. 260–61
8. Alexander Roberts and James Donaldson, *The Ante-Nicene Fathers,* vol. II, Fathers of the Second Century, Clement of Alexandria, *The Stromata,* ch. XVI (Grand Rapids, Eerdmans, 1956), pp. 550–51.
9. Alexander Roberts and James Donaldson, *The Ante-Nicene Fathers,* vol. IV, Origen, *De Principiis* 1.5.4 (Grand Rapids: Eerdmans, 1951), p. 258.
10. Homily 25 on Matthew. Cited by Martin Chemnitz, *An Examination of the Council of Trent,* vol. I, (St. Louis: Concordia, 1971), pp. 157–58.
11. *A Library of the Fathers of the Holy Catholic Church, The Catechetical Lectures of S. Cyril* 4.17, (Oxford: Parker, 1845), p. 42.
12. Ibid., Lecture 16.2, p. 203–4.
13. Philip Schaff and Henry Wace, *Nicene and Post-Nicene Fathers,* First Series, vol. IX, Saint Chrysostom, *Homilies on the Statues,* Homily I.14 (Grand Rapids: Eerdmans, 1956), pp. 336–37.
14. *A Library of the Fathers of the Holy Catholic Church, The Homilies of S. John Chrysostom,* 2 Timothy, Homily 9, (Oxford: London, 1843), p. 250.
15. Philip Schaff and Henry Wace, *Nicene and Post-Nicene Fathers,* Second Series, vol. IX, Hilary of Poitiers, *On the Councils,* pp. 29–30.
16. *De Bono Viduitatis,* ch. 2. Cited in *An Examination of the Council of Trent,* by Martin Chemnitz, vol. I (St. Louis: Concordia, 1971), p. 152.
17. *The Unity of the Church,* ch. 3. Cited by Martin Chemnitz, *An Examination of the Council of Trent,* vol. I (St Louis: Concordia, 1971), p. 157.
18. *The Fathers of the Church, Saint Jerome, Against Rufinus,* Book II.27 (Washington, D.C.: Catholic University, 1965), p. 151.
19. Philip Schaff and Henry Wace, *Nicene and Post-Nicene Fathers,* Second Series, vol. VI, St Jerome: Letters and Select Works, *Prefaces to Jerome's Works, Proverbs, Ecclesiastes and the Song of Songs* (Grand Rapids: Eerdmans, 1954), p. 492.
20. Philip Schaff and Henry Wace, *Nicene and Post-Nicene Fathers,* Second Series, vol. I, Eusebius, *Church History,* V.28.3–4 (Grand Rapids: Eerdmans, 1952), pp. 246–47.
21. Philip Schaff and Henry Wace, *Nicene and Post-Nicene Fathers,* vol. IV, Athanasius, *Letter* 56.1, (Grand Rapids: Eerdmans, 1953), p. 567.
22. Ibid., *Letter* 60.6, pp. 576–77.
23. Philip Schaff and Henry Wace, *Nicene and Post-Nicene Fathers,* vol. IV, Athanasius, *Letter* 56.1, p. 567; *Letter* 60.6 (Grand Rapids: Eerdmans, 1953), pp. 576–77.
24. Philip Schaff and Henry Wace, *Nicene and Post-Nicene Fathers,* Second Series, vol. IX, John of Damascus, *Exposition of the Orthodox Faith,* Book I, ch. I (Grand Rapids: Eerdmans, 1955), p. 1.

Appendix 2

1. Philip Schaff, *The Creeds of Christendom*, vol. II, *Dogmatic Decrees of the Vatican Council*, ch. 4 (New York: Harper, 1877), pp. 266–71.
2. *The Documents of Vatican II*, Walter M. Abbott, S.J., General Editor (Chicago: Follett, 1966), pp. 47–49.

Appendix 3

1. Philip Schaff, *A History of the Christian Church*, vol. VI (Grand Rapids: Eerdmans, 1910), pp. 25–27.

Appendix 4

1. Dogmatic Decrees of the Vatican Council as found in Philip Schaff, *The Creeds of Christendom*, vol. II, chs. 1, 2, 3 (New York: Harper, 1877), pp. 239–46.
2. *The Documents of Vatican II*, Walter M. Abbott, S.J., General Editor (Chicago: Follett, 1966), pp. 38, 40, 43–44.

Appendix 5

1. Philip Schaff and Henry Wace, *Nicene and Post-Nicene Fathers*, Second Series, vol. IX, St. Hilary of Poitiers, *On the Trinity*, Book VI.36–37 (Grand Rapids: Eerdmans, 1955), pp. 111–12.
2. Allan Menzies, *Ante-Nicene Fathers*, vol. X, *Origen's Commentary on Matthew*, chs. 10–11 (Grand Rapids: Eerdmans, 1951), p. 456.
3. *Commentary on Isaiah* IV.2, M.P.G., vol. 70, Col. 940.
4. *Commentary on Zacharias*. Cited by J. Waterworth, S.J., *A Commentary* (London: Thomas Richardson, 1871), p. 143.
5. *Commentary on the Psalms*, M.P.G., vol. 23, Col. 173, 176.
6. *Commentary on Matthew* 7.25, M.P.L., vol. 26, Col. 51. Cited by Karlfried Froehlich, *Formen der Auslegung von Matthaus 16,13–18 im lateinischen Mittelalter*, Dissertation (Tubingen, 1963), p. 49 n200.
7. *Epistle 65.15, Ad Principiam*. Cited by J. Waterworth S.J., *A Commentary* (London: Thomas Richardson, 1871), p. 109.
8. *Commentary on Amos* vi.12–13. Cited by J. Waterworth, S.J., *A Commentary* (London: Thomas Richardson, 1871), pp. 112-13.
9. Philip Schaff and Henry Wace, *Nicene and Post-Nicene Fathers*, vol. VI, St. Jerome, *Against Jovinianus*, Book 2.37 (Grand Rapids: Eerdmans, 1954), p. 415.
10. Ibid., *Against Jovinianus* 1.26, p. 366.
11. Discourse 32.18, M.P.G., vol. 36, Col. 193–94.
12. *Panegyric on St. Stephen*, M.P.G., vol. 46, Col. 733.
13. Philip Schaff, *Nicene and Post-Nicene Fathers*, Letters of Athanasius, *Letter* 29 (Grand Rapids: Eerdmans, 1953), p. 551.

14. *A Library of the Fathers of the Holy Catholic Church,* Select Treatises of S. Athanasius, Discourse IV, Subject IX.11 (Oxford: Parker, 1844).
15. Commentary on Ephesians, M.P.L., vol. 17, Col. 380.
16. *In Ev. Marc.* ch. 3. Cited by J. Waterworth S.J., *A Commentary* (London: Thomas Richardson, 1871), pp. 133-34.
17. *Homily of the Nativity.* Cited by J. Waterworth S.J., *A Commentary* (London: Thomas Richardson, 1871), p. 148.
18. *Adversus Haereses* 59.7, M.P.G., vol. 41, Col. 1029.
19. Philip Schaff, *Nicene and Post-Nicene Fathers,* vol. XIII, Aphrahat, *Select Demonstrations,* Demonstration I.2-6, 13, 19 (Grand Rapids: Eerdmans, 1956), pp. 345-47, 350, 352.
20. Vol. III, Theodoret, *Epistle* 146, p. 318.
21. Ibid., vol. III, Theodoret, *Epistle* 78, To Eulalius, p. 273.
22. *Commentary on Canticle of Canticles* II.14, M.P.G., vol. 81, Col. 108.
23. *A Library of the Fathers of the Holy Catholic Church,* (Oxford: Parker, 1850), vol. 31, S. Gregory the Great, *Morals on the Book of Job,* Book XXXV.13, p. 670. M.P.L., vol. 94, Col. 222.
24. *Expositions in the Psalms,* Psalm 45.5, M.P.L., vol. 70, Col. 330.
25. *Expositions in the Psalms,* Psalm 86.1, M.P.L., vol. 70, Col. 618.
26. *Dialogue on the Life of John Chrysostom,* M.P.G., vol. 47, Col. 68.
27. *Oratio* XXV.4, M.P.G., vol. 85, Col. 296-297.
28. *Commentary on Canticle of Canticles,* M.P.G., vol. 87 (ii), Col. 1693.
29. *Allegories in the New Testament,* M.P.L., vol. 83, Col. 117-118, Numbers 135, 136, 148.
30. *Etym.* VII.2, M.P.L., vol. 82, Col. 267.41.
31. *Homily on the Transfiguration,* M.P.G., vol. 96, Col. 554-555.
32. *Homily on the Transfiguration,* M.P.G., vol. 96, Col. 548.

Appendix 6

1. Philip Schaff and Henry Wace, *Nicene and Post-Nicene Fathers,* Second Series, vol. XII, *Epistles of Gregory the Great,* Book V, Epistle 18 (Grand Rapids: Eerdmans, 1956), pp. 166-69.

Appendix 7

1. Philip Schaff, *The Decree of Pope Pius IX on the Immaculate Conception,* in *The Creeds of Christendom,* vol. II (New York: Harper, 1877), pp. 211-12.
2. *The Documents of Vatican II,* Walter M. Abbott, S.J., General Editor (Chicago: Follett, 1966), pp. 88, 90.
3. *Munificentissimus Deus, Selected Documents of Pope Pius XII* (Washington: National Catholic Welfare Conference), 38, 40, 44-45, 47.
4. *The Documents of Vatican II,* Walter M. Abbott, S.J., General Editor (Chicago: Follett, 1966), pp. 88, 90.

Appendix 8

1. J. B. Lightfoot, *The Apostolic Fathers*, The Teaching of the Apostles 9 (Grand Rapids: Baker, 1989), pp. 126–27.
2. *The Fathers of the Church, Saint Justin Martyr,* Dialogue with Trypho 70 (Washington, D.C.: Catholic University, 1948), p. 262.
3. Alexander Roberts and James Donaldson, *The Ante-Nicene Fathers*, vol. II, *Theophilus to Autolycus*, Book III, ch. IV (Grand Rapids: Eerdmans), p. 112.
4. Alexander Roberts and James Donaldson, *The Ante-Nicene Fathers*, vol. II, Clement of Alexandria, *The Instructor,* Book II, ch. II (Grand Rapids, Eerdmans: 1951), p. 245.
5. *A Library of the Fathers of the Holy Catholic Church, The Epistles of S. Cyprian, Epistle* 63. 4, 7, 9–10 (Oxford: London, 1844), pp. 184, 187–89.
6. *Demonstratio Evangelica* VIII. i.76–80. Cited in Darwell Stone, *A History of the Holy Eucharist,* vol. I (London: Longmans, Green, 1909), pp. 62–63.
7. *Festal Epistles* IV.19. Cited in Darwell Stone, A History of the Holy Eucharist, vol. I (London: Longmans, Green, 1909), p. 90.
8. Philip Schaff and Henry Wace, *Nicene and Post-Nicene Fathers,* vol. VIII, St. Augustin, *Exposition on the Psalms* III.1 (Grand Rapids: Eerdmans, 1956), p. 5.
9. Ibid., vol. II, *The City of God* 10.6.5., p. 183.
10. Ibid., vol. II, *The City of God* 10.21.25, p. 473
11. Ibid., *The City of God* 10.21.20, p. 467.
12. Ibid., vol. VII, St. Augustin, *Homilies on the Gospel of John*, Tractate 26.12; 26.19, pp. 172–173.
13. Ibid., vol. VI, St. Augustin, *Homilies on the Gospels*, Sermon 81.1, p. 501.
14. Ibid., vol. VI, Sermon 62.5, p. 448.
15. Ibid., vol. VII, Tractate 25.12, p. 164.
16. Ibid., vol. VII, Tractate 26.18–19, p. 173.
17. Ibid., vol. II, *On Christian Doctrine* 3.16.24, p. 563.

Appendix 9

1. J. B. Lightfoot, *The Apostolic Fathers,* The Didache 14 (Grand Rapids: Baker, 1989), p. 128.
2. Thomas B. Falls, *Saint Justin Martyr, Dialogue with Trypho* 70, 41, 117 (Washington, D.C.: Catholic University, 1948), pp. 262, 209, 328.
3. Alexander Roberts and James Donaldson, *The Ante-Nicene Fathers* vol. IV, Origen, *Against Celsus,* Book VIII, Ch. XXI (Grand Rapids: Eerdmans), p. 647.
4. Eusebius, *Demonstratio Evangelica* I.x.28–38. Cited in Darwell Stone, A History of the Eucharist, vol. 1 (London: Longmans, Green, 1909), pp. 110–11.
5. Philip Schaff and Henry Wace, *Nicene and Post-Nicene Fathers,* vol.

NOTES FOR PAGES 198–213

XIV, Saint Chrysostom, *The Epistle to the Hebrews*, Homily 17.6 (Grand Rapids: Eerdmans, 1956), p. 449.
6. Ibid., *The Epistle to the Hebrews*, Homily 11.4–5, pp. 419–20.
7. Philip Schaff, *Nicene and Post-Nicene Fathers*, vol. IV, St Augustin, *Reply to Faustus the Manichean* VI.5 (Grand Rapids: Eerdmans, 1956, p. 169.
8. Ibid., *Faustus* 20.18, p. 261.
9. Ibid., *Faustus* 20.21, p. 262.

Appendix 10

1. Thomas Aquinas, *Summa Theologica of St. Thomas Aquinas*, vol. 3 (Westminster: Christian Classics, 1981), pp. 1163, 1165, 1167, 1180, 1184, 1185, 1193.

Appendix 11

1. *Luther's Primary Works*, Edited by Henry Wace and C. A. Buchheim, *Concerning Christian Liberty* (London: Hodder & Stoughton, 1896), pp. 275–77, 288.
2. *The Library of Christian Classics*, John McNeill, ed., vol. XX, *Calvin, The Institutes of the Christian Religion*, (Philadelphia: Westminster, 1960), pp. 797–98, 816. Book III, ch. 16.1, 17.12.

Appendix 12

1. J. B. Lightfoot, *The Apostolic Fathers, The Epistle of S. Clement to the Corinthians*, 49, 32 (Grand Rapids: Baker, 1989), pp. 34, 26.
2. Ibid., *The Epistle of S. Polycarp*, 1, p. 95.
3. Ibid., *The Epistle of S. Ignatius, To the Trallians* 2, p. 73; *To the Philadelphians*, 8,5, pp. 81, 80.
4. Thomas B. Falls, *Saint Justin Martyr, The First Apology* 32; *Dialogue with Trypho* 13, 23, 35, 92 (Washington, D.C.: Catholic University, 1948), pp. 69, 166, 183, 202, 294–95.
5. Alexander Roberts and W. H. Rambaut, trans., *The Writings of Irenaeus: Against Heresies*, 4.2.7; 4.5.5; 4.9.1; 4.6.7 (Edinburgh: T. & T. Clark, 1874), pp. 382, 388, 399–400, 393.

Appendix 13

1. Philip Schaff, *The Creeds of Christendom*, vol. II, pp. 92–97, 99–100, 104–8, 112-13, 115, 117.

Index

Albertus Magnus, 76
Ambrose
  and the eucharist, 120
  and original sin, 76
  on the rock of Matt. 16, 50, 220 n.15
Ambrosiaster
  and the eucharist, 120
  on the rock of Matt. 16, 178
Anastasius, 11
Anathemas
  of the Council of Trent, 90, 122, 212–13, 226 n.7
  of Vatican I, 163, 169, 170, 172
Anselm, 76
Antinomianism, 143
Aphraates
  on the rock of Matt. 16, 179
Apocrypha (the)
  and Christ, 8
  and the Fathers, 9–11, 12, 14
  and the Hebrew canon, 8–9
  and Josephus, 9
  and the Septuagint, 9
  its contents, 7
  not inspired, 14
  the rule of Jerome, 10–11, 12
Apostolic tradition
  and oral tradition, 24—25
  and Scripture, 23–25
  content of, 25
Aquinas, Thomas, 134, 200–1
Arian heresy, 64
Asceticism, 77–79, 108–9, 146
Assumption (of Mary)
  and the Fathers, 81–82
  and Vatican II, 189–90
  decree of Pius XII, 188–89
  definition of, 81, 188–89
  origin of the teaching, 82
  papal condemnation of, 82–83
Athanasius
  and the canon, 9–10
  and the eucharist, 120, 193
  on the rock of Matt. 16, 177–78
  on scripture and tradition, 161
Atonement (of Christ)
  once for all, 128–30
  and forgiveness of sins, 108, 116, 129
  and indulgences, 110
  and justification, 138–39
  and purgatory, 112
  undermined by penance, 102
Augustine
  and immolation, 123
  and original sin, 76
  and purgatory, 115
  and pope Zosimus, 58
  and repentance, 98
  on the apocrypha, 12–13
  on authority of Scripture, 25, 159–60
  on the eucharist, 120–21, 193–95
  on the rock of Matt. 16, 47–48
  on sacrifice, 123, 125–26, 198–99, 230, n.28–29
  the *Retractations*, 66
Authority
  of the Church, 147–48

INDEX

of general councils, 58, 60–61
of Scripture, ix, 1–7, 15–18
of tradition, 16–17
Roman Catholic teaching, x, 34
to preach the gospel, 41

Baptism, 95–99
and circumcision, 97
and the fathers, 95–96
and repentance and faith, 97
its biblical meaning, 96–97
Basil of Seleucia
on the rock of Matt. 16, 181
Basil the Great
and the canon, 10
and the sinlessness of Mary, 75
on the penitential discipline, 226–27 n.10
on Scripture and tradition, 27–28
Bede, 76
Bernard of Clairvaux, 76
Binding and Loosing, 39–42, 101, 103
and the gospel, 39–42
Bonaventura, 76
Boniface VIII (pope), 68, 165–67
and the bull *Unam Sanctam*, 165–67

Cajetan, Cardinal
on the canon and the apocrypha, 12
Calvin, John
justification and sanctification, 203–4
spiritual partaking of Christ, 130
Canon (Old Testament)
and Cardinal Cajetan, 12
and Councils of Carthage and Hippo, 8, 11, 13
and Josephus, 8–9
and the Septuagint, 9

and the Council of Trent, 8
and the Fathers, 9–13
Alexandrian, 9
Hebrew, 8–9
Protestant teaching, 7
Roman Catholic teaching, 7
Cassiodorus
on the rock of Matt. 16, 181
Catalogus Liberianus, 45
Celestius, 65
Celibacy, 77–78
Chrysostom, John
and the eucharist, 120, 127, 198
on the rock of Matt. 16, 50–51, 220 n.16
on Scripture, 158–59
Church (the), 147–48
and unity, 148
and truth, 147–48
its spiritual nature, 147
its purpose, 148
Clement of Alexandria
and the penitential discipline, 105
and purgatory, 114
on the eucharist, 119, 125, 192
on Scripture, 157
Clement of Rome
and the eucharist, 125
and justification, 104, 205
and the eucharist, 125
and the priesthood, 93
Confession, 99–106
and absolution, 104–5, 108
and the Fathers, 104
and the Old Testament priesthood, 102
historical development of, 99–100, 104–6, 108
Roman Catholic teaching, 99–100
Scriptural teaching, 101–3
Consubstantiation, 122
Co-Redemptrix
papal teaching, 86

[237]

Council of
  Basel, 68
  Carthage, 8, 11, 13, 58–59
  Chalcedon, 59, 61
  Constance, 68, 223
  Constantinople, 61
  Ephesus, 73
  Fifth Ecumenical, 65–66
  Hippo, 8, 11, 13
  Nicea, 58, 61, 105
  Sardica, 58–59
  Sixth Ecumenical, 67, 222–23
  III Toledo, 105
  Trent, 8, 13, 27, 32, 90, 108, 117, 122, 208–13, 226 n.7, 231–32 n.10
  Vatican I, 30, 34–35, 43, 56, 63, 168–72
  Vatican II, 163–64, 172–73
Councils
  and the bishops of Rome, 58, 60–61, 65–70
Cyprian
  and the bishop of Rome, 59
  and the chair of Peter, 49–50
  and penance, 105, 227 n.13
  and the priesthood, 94–95
  and the rock of Matt. 16, 49
  and sacrifice, 126
  on the eucharist, 192
  on Scripture and tradition, 156–57
Cyril of Alexandria
  on the rock of Matt. 16, 175
Cyril of Jerusalem
  and the canon, 9
  and baptism and repentance, 98
  and the eucharist, 120
  on Scripture, 26, 158

Development of Doctrine, 18–19
  and the gospel, 19
Didache The
  and the eucharist, 118, 191
  and the priesthood, 93
  and sacrifice, 125, 196

Donation of Constantine, 62
Dulia, 73, 87

Ecumenism
  and the gospel, 149
Epiphanius
  and the assumption of Mary, 81, 224 n.9
  and the canon, 10
  on the rock of Matt. 16, 179
Eucharist, 117–32
  and the atonement of Christ, 128–29
  and John 6, 130
  Roman Catholic teaching, 117
  views of the Fathers, 118–27, 191–99
Eugenius IV (pope), 68
Eusebius of Cesarea
  and the eucharist, 119–20, 192–93
  and sacrifice, 125, 197–98
  and the authority of Scripture, 160–61
  on the rock of Matt. 16, 175–76
Eustathius of Antioch
  and the eucharist, 120
ex cathedra, 63
excommunication, 104
exomologesis, 98, 104, 107

Faith, 20–21, 130, 133–37, 152
  and intellectual assent, 134–36
  and justification, 20, 136
  and repentance, 20, 133–34
  and salvation, 133
  Thomas Aquinas, 134, 200–1
  and works, 20–21, 134
  definition of, 133
  historical corruption of, 134–36
  object of, 133
  Roman Catholic teaching, 134–35

INDEX

Formula of Hormisdas
and papal infallibility, 55

Galileo
and papal infallibility, 69
Gelasius I (pope), 82–83, 120
Glossa Ordinaria
and papal infallibility, 54
Gnosticism, 24–25, 150
and oral tradition, 24–25
Gospel (the), 15–16, 18–21, 148, 151–52
a completed message 18
and the theory of development, 18–19
and unity, 148
Grace
and imputed righteousness, 138
and justification, 137–38
and works, 138
Roman Catholic teaching, 107–8, 141–42
Greek philosophy, 114–15
and Roman Catholic Tradition, 150
Gregory of Nazianzen
and the canon, 10
and the eucharist, 120
on the rock of Matt. 16, 177
Gregory of Nyssa
and the eucharist, 120
on the rock of Matt. 16, 177
Gregory of Tours
and the assumption of Mary, 82
Gregory the Great (pope)
and the canon, 11
and John of Constantinople, 62, 184–86
and the immaculate conception, 76

Hilary of Poitiers
and the canon, 10
and the sinlessness of Mary, 75
on the rock of Matt. 16, 174

on the authority of Scripture, 161
Hippolytus
on the authority of Scripture, 156
Honorius (pope), 67, 222–23
condemnation for heresy, 222–23
Hormisdas (pope), 55, 83
Hugo of St. Victor, 76
Hyperdulia, 73, 87

Ignatius of Antioch
and the eucharist, 118
letters to churches, 57
on justification, 205–6
on the priesthood, 93
Immolation
definition of, 122
and the Council of Trent, 122–23
and the Fathers, 122–23
Indulgences, 99, 104, 109–10
Infallibility (papal)
and patristic interpretation, 53–55
contrary to history, 56–71
Roman Catholic teaching, 34–35, 63, 162–64
Irenaeus
and the apostolic tradition, 23–25
and the church of Rome, 57–58
and the eucharist, 118
and the sinlessness of Mary, 75
and gnostic oral tradition, 24–25, 57
and unanimous consent, 218 n.17
on the authority of Scripture, 155
on justification, 206–7
on Mary, 72
Isidore of Seville
and Mary, 81
on the rock of Matt. 16, 182

[239]

Jerome
- and the apocrypha, 10–13, 160
- and the canon, 10–14, 160
- and the eucharist, 120
- and Mary, 81
- on the rock of Matt. 16, 176–77

Jesus
- and the apocrypha, 8
- and the Jews, 145, 151
- and prophecy, 6
- and Scripture, 5

Johannes Teutonicus
- and papal infallibility, 54

John of Damascus
- and the canon, 11
- on the authority of Scripture, 161
- on the rock of Matt. 16, 182–83
- and tradition, 16–18

Josephus
- and the Old Testament canon, 8

Justin Martyr
- and the eucharist, 118, 192, 228 n.2–3
- and sacrifice, 125, 196–97, 229 n.23
- on justification, 206

John 21:15–17
- interpretation of the fathers, 53–55

Judaizers
- and Roman Catholicism, 147

Justification, 20–21, 136–44
- and assurance of salvation, 139
- and eternal life, 136–37, 139
- and the Council of Trent, 208–13
- and the Fathers, 205–7
- and faith, 136–37
- and grace, 137
- and imputed righteousness, 138, 143
- and the law, 137–39
- and the merits of Christ, 138–39
- and sanctification, 140, 202–7
- and works, 20–21, 136–39
- eternal nature of, 139
- definition of, 138

Keys (the), 39–43

Latria, 73, 87
Legalism, 146
Leo I (pope), 52, 76
Leo II (pope)
- condemnation of pope Honorius, 67

Leontius of Byzantium
- and the canon, 11

Liber Pontificalis, 62
Liberius (pope), 64
Lord's Supper (the), 129–32
- and the Passover, 131–32
- commemoration of Calvary, 129–30, 132

Luke 22:32
- interpretation of the fathers, 53–55

Macarius of Egypt
- and the eucharist, 120

Magisterium, 26, 48, 150
Marius Victorinus,
- and the sinlessness of Mary, 75

Martin V (pope), 68–69
Mary, 72–89
- and the Fathers, 75–76, 81–82, 101, 103
- assumption of, 81–85
- immaculate conception of, 73–77
- mediatorial role of, 85–88
- parallels to Christ, 88
- perpetual virginity of, 77–80
- *theotokos*, 73

Mass (the)
- sacrificial nature of, 117, 122–23

INDEX

and Malachi 1:11, 124
Matthew 16:18–19
  views of the Fathers, 46–53,
    174–83
Mediatrix, 72, 85–86, 190
  papal teaching, 86
Melito of Sardis
  and the canon, 9
Monotheletism (heresy of)
  definition of, 222 n.14
  and pope Honorius, 67

Nicholas I (pope), 62, 83–84
Nilus of Ancyra
  on the rock of Matt. 16, 182

Origen
  and celibacy, 77
  and the canon, 8, 14
  and the eucharist, 119, 125,
    197
  and the sinlessness of Mary,
    75
  on the authority of
    Scripture, 157–58
  on the rock of Matt. 16, 51,
    174

Pacian
  and the penitential
    discipline, 105
Palladius of Hellenopolis
  on the rock of Matt. 16, 181
Papacy
  and Vatican I, 34–35, 46,
    168–72
  and Vatican II, 172–73
  appeal to scripture, 35–36,
    53
  historical tests, 56–71
  infallibility, 34–35, 63, 162–
    64
  Peter and the rock, 36
  primacy, 34–36, 168–73
Passover (the), 131–32
Paul V (pope), 69
Paul of Emessa
  on the rock of Matt. 16, 178

Penance
  Roman Catholic teaching,
    99, 107, 226 n.7
  corruption of repentance,
    107–9, 136
  and the Fathers, 104–7,
    226 n.10
  and the Council of Nicea,
    105
  and the Council of III
    Toledo, 106
  and satisfaction for sin, 107
Perpetual virginity (of Mary),
    77–81
  and Jewish culture, 80–81
  contradictory to Scripture,
    77–80
Peter (apostle)
  interpretation of the rock, 37
  position in the early church,
    43–46
Peter Lombard
  and the meaning of the
    mass, 123
  on the nature of confession,
    108
Philo
  and the Old Testament
    canon, 9
Pius IX (pope), 43, 187–88
  and the immaculate
    conception, 187–88
Pius XII (pope)
  and the assumption of Mary,
    84, 188–89
Platonism, 114, 150
Polycarp
  and the priesthood, 93
  on justification, 205–6
Priesthood, 91–95
  and Christ, 92
  and the Fathers, 93–94
  and the first century church,
    93
  and scripture, 91–92
Protestantism
  and the apostolic tradition,
    149

Pseudo–Isidorian Decretals, 62
Purgatory, 99, 104, 110–16
   and the early church, 114
   and Scripture, 110–13
   its origin, 114–16

Radbertus
   and the eucharist, 127
Redemption, 40–41
Reformation (the)
   and ecumenism, 149
   and the gospel, 149
   and historic Christianity, 149
Repentance, 20, 97–102, 108, 131
   and penance, 102, 136
   meaning of, 100
Rock (the)
   Peter's interpretation, 36–37
   Protestant teaching, 53
   Roman Catholic teaching, 36, 52
   teaching of the Fathers, 46–52
   teaching of Scripture, 373–79
Rufinus
   and the canon, 10

Sacraments
   baptism, 95–96
   confession and penance, 99–109
   eucharist, 117–32
   means of salvation, 90
   ordination and priesthood, 91–95, 101
   Roman Catholic teaching, 90–91
Sacramentalism, 146
Sacrifice
   of Christ, 108, 128–29
   and the eucharist, 129
   and the Fathers, 125–27, 196–99
   and the Lord's Supper, 129–32
   and Roman Catholic teaching, 122–24
   and the Reformation, 124, 130
Salvation
   and the church, 151–52
   and justification, 139
   and repentance, 133–34
   and sanctification, 140, 143
   and union with Christ, 139
   assurance of, 139
   eternal nature of, 139
   foundation of, 133
   meaning of, 139–40
   source of, 133, 151–52
Sanctification
   and justification, 140
   and the Reformers, 140, 202–3
   and salvation, 20, 134, 143
   Roman Catholic teaching, 141–43
Scripture
   and the Apostolic tradition, 23–24
   and Christ, 5–6, 145, 151
   and the Fathers, 22–23, 155–61
   and Paul, 15–16
   and Peter, 1–2
   authority of, 1, 15–18, 151
   inspiration of, 1–2, 6–7
   judge of tradition, 15–18
   Roman Catholic teaching, ix–x, 3, 15–16, 122
   sufficiency of, 2–4
Shepherd of Hermas
   and the penitential discipline, 105
Sola scriptura, 3, 14, 18, 84
   a biblical principle 15–18
   a historical principle 26, 32, 84, 155–61
   meaning of, ix
Stephen I (pope)
   and heretical baptism, 59–60
Stoicism, 150
Supererogation (works of), 109

Tertullian

INDEX

and the apostolic tradition, 23, 25, 27
and the authority of Scripture, 84, 155–56
and the eucharist, 119
and penance, 104–5, 227 n.13
and the priesthood, 94
and the sinlessness of Mary, 75
and tradition, 27
on the rock of Matt. 16, 219 n.9

Theodoret
and the eucharist, 120
on the rock of Matt. 16, 180

Theophilus
and the eucharist, 192

Theophylact
on the rock of Matt. 16, 51

Theotokos, 73

Tradition
and the Fathers, 22–30
and inspiration, 17
and the gnostics, 24–25
and Jesus, 16, 145
and the Jews, 17, 145–47
and Scripture, 15–21
concept of in the early church, 23
its biblical meaning, 15
Roman Catholic teaching, ix–x, 15–16, 22
warnings against, 16

Tradition of Roman Catholicism
and error, 151
and the Jews, 145–147
contrary to history, 7–14, 19, 22–33, 31–33, 47–55, 71, 75–77, 81–85, 93–94, 99–100, 104–10, 114–16, 119–22, 125–27, 134–35, 150–51
contrary to Scripture, 2–6, 15–17, 37–43, 76–80, 85–89, 91–92, 107–8, 110–14, 116, 123–24, 128–32, 133–34, 137–44, 150
undermines the gospel, 71, 88–89, 96–97, 110, 116, 129–44, 150–52

Transitus literature, 82–83
and the assumption of Mary, 82
papal condemnation of, 83

Transubstantiation, 117
and the Fathers, 120

Treasury of merit, 109–10

Trent (Council of)
on confession and penance, 226 n.7
on justification, 208–13
on the sacraments, 90
on the sacrifice of the mass, 122
on unanimous consent, 30

Unanimous Consent, 29–32, 55, 150
and the Council of Trent, 30
and Irenaeus, 29, 218
and Vincent of Lérins, 29
and Vatican I, 30

Unity
and Protestantism, 148–49
and truth, 148–49
and uniformity, 149
its foundation, 148

Urban VIII (pope), 69

Vatican I
on papal infallibility, 34–35, 162–63
on papal primacy, 34–35, 43–44, 168–72
on unanimous consent, 30

Vatican II
and the sacrifice of the mass, 124
on the assumption of Mary, 189–90
on the immaculate conception, 188
on papal infallibility, 163–64

on papal primacy, 172–73

Vigilius (pope), 65–66
Vincent of Lérins
   and the apostolic tradition,
      28–29
   on original sin, 223–24 n.4
   on unanimous consent, 29

Zosimus (pope), 58, 65
Zwingli
   and the eucharist, 122